An Idiot Abroad

ALSO BY KARL PILKINGTON

THE WORLD OF KARL PILKINGTON
HAPPYSLAPPED BY A JELLYFISH
KARLOLOGY

An Idiot Abroad

The Travel Diaries of Karl Pilkington

With Ricky Gervais and Stephen Merchant

Photography by Rich Hardcastle and Freddie Clare
Illustrations by Dominic Trevett

CANONGATE
Edinburgh · London · New York · Melbourne

mentornmedia

PUBLISHED BY CANONGATE BOOKS IN 2010

7

FOR ACKNOWLEDGEMENTS, PLEASE SEE PAGE 284

FIRST PUBLISHED IN GREAT BRITAIN IN 2010 BY CANONGATE BOOKS LTD,
14 HIGH STREET, EDINBURGH EH1 1TE

WWW.MEETATTHEGATE.COM

BRITISH LIBRARY CATALOGUING-IN-PUBLICATION DATA
A CATALOGUE RECORD FOR THIS BOOK IS AVAILABLE
ON REQUEST FROM THE BRITISH LIBRARY

ISBN 978 1 84767 9 260

BOOK DESIGN BY LUKE BIRD AND CANONGATE BOOKS
REPRODUCTION BY SYNTAX, EDINBURGH

PRINTED AND BOUND IN ITALY BY GRAPHICOM

CONTENTS

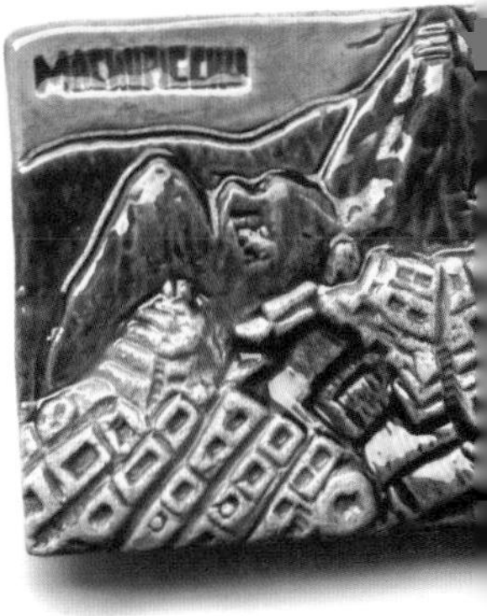

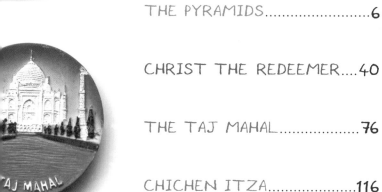

INTRODUCTION

KARL PILKINGTON

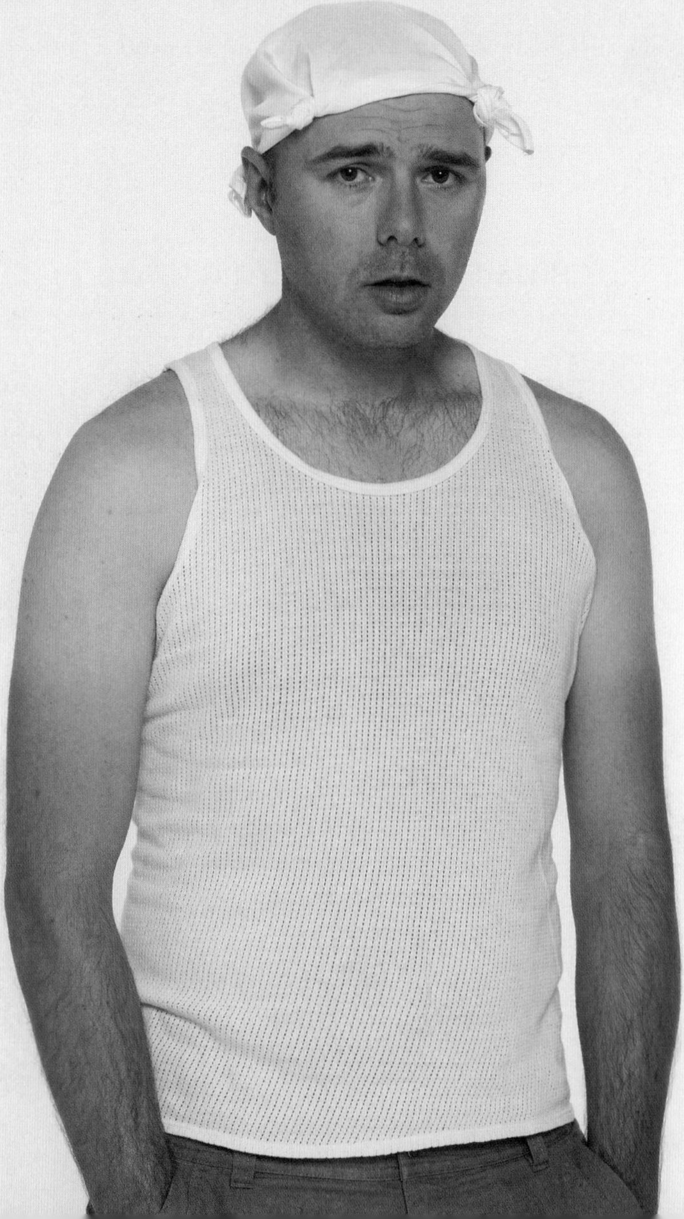

'HE IS – I DON'T KNOW THE POLITICALLY-CORRECT TERM – A MORON. A COMPLETELY ROUND, EMPTY-HEADED, PART-CHIMP MANC.'

RICKY GERVAIS

'HE'D 'VE BEEN HAPPIER IN MEDIEVAL TIMES IN A VILLAGE WHERE YOU DIDN'T TRAVEL BEYOND THE LOCAL COMMUNITY.'

STEPHEN MERCHANT

HE'S A REAL, GENUINE FREAK THAT WE HAVE OFTEN THOUGHT WE WOULD LIKE TO INTRODUCE TO THE WORLD, LIKE TWO VICTORIAN SHOWMEN, LIKE P.T. BARNUM AND HIS FAT FRIEND WHO ARE JUST SAYING, 'LOOK, YOU MUST COME AND OBSERVE THIS WONDER OF THE WORLD!'
I MEAN, HE IS – I DON'T KNOW THE POLITICALLY-CORRECT TERM – A MORON. A COMPLETELY ROUND, EMPTY-HEADED, PART-CHIMP MANC.
IN MANY REGARDS WE'VE OFTEN DESCRIBED HIM – AND IT'S APPROPRIATE – AS BEING LIKE SOME KIND OF REAL-LIFE HOMER SIMPSON.
YES.
HOMER IS ARROGANT AND YET AN IDIOT. SMALL-MINDED, PETTY. BUT AT HIS CORE A GOOD PERSON.
AND LOVABLE. ABSOLUTELY LOVABLE. HE'S GOT CHILD RIGHTS BECAUSE HE SAYS THE MOST AWFUL THINGS SO NAIVELY AND SWEETLY. THINGS LIKE 'CHINESE PEOPLE DON'T AGE WELL ...' I GO, 'WHAT?' HE GOES, 'THEY DON'T AGE WELL.' HE SAYS, 'YOU LL NEVER SEE A THIRTY-FIVE-YEAR-OLD ONE.' I GO, 'WHAT DO YOU MEAN?' HE WENT, 'WELL, THEY'RE GOOD-LOOKING WHEN THEY'RE YOUNG BUT THEN THEY AGE OVERNIGHT. THEY'RE LIKE A PEAR.' I MEAN, RACISM. LIKE, YOU KNOW...
IT'S NOT RACIST. IT'S JUST IGNORANT.

IT'S JUST IGNORANCE, HE THINKS THAT. I WENT, 'WELL, SOME OF THE OLDEST PEOPLE IN THE WORLD ARE CHINESE'. HE WENT, 'ARE THEY THOUGH?' HE THINKS THEY MIGHT BE LYING. HE THINKS THESE OLD CHINESE BOYS MIGHT BE THIRTY-FIVE BUT LYING ABOUT THEIR AGE 'COS THEY DON'T AGE WELL. I MEAN, HE'S AN IDIOT. I MEAN, HIS THEORIES, HIS OUTLOOK ON LIFE. HE REALLY WOULD NEVER GO AWAY IF IT WASN'T FOR HIS GIRLFRIEND.
HE'D'VE BEEN HAPPIER IN MEDIEVAL TIMES IN A VILLAGE WHERE YOU DIDN'T TRAVEL BEYOND THE LOCAL COMMUNITY. THAT WOULD'VE BEEN FINE FOR HIM.
YEAH, MAKING UP HIS OWN THEORIES ABOUT THE MOON.
TERRIFIED BECAUSE HE DOESN'T KNOW WHERE IT GOES DURING THE DAY.
YEAH, HE'S QUITE REMARKABLE. SO I THINK WE SHOULD BROADEN HIS OUTLOOK. AND THEY SAY TRAVEL BROADENS THE MIND. SO I JUST THINK IT'D BE AMAZING TO SEND HIM ROUND THE WORLD...
WELL, YEAH. I MEAN, HE'S TRAVELLED, BUT IT'S ONLY BEEN TO PLACES LIKE MAJORCA. SOMEWHERE SAFE, A LITTLE TWO-WEEK PACKAGE HOLIDAY.
IF IT WASN'T FOR HIS GIRLFRIEND, HE WOULDN'T DO ANYTHING. HIS JOB AT HOME IS WASHING-UP. HE LOOKS FORWARD TO THAT BECAUSE THAT'S SOMETHING HE'S DONE. OFTEN I CALL HIM AND HE SAYS, 'I'M WASHING-UP' LIKE IT'S A BIG EVENT. ONE DAY HE'D STARTED A DIARY AND HE DID THE WASHING-UP AND TOOK HIS GIRLFRIEND'S SHOES TO THE COBBLERS. NOW I HADN'T HEARD THE WORD 'COBBLERS' IN AGES...

I DIDN'T REALISE COBBLERS STILL EXISTED. I THOUGHT THEY WERE ONLY IN FAIRYTALES.
YES, EXACTLY. AND SHE MAKES HIM GO ON HOLIDAY. WHEN SHE BOOKS A HOLIDAY HE GOES, 'OH, I GOTTA GO OR I'D JUST STAY AT HOME ALONE', AND WHEN HE DOES THAT HE FORGETS TO EAT. ONCE, RIGHT, SOMEONE AT THE RADIO STATION WHERE HE USED TO WORK SENT US AN EMAIL THAT KARL HAD SENT BY MISTAKE, RIGHT? IT WAS AN EMAIL FROM HIS GIRLFRIEND. SHE WAS OUT THAT NIGHT AND SO, IN DETAIL, SHE WAS TELLING HIM WHERE THE QUICHE WAS IN THE FRIDGE, CUT IT UP IN SLICES AND SHE EVEN PUT 'EAT' ON IT.
DIDN'T HE TRY AND PUT FISH FINGERS IN A TOASTER OR SOMETHING?
YEAH, HE DID THAT ONCE. NO, SAUSAGES.
SAUSAGES.
YEAH, SHE CAME HOME GOING, 'WHAT ARE YOU DOING?' HE'D FORGOT TO DRINK SO HE'D HAD KIDNEY STONES. I MEAN, HE IS...
HE'S A TYPICAL LITTLE ENGLANDER AND HE DOESN'T LIKE GOING OUT OF HIS COMFORT ZONE. THAT'S KEY. YOU KNOW, HE'S GOT EVERYTHING AROUND HIM THAT HE'S HAPPY WITH AND HE'S COMFORTABLE WITH. EVEN WHEN HE GOES ON HOLIDAY, YOU KNOW, HE'S THE SORT OF PERSON WHO PACKS SOME TEABAGS. HE'S NOT COMFORTABLE GOING BEYOND THINGS HE DOESN'T UNDERSTAND. AND HE THINKS HE'S NOT INTERESTED. WHAT EXCITES US IS THE IDEA OF FORCING HIM TO GET OUT THERE. WE'D LIKE TO SEE HIM GO OUT INTO THE WORLD, EXPERIENCE OTHER CULTURES, OTHER PEOPLES, AND SEE IF, IN ANY WAY, WE CAN CHANGE HIS OUTLOOK ON THE WORLD.

YEAH. CAN I JUST SAY THAT I'VE GOT TO ADMIT THAT STEPHEN'S MOTIVES ARE A LOT PURER THAN MINE. HE WANTS KARL TO ENJOY IT...
I'VE TRAVELLED. I'VE BEEN TO MANY EXOTIC PLACES. I GENUINELY THINK TRAVEL BROADENS THE MIND. I'VE BECOME A RICHER PERSON FOR IT...
I WANT HIM TO HATE IT. I WANT HIM TO HATE EVERY MINUTE OF IT FOR MY OWN AMUSEMENT. THAT'S IT. I THINK WE'VE GOTTA SEND HIM ECONOMY. I THINK WE'VE GOTTA PUT HIM UP IN SHACKS AND AWFUL HOTELS. I THINK WE'VE GOTTA EXPOSE HIM TO SOME OF THE MOST MIND-BLOWING DEGRADATION THAT WE CAN. AND THAT'LL BE FUNNY. NOTHING IS FUNNIER THAN KARL IN A CORNER BEING POKED BY A STICK. I AM THAT STICK AND NOW I HAVE THE MIGHT OF SKY BEHIND ME. THIS IS ONE OF THE FUNNIEST, MOST EXPENSIVE PRACTICAL JOKES I'VE EVER DONE. AND IT'S GONNA BE GREAT.
I'M HOPING AS WELL THAT HE'LL BE POKED BY SOME REAL STICKS.
I KNOW. WHAT COUNTRY DO THEY POKE YOU WITH STICKS?
THERE'S GOTTA BE A COUNTRY WHERE THEY POKE YOU WITH STICKS...
THERE'S BOUND TO BE. THERE'S BOUND TO BE ONE OF THEM WEIRD LITTLE COUNTRIES WHERE, IF YOU SEE A MAN WITH A ROUND HEAD, YOU'RE ALLOWED TO POKE HIM WITH A STICK. ONE OF THOSE UNREPEALED LAWS. JUST FIND ME THAT COUNTRY!

CHAPTER ONE

THE PYRAMIDS

'ASCENDING THE PYRAMID, I COULD NOT BUT THINK OF WATERLOO BRIDGE IN MY DEAR NATIVE LONDON – A BUILDING AS VAST AND AS MAGNIFICENT, AS BEAUTIFUL, AS USELESS AND AS LONELY.'

WILLIAM MAKEPEACE THACKERAY

'I REALLY CAN'T BELIEVE WHAT A STATE THE PYRAMIDS ARE IN. I THOUGHT THEY HAD FLAT RENDERED SIDES, BUT WHEN YOU GET UP CLOSE, YOU SEE HOW THEY ARE JUST GIANT BOULDERS BALANCED ON TOP OF EACH OTHER, LIKE A MASSIVE GAME OF JENGA THAT HAS GOT OUT OF HAND.' KARL PILKINGTON

EGYPT
NILE
Taj Al Sultan
Al Hakim Mosque
KFC
Peace and quiet
Al Azhar Park
GIZA
Pizza Hut
Sphinx
Windsor Hotel
Egyptian Museum
Golden Nile Floating Restaurant
NILE
desert

FRIDAY 17TH OCTOBER

My Seven Wonders experience started today with a trip to get my injections. I've never had to have an injection to go on holiday before. I don't tend to go to extreme places normally. I like my holidays to be the same as being at home but in a different area. The time we were in the Cotswolds and could only get whole milk instead of semi-skimmed was almost enough to make me turn around and go back home, so this is going to be a challenge for me.

I was booked into a clinic off Tottenham Court Road in London, which seems a bit odd, as this area is mainly known for its electrical shops. It would be like going to Chinatown for a curry. They told me I had to have six injections – Tetanus, Typhoid, Yellow Fever, Rabies, Hepatitis A and B. I asked if I could have the injections in my arse, as I have just moved house and need to be able to use my arms when they deliver my new washing machine. (I'm guessing this isn't a problem Michael Palin has ever had to worry about.) The nurse said she had never been asked to put injections into an arse cheek and said I was worrying too much and that my arm should be fine.

She gave me the jabs and said I was covered for every worst-case scenario, including being bitten by a dirty chimp. I told her this is why we have over-population problems. Why are idiots who annoy dirty chimps being protected?

SATURDAY 18TH OCTOBER

Good job I didn't have the injections in my arse, as I had to sit on it all day waiting for the washer/dryer to be delivered. They gave me a window of 8 a.m. to 6 p.m. That window has a name. It's called Saturday.

I was up at 7.50 a.m. It turned up at 5.40 p.m.

My arm ached after fitting the machine into the kitchen.

MONDAY 23RD NOVEMBER

I did some filming today with Ricky and Steve. They told me the places I would be visiting: Egypt, Brazil, India, Mexico, China, Jordan and Peru. I have to confess, these are all places I've never really fancied visiting. If it wasn't for the Wonders I doubt most people would go to these destinations. Me and Suzanne mainly go to the Cotswolds, Devon, Spain or Italy. I'm not a proper traveller. I don't like to be challenged or have too much of a change and prefer a week away just to relax rather than broaden my mind. I'm not very adventurous. Maybe I'd see the Wonders if time travel was possible but then I also had a really nice time in Majorca back in 2007 in a villa with four bedrooms and its own swimming pool which was only £300 for the week, so I'd probably just end up using the time machine to go back to that holiday as I know I enjoyed it, plus I wouldn't have to pay again as I paid for it back then.

Steve told me that some of the areas we would be visiting are quite dangerous. Krish, the producer, said I shouldn't worry, as we will have a man with a gun protecting us at some of the locations. Being attacked by a dirty chimp with rabies doesn't seem such a worry anymore.

WEDNESDAY 25TH NOVEMBER

I had to go and get my medical done to make sure I was fit enough for the challenge of travelling around the Seven Wonders of the World. It was a really posh clinic on Harley Street. I knew it was a classy place, as the waiting room had all the same style chairs, which is rare. Most doctors I have been to have loads of different styles that have been bought at various times. It always reminds me of Christmases at home when we'd borrow chairs from various neighbours so we could seat everyone for dinner.

They say you can tell the quality of a doctor's by the magazine selection. The place on Harley Street had loads. They had every magazine you could wish for and some that you wouldn't. One of which was *Boyz*, a gay magazine. I was the only one in the waiting room so thought I would have a flick through it to see what gays like to read about. There wasn't much reading to be done, as it was just picture after picture of half-naked men (mainly the lower half) dressed as mechanics, farmers and plumbers with their tackle out. I've never understood what gay blokes get from looking at these pictures, as they have knobs of their own to look at. Other than the pictures there was the odd bit of text that was always a pun on the knob and bollocks. The main one I remember was Suckcocko. The puzzle was exactly the same as a normal Suduko, just with the knob twist to its name.

I had my medical. The doctor said I was in good shape for my age. It's the first time someone had ever brought my age into my health. It made me feel quite old.

WEDNESDAY 9TH DECEMBER

I was picked up at 4.30 a.m. and taken to the airport for our flight to Cairo. Six hours later we were on the road to our hotel. I hadn't been told anything about who or what I'd be meeting, eating or seeing. Apparently that's the way each trip is going to work, which I know will annoy me, as I don't really like surprises. Not big ones anyway. Just having a pack of Revels holds enough of a surprise for me.

The first thing that hit me about Egypt was the traffic. It was mental. There was a song in the 1980s by a girl group called The Bangles who sang 'Walk like an Egyptian' yet no one seems to be walking anywhere here – everyone is driving. They make every three-lane road into a six-lane road, and cram so many people into their cars it's ridiculous. Passengers are squashed up against the windows like those Garfield cats that people used to stick on their car windows in the 1980s. The horns are in constant use, but this might be because there are so many people crammed into the car someone's arse is accidentally pressing against the horn.

It was a long journey to the hotel. As we drove, all the nice hotels seemed to disappear until we finally pulled up at a place called The Windsor. It is one of the oldest hotels in Cairo and it is situated in one of the roughest areas. It even has a security scanner at the entrance, as if to prove how dodgy the area is. As I walked through, my belt set off the bleeper. It was enough to startle me, but it didn't seem to wake the security man.

As well as being one of the oldest hotels, it had the staff to match. You wouldn't get people of this age working in hotels in England. An old fella brought my case from the coach. We were parked right outside the entrance, but it took the old fella the same amount of time it took me to fill out all the forms and collect my key. It reminded me of the time I was moving flats and I found a company that did removals and was cheaper than everyone else. They charged £10 an hour. I realised what an error I had made when the man turned up. He must have been close to 70 years old. It took him 30 minutes to climb the stairs to our third-floor flat. He had a sweat on just bringing us the empty boxes. It cost a fortune in the end.

Another man took me to my room. I was on the second floor, just where the cleaners congregated. I couldn't believe it. Not the fact that it's where they congregated, but the fact that the hotel had cleaners. It was also clearly a bit of a storage area, as there was a piano outside my door and five TV sets stacked on top of the wardrobe in my room.

I was given the full tour of the room: 'Telephone there. Bathroom here.' He said one or two other things, but I could not hear properly due to the creaking of the floorboards and the noise of the traffic outside. There were two beds separated by a fluorescent tube light on the wall that, once you switched it on, showed up all the damp stains on the walls in their full glory.

I wandered downstairs to meet up with the crew and bumped into the owner outside. I don't know if he was waiting to meet me to check if everything was okay or if he was about to have his piano lessons. He was in his late sixties and looked smart but tired. He was keen to tell me that Michael Palin had stayed here once. If these are the sorts of places Palin stayed in, no wonder he went round the world in 80 days. He was obviously keen to get home as soon as poss.

WINDSOR
HOTEL

The owner then introduced me to his dad, who was in his nineties, at least. I wish I hadn't met him, as it would have made asking for a better room a lot easier.

At 4 p.m. we ordered food. Most of us asked for chicken kebabs, apart from Jan, our cameraman, who is more of a hardened traveller than the rest of us. When we were talking about the worst places we had visited on the coach ride into Cairo and I had said a week in Lanzarote was pretty grim, Jan announced he had done three months in Antarctica.

Finally, at 5.30 p.m. our food was brought to the table. It actually left the kitchen at about 5.22, but all the staff were quite old and shuffled slowly from the kitchen to our table.

Went to bed. Nodded off counting the car horns outside.

THURSDAY 10TH DECEMBER

I met Ahmed this morning. He's a local lad who is an expert on the Pyramids and Egyptian history in general. I was worried that I wouldn't be able to understand him, but his English was better than mine. He may as well have talked Egyptian to me, as the English words he used went right over my head. One of the words he used was 'tintinnabulation', which he told me means a ringing or tinkling sound.

He took me to a mosque. Praying and religion are a big deal in Egypt. Ahmed prays five times a day. I would never keep to it if I lived here. I struggle having my five fruits a day. Religion has never been a big part of my life. I wasn't christened. My mam told me not to tell many people about not being christened, as she said I would be a prime target for witches. To this day I don't know what she meant by that.

Ahmed told me about how he believes that after death you go to a place that is perfect in every way. I said I'm quite happy with my life as it is now. In Ahmed's perfect world he listed not having to use the loo. I told him going to the toilet is one of my favourite parts of my day. It's proper 'me time' where I get to clear my head and think about things with no other disturbances, but after seeing the toilets in Egypt

I can understand why he thinks this way. They are just holes in the ground with a hose for cleaning up.

We then went off to old Cairo to see the market.

The markets are made of up tiny, rough roads, crammed with motorbikes and vans. The stalls themselves sell mostly clothing, cotton and wool. 'How can I take your money?' was a popular shout from most of the store owners as I browsed at the wide selection of tat on offer.

I wanted to buy a gown for Ricky, as he likes to slob out when he's at home. Most days he has his pyjamas on by 5 p.m. I found one pretty quickly, but it took 45 minutes to get the price I wanted. I wish they just had price tags on the products to save the hassle of haggling. If you nipped out for bread and milk you could be gone for hours. The only good thing about this way of buying products is that you would never have that awkward situation when you're a penny or two short and have to ask a shopkeeper to let you off.

We passed a man with crates full of living rabbits and pigeons. They were being sold as food. I've never eaten rabbit but I've never had one as a pet either. I like the way you could get one as a pet though and eat it if you found it too much trouble to look after. I think we'd eat guinea pig too if they weren't so expensive.

The new market was also full of tourist tat. Headscarves, ashtrays, toy camels, plastic pyramids. Even though I had no intention of buying anything when I set out for the market this morning, by the time I left I had purchased a plastic cat and an eagle for me mam. I'm hoping she will find it handy, as she used to have two birds. But one died, so she replaced the dead one with a pebble with one of the dead bird's feathers glued on it so Kes, the other bird, still feels like he has company. I figured that the eagle from the market would make a good replacement.

I stopped to have a cup of tea, but it wasn't very relaxing, as I was constantly hassled by people trying to sell me wallets, glasses, lighters, fags, necklaces, rings and watches.

I witnessed the call to prayer for the first time today. It's something that can't go unnoticed. It's the only time the car horns are drowned out, by the singing of prayers from different parts of the city.

Everything comes to a halt. The only time I experienced something like this was when I worked at a printer's when I was eighteen. All the printers and packers and guillotine workers all stopped at 11 a.m. to listen to 'Our Tune' with Simon Bates on Radio 1.

During the call to prayer each area of the city tries to be louder than the other. Everyone seems to get involved, and they may as well, as there is no escaping it. It makes you think about religion even though you weren't thinking about it, in the same way I'd suddenly fancy an ice-cream when the ice-cream man's chime would sound. The only time I was aware of religion growing up was when *Songs of Praise* came on the telly on a Sunday evening. This was always my cue to go and have my bath for the week ahead.

FRIDAY 11TH DECEMBER

Ricky called last night. He was moaning 'cos I hadn't been in touch. He said he had left loads of messages asking me to call him, but I can't access them, as I've been locked out of my phone after entering the wrong security code more than four times. I told him I could still get texts, but that they cost me around 70p to receive them.

Ahmed took me to the Cairo Museum today. I hated it. It was exactly what I thought it would be like. I've never enjoyed museums. I had also seen a lot of this stuff at the Millennium Dome when there was a King Tut exhibition on. I didn't want to go to that either, but Suzanne, my girlfriend, had arranged for us to see her brother there. It was like the Cairo Museum. Box after box of some old ornament painted gold. Even the corpse of King Tut was in a box. Most people were more impressed by the fact that Jilly Goolden, the wine critic, was having a tour.

Ahmed told me they were expanding the museum so it could fit more tourists inside, but I think this will just encourage the museum people to put even more old boxes on display. It's interesting to see that people had so much clutter even thousands of years ago. The only way to get

WHAT ABOUT EMAIL? YOU GOT EMAIL ON YOUR PHONE?'
YEAH, BUT I DON'T REALLY WANNA ANSWER THEM 'COS THEY'RE LIKE 70 PENCE A TIME OR SOMETHING. I GOT AN EMAIL FROM OXFAM, SAYING IF I WANTED TO BUY SOME GOAT AGAIN. THAT'S COST ME A QUID.
EVEN IF YOU DON'T ANSWER IT OR RETRIEVE IT?
IF IT GETS TO MY PHONE, I'M CHARGED FOR IT. THAT IS IT. SO DON'T START SENDING PICTURES OF YOUR HEAD AND THAT.
YOU'RE AN IDIOT THEN, BECAUSE NOW I'M GONNA SEND YOU A MESSAGE OR AN EMAIL EVERY COUPLE OF MINUTES. WHY DO YOU TELL ME THESE THINGS?
DUNNO.
Gervais

rid of it all was to bury it, and then some archaeologist went and dug it all up. Humans have always been hoarders of tat. I think that's why lofts were invented; it's somewhere to stick all the crap we collect in our lives rather than bury it.

Ahmed explained how many of these items were made for the kings to take into their next lives. This would annoy me if I lived back then and people kept saying, 'Hey, King Karl, I've got you a lovely gift.'

'Have you? Let's have a look.'

'No, it's for when you're dead.'

'Well, I'd rather see it now, if I'm honest.'

'No, it's all wrapped for when you're dead.'

'Will you stop going on about me being dead!'

Surely I should choose what I'm going to be surrounded with in my next life? At least then I'd have time to have a chariot boot sale to get rid of my least favourite things.

I left the museum, as I couldn't take anymore. It was too busy for me, with people pushing and shoving. There were even some people there with babies in prams screaming their heads off. It's not a great place to take a baby, is it?

I noticed there was a KFC outside, so I had one, as I needed something that reminded me of home. I went to place my order, but the girl behind the counter pointed to a note on the counter. The note informed customers that it was a deaf KFC. I was confused. Did this mean they only served deaf people? The girl behind the counter pointed out the menu. There were instructions on how to place an order, which basically involved pointing to the items you wanted, which is the way I normally order my food when I'm abroad anyway. It was quick and easy and quite a good idea, as I was worried that no one would speak English and I wouldn't be able to order a Zinger Meal. It turned out that not speaking meant life was a lot easier.

It was nice to be in a fast food restaurant that didn't have dance music blasting out of the speakers and staff yelling at each other like they are working on the floor of the Stock Exchange. Service was fast and friendly, due to the fact the staff weren't stood around gabbing by the milkshake counter as they normally do in most fast food chains. I saw a man using a videophone to chat to someone using sign language. I've never thought about videophones being used for the deaf. We used to watch a lot of TV with subtitles when I was younger, not 'cos anyone in our family was deaf but 'cos my dad worked nights so we all had to be quiet.

Suzanne called today. She was annoyed, as the boiler was playing up at home and she asked me to sort it before I left. I always have problems with boilers.

Ricky sent me a text that just read: '70p.'

SATURDAY 12TH DECEMBER

I wore the jellabiya that I bought for Ricky last night. I wanted something comfy to relax in so opened it and tried it on. I ended up sleeping in it too. That's the good thing with the local dress – it's so light and comfy. If you lived and worked here you could wear them as pyjamas and then just get up at five to nine, roll out of bed and go to work in them. I think this is the reason you see doctors wearing those light blue pyjamas. Same thing – wear them in bed, and if you're on call and get woken in the night, you can go straight to work.

The only problem with wearing a jellabiya is there is no waistline, so it's impossible to know if you're putting on weight.

Steve called last night. I told him the museum visit was a waste of time. He was annoyed with me but said he had arranged for me to go on a Nile cruise. I can't say I was looking forward to it. I don't like the idea of being trapped in a space with a lot of other people and having no way of leaving. I told Steve it sounded too much like organised fun, but I had no other plans, so I went along with it.

I met the manager. A smart man in his late fifties or early sixties with jet-black dyed hair and mascara, he gave me a quick tour of the massive boat, which was set over three floors. He introduced me to his captains and cooks and then finally to a quiet man whose job it was to dive into the Nile to collect any items that are dropped by the guests. The manager explained how he has dived to collect cameras, watches and jewellery for careless guests. As the manager spoke about other items he has rescued, he stood there all in black with his polo-neck jumper tucked in his trousers like a baddie in one of the *Bourne Identity* films. I asked if I could throw something in the Nile for him to collect later. The manager agreed. I was quite excited about it and went to eat.

The food was good. I had soup to start then turkey and veg, followed by some chocolate cake.

The entertainment I had to sit through consisted of a man who whizzed round on the same spot for fifteen minutes, an Egyptian comedian who had an annoying voice, and a belly dancer. I have never been into this sort of entertainment. I've never been to a strip club or lap-dancing place, so I didn't know what was the best thing to do. Is it more polite to

TRYING RICKY'S JELLABIYA ON FOR SIZE.

IT TURNED OUT I WAS THE ONLY ONE BOOKED ON THE OFFICIAL WINDSOR HOTEL TOUR OF CAIRO.

I WAS TOLD IT WOULD STOP ME HEAD GETTING BURNT.

look at the woman's babajangers and arse, as she dances around shaking everything, or is that pervy? But if I just kept my head down and showed more interest in the turkey on my plate, would that be an insult to her? In the end I did a bit of both.

Once the dancing was over I went to find the manager and his diving friend. I asked if he was sure it was okay for me to throw something in. He said yes, it was, no problem. I asked the manager to check with the diver that he was happy, but the manager just said that if he asks the diver to do something, he does it. I said I wanted to throw my Egyptian mobile phone in the river, but the manager was not happy for me to do that. We ended up agreeing that we would throw in a salt-and-pepper pot. But before we threw it in, he wanted to wrap it in bright pink gaffa tape so it was more visible in the dark, muddy waters of the Nile.

I started to doubt the man's ability to retrieve the salt-and-pepper pot and asked again if the diver was happy to do this for us. The manager spoke on his behalf again and said, 'Of course.'

I was just about to chuck the salt-and-pepper pot when the manager asked me to wait, as the boat needs to stop nearer to the edge where the current of the river is not as strong and the water isn't so deep. It all started to sound like a made-up job. The baddie from *The Bourne Identity* then got off the boat and pointed to where he wanted me to throw it. So, hang on, the diver can only retrieve items if passengers drop them overboard close to the edge where the current is not strong and if they happen to have wrapped them in pink gaffa tape and have let the diver know before dropping them?

An argument then broke out between the manager and the diver. I asked what was wrong. The manager said the diver didn't want to do it. I said it wasn't a problem. I said I wouldn't have asked if he hadn't brought it up. It all put a bit of a dampener on the night. I just think the manager wanted to impress us so much he was willing to throw a member of staff overboard for us.

I said I enjoyed the turkey and left.

Strange night.

SUNDAY 13TH DECEMBER

I went into Cairo today and started to feel a rumble in the belly. I was told there was a toilet in the market. It turned out to be one of those public toilets you have to pay to use, but I didn't mind, as I felt like I was going to get my money's worth the way my belly was feeling.

Trouble was, I didn't have any money on me to give to the old man at the entrance so I just walked past him. I opened the first cubicle to find a traditional Egyptian toilet. I then looked in cubicles two and three with no joy. I was close to using the urinal when cubicle four saved the day. It had a westernised toilet. I rushed in, shut the door and went to sit down when I noticed it wasn't a complete westernised toilet. There was no bloody paper, just a tap with a hose attached. I contemplated giving it a go, but I really can't see how you can clean yourself properly using just a hose. It's the equivalent of trying to wash your car with just a hose. You can't. You'd end up just spraying off the mud flaps. You need a sponge. I turned to leave but couldn't, as there was no bloody handle on the door. I was locked in. I banged on the door but no one came. The man on the front door couldn't hear me banging, probably due to the call to prayer. I'm glad I didn't pay to use the place. It stank, had no toilet paper and no handle. I tried to call Krish or Christian but I had no phone signal. I couldn't even sit down, as there was no toilet seat.

I was there for about ten minutes before someone opened the door to use the toilet. 'No handle,' I said. He was English and told me you have to pay to use the toilet and in return you get the handle. I've never heard anything like it.

'Why doesn't he just sell toilet paper 'cos there's none in there,' I said.

The English guy whipped out a roll from his bag and said he never leaves the hotel without it. 'I keep it in my bum bag.'

Never has the name 'bum bag' been so appropriate.

In he went. I thought about waiting for him to finish and asking if I could borrow a few sheets but I didn't fancy hanging around. Where's an Andrex puppy when you need one?

I rejoined Krish and Christian, who hadn't even noticed I'd been gone for 30 minutes. They had been busy sorting out where we were going to eat.

'What sort of place do you fancy going to?' asked Krish.

I wasn't fussed. 'Just somewhere with toilets,' I said.

I was taken to a fancy place run by a man called George.

George, the owner, told me he would give me a proper traditional taste of Egypt, which worried me. What I'd seen of Egyptian food so far consisted of brown/beige mush that you dip bread into. I'm not a fan of this type of food. Humous and couscous doesn't seem like a proper meal to me.

I used the toilets. They were nice and clean, and had handles and everything. Fancy.

We had to wait for 40-odd minutes before the dishes came to the table. George sat with me whilst I ate. It all looked okay. I just had a mouthful of each and asked questions later. It turned out I'd tried an ox's brain, tongue and eye, and its knob and bollocks. Why would anyone want to eat this? Why would you take a big animal like an ox and eat either end of the beast but not the nice meaty bit in-between?

I suppose I came to Egypt to experience new things, and this was a first for me. I would normally be eating beef and veg on a Tuesday.

My stomach was a lot quieter than it was this morning. I think eating all that odd food had sent it into shock, so before I went to bed I had some Jaffa Cakes I'd brought with me to try and give my stomach something it was used to.

MONDAY 14TH DECEMBER

I met a local man today. His name was Mahmoud. He's 22 years old and makes his living from giving camel rides close to the Pyramids. He invited me round to his house. His front door was open to anyone – even his camel. This seems a bit odd, when I'm not even allowed to keep a cat in my flat due to the rules in my lease.

On my arrival I used the toilet, as I don't think the knob and bollock

EGYPTIAN LUNCH AT PIZZA HUT. 7-INCH CHICKEN SUPREME THAT COMES WITH A SIDE ORDER OF COUSCOUS. I LEFT THE COUSCOUS.

THE CAMEL ISN'T THE ONLY THING THAT LOOKS LIKE IT'S GOT THE HUMP.

30 MINUTES LATER I WAS DOING WHEELIES ON IT.

I had eaten yesterday agreed with me. The toilet seemed to be in use. By a chicken. Mahmoud chased it out. I was going to explain to him that a supermarket I worked at got a warning from Health and Safety for storing Pot Noodles in the staff toilet, but he was struggling to understand my accent as it was. I asked if there was somewhere to wash my hands. He pointed to the sink in the kitchen that was occupied by another chicken, a dead plucked one this time, surrounded by floating carrots and potatoes. He didn't seem to mind that I rinsed my hands over his dinner.

Mahmoud's wife was sat on the kitchen floor cutting potatoes. He explained how he could have four wives but he has just the one at the moment. I asked if he would go for a totally different kind of woman for wife number two. That's how I would do it. I said Snow White had seven midgets and she had every characteristic covered. I wondered if that's how he would choose his wives. He said he's after a stronger one. He said it like he was talking about buying a new car.

That made things a bit awkward, so we left the house to take a camel ride to see the Pyramids.

I've never been on a camel before. They are not very comfy animals to ride. They have a lump in them for a start. Plus I was nervous, as the last time I rode an animal it was a horse at a fête when I was younger and it bolted after a woman put her fag out on its arse. I slid underneath and got kicked in the head.

Mahmoud led us along some pretty busy roads, which didn't make us very popular, as we held the traffic up. We eventually got to the desert but couldn't see much due to the sandstorm. My face was being battered by tiny grains of sand. The way Egyptians like to make money out of everything I'm surprised the tourist board hasn't advertised it as 'A day out in a sandstorm. The ultimate exfoliating experience.'

The plan is to get a closer look tomorrow.

TUESDAY 15TH DECEMBER

I went to the Pyramids site again, this time by van. It was heaving today. We were there early, but we still weren't the first. Coachloads of people were entering. The first thing you see is the Great Sphinx. I'm not a fan of this sort of thing – a lion's body with a human head. A few men were selling models of it. The problem is, the nose is missing from the Sphinx, which means all the models they were selling also had the nose broken off, which just makes it look like a damaged ornament.

I really can't believe what a state the Pyramids are in. I thought they had flat rendered sides, but when you get up close, you see how they are just giant boulders balanced on top of each other, like a massive game of Jenga that has got out of hand. I was told how it was only one of the Pyramids that was a Wonder of the World, even though there are three of them, which is odd, as they all look the same. It's the Great Pyramid that's the official Wonder. I'd be annoyed if I was the builder who built one of the other two if my workmate was getting all the praise for building the 'Great One'. It wouldn't surprise me if it was one of the other builders who knocked the nose off the Sphinx in anger after hearing that news.

I'm sorry to say they didn't look as impressive as they do in the photos I've seen of them. They always look like they are sat in the middle of a desert with nothing around them, but in reality you can see a lot of blocks of flats in the background and the Pizza Hut at the entrance and there is a lot of rubble around them too.

I'm coming back tomorrow to get a tour with a guide.

WEDNESDAY 16TH DECEMBER

We went to see the Pyramids again today. I was meant to meet up with Dr Hawass, who is the main man who looks after the Pyramids site, but he cancelled last-minute, as he was ill, so I got a tour from a man called Aladin. He knows everything there is to know about the Pyramids.

KARL'S FACTS

THERE ARE ACTUALLY 118 PYRAMIDS IN EGYPT, NOT JUST THE THREE EVERYONE TALKS ABOUT.

THE 'GREAT PYRAMID' IS BUILT FROM ABOUT 2.3 MILLION STONE BLOCKS, WEIGHING AN AVERAGE OF 2.5 TO 15 TONNES EACH. IT'S ESTIMATED THAT THE WORKERS WOULD HAVE HAD TO SET A BLOCK EVERY TWO AND A HALF MINUTES.

THE GREAT PYRAMIDS NOW STAND A FULL THREE MILES SOUTH OF THE SPOT WHERE THEY WERE ORIGINALLY BUILT OWING TO THE AMOUNT THAT THE EARTH'S SURFACE HAS SHIFTED IN THE LAST 4,500 YEARS.

EVEN THE BUILDERS HAD TOMBS.
WHEN AN AMERICAN WOMAN WAS THROWN FROM HER HORSE IN GIZA, THE STUMBLING BLOCK TURNED OUT TO BE THE TIP OF AN ENORMOUS BUILDERS' NECROPOLIS, CONTAINING OVER 600 TOMBS.

He loves them, which I find odd 'cos it's not like he's a project manager who comes every day and sees the development of them – they've looked like this for years and they'll not change or be done up.

Aladin began by raving about how the Pyramids were built. I don't enjoy tours like this. They are more like a history lesson. Too many dates were being mentioned. I watched other people who were on tours and their faces also looked disappointed and uncertain – as if they weren't sure what they were meant to do now they'd seen the Pyramids. It's the same sort of feeling you get when you visit someone in hospital and you've had the smalltalk and given them their grapes and you want to leave, but feel like it's too early to go. That's how I felt.

THURSDAY 17TH DECEMBER

I was told by Krish that I'm going to meet a couple today who actually have a use for the Pyramids and that we'll be going inside one finally. It's probably the first time I've been excited since I've been in Egypt.

I went to meet them at their apartment. They were called Andrew and Seija. They run something called Galactic Light and go into the Pyramids quite often, as they explained, 'to connect with the powers of the Cosmos, the Unity or the Christ Grid around the planet, and Atlantis. As the great Pyramid is the focal point of the whole Grid system, it is connected to all sacred monuments around the Globe, as well as to the centre of our Galaxy and the centre of the planet Earth. It is an amazing, magnificent monument transcending space and time.'

That lost me a bit. I just wanted to see what one looked like inside after being disappointed by its lack of kerb appeal.

They had a nice apartment though, with a great view of the Pyramids from the toilet. They taught me how to relax and went through some mantras that we would be doing once we were inside the Pyramid.

All was going quite well, and I was starting to feel quite calm, until the call to prayer began. There was a speaker right outside their living-room window that blasted out the prayer for a good 20 minutes.

CONTRARY TO POPULAR BELIEF, NOT A SINGLE MUMMY HAS BEEN FOUND INSIDE THE PYRAMIDS. MUMMIES HAVE MOSTLY BEEN FOUND IN THE VALLEY OF THE KINGS.

DEBUNKING ANOTHER POPULAR MYTH, THERE ARE NO HIEROGLYPHICS, OR ANY FORM OF WRITING, IN THE GREAT PYRAMID.

This really was the main thing that put me off living in Egypt. I asked Andrew if they were aware of the speakers when they bought the place. I bet the estate agent got them in and out way before any call to prayer took place. After I had learnt a few chants, we had burgers and chips and headed for the Pyramids. It was the end of the day, but we had permission to be there after all the other tourists had left. It was quite eerie. There were no coaches or camels or people selling tat, and it was dark.

The Pyramids

We entered the Pyramids and made our way up some steep steps that Andrew and Seija said were around 150 metres tall. We then had to squeeze through a small gap on our knees to get into a place called the King's Chamber. I'm not that good with guessing sizes but I'd say you could get 50 people in there at a push.

The walls were a pinkish granite that looked impressive, but the stone coffin at the end of the room looked a bit of a mess. The stone looked like it had been cut roughly. It was as if by this point in the construction

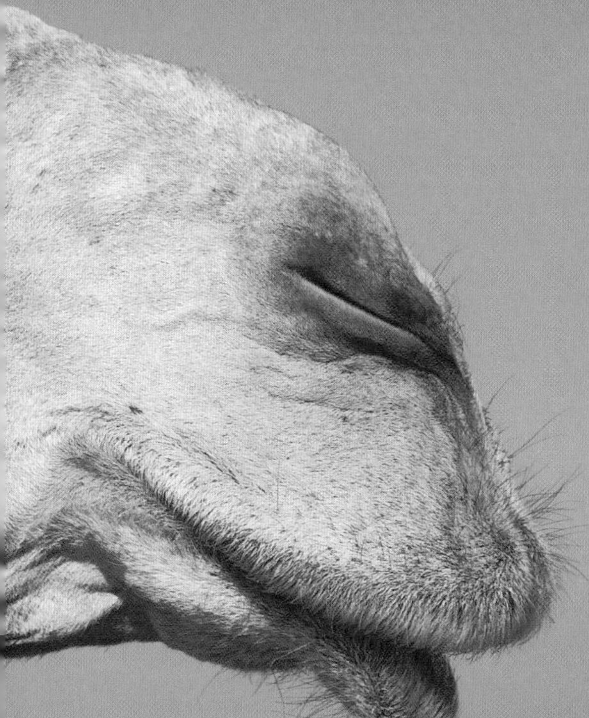

(23 years in) everyone had had enough and rushed to complete it. It's like when you have an extension done on your house and you end up with a snag list of jobs like cracked plaster or loose plug sockets that take longer to get done than the extension itself.

The lid was missing from the stone coffin and so was the mummy.

Andrew and Seija lit some candles, which wasn't that clever, as it was roasting in there already, with no ventilation, and there were no fire escapes, but I didn't say anything, as I didn't want to ruin the mood. They started the mantra. Seija then led me towards the stone coffin and made me get in it. I didn't know this was the plan, but as they led me, they chanted the mantra all the way so I couldn't stop to ask what was happening. It was one of the weirdest experiences of my life. I lay there, as still as I could, in a 4,000-year-old coffin while two strangers chanted over me. I was in there for about five minutes in all, and then Seija and Andrew pulled me out so that Seija could have a go.

Before we left, Seija asked if I felt any cosmic powers. I wanted to say yes, but I hadn't, so I decided to be honest with her. She seemed disappointed by this news.

As weird as it all was, it was an amazing final experience, and it did make my trip to Egypt and the Pyramids all worthwhile. How many people can say they've lain in a candle-lit coffin in the middle of the King's Chamber in one of the Great Pyramids?

It was also the only time I had been in Egypt when I couldn't hear the call to prayer or beeping of car horns or even, as Ahmed would say, any sort of tintinnabulation.

CHAPTER TWO
CHRIST THE REDEEMER

'FEAR NO ANTICLIMAX: CLIMBING THE STATUE IS A STUNNING EXPERIENCE BY DAY, AND NOTHING SHORT OF MIRACULOUS AT NIGHT.'
THE ROUGH GUIDE TO BRAZIL

'I'M PRETTY SURE IF IT WAS PLONKED ON A ROUNDABOUT IN STRETFORD, NEXT TO THE ARNDALE CENTRE, IT WOULDN'T GET A LOOK-IN.' KARL PILKINGTON

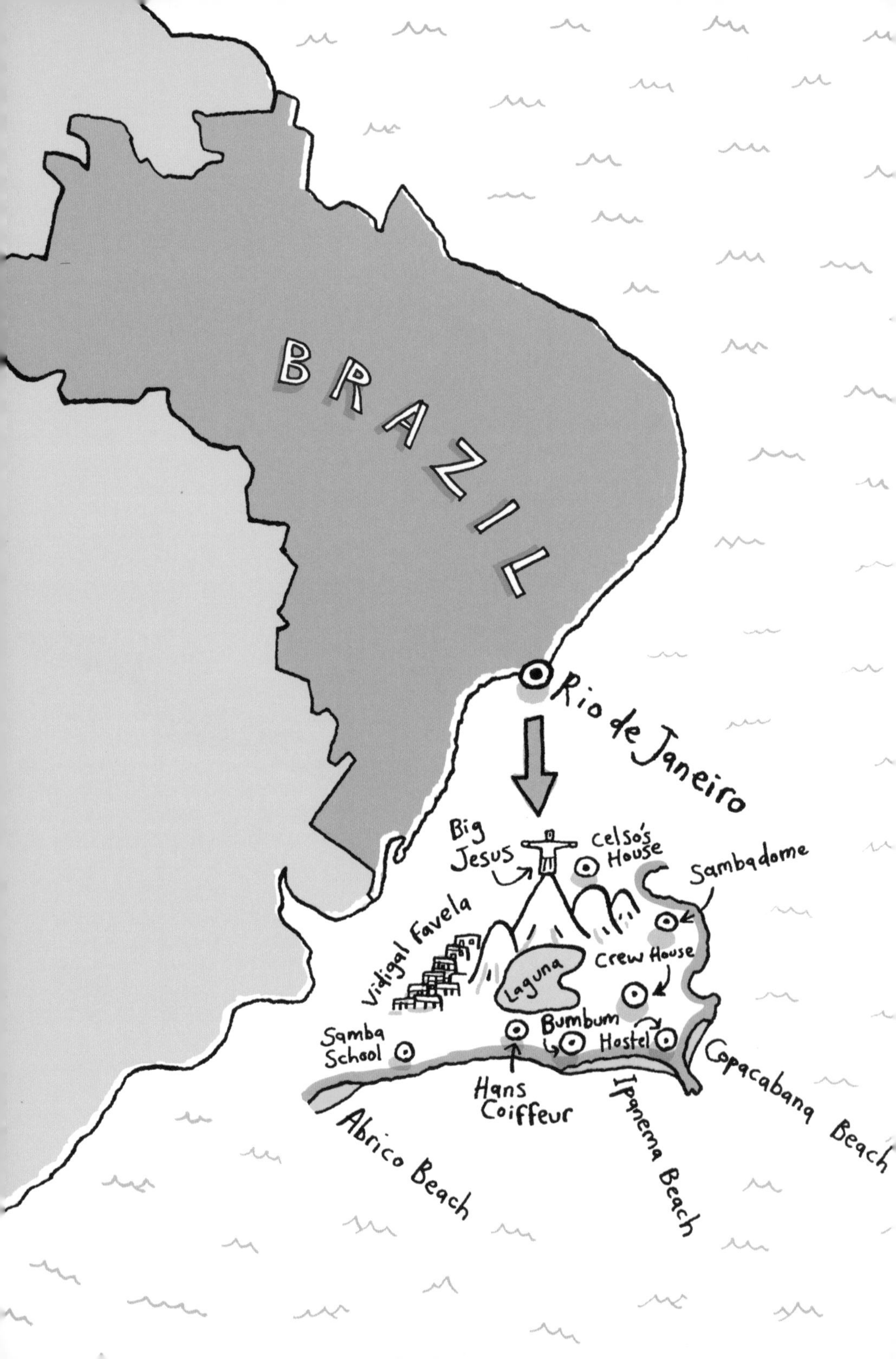
BRAZIL
Rio de Janeiro
Big Jesus
Celso's House
Sambadome
Vidigal Favela
Laguna
Crew House
Samba School
Bumbum
Hostel
Hans Coiffeur
Copacabana Beach
Abrico Beach
Ipanema Beach

TUESDAY 9TH FEBRUARY

The heat as we left the airport this afternoon was mental. I never normally sweat on my head but today I was dripping. Even my ears were sweating. Ricky and Stephen told me that all this travelling was going to bring me new experiences, but sweaty ears were not on my list.

As we drove in the sunshine past the golden sands of Ipanema beach I was doing a bit to camera about how much I thought I was going to enjoy my time in Rio. Then I got to my destination, Hostel Piratas de Ipanema, and my heart sank.

'The rules of the hostel are to clean the kitchen after you've used it,' said Fredericko, the owner, before I'd even put my bags down.

'You'd best go through the rules again with the bloke who used it last then,' I said.

The place was well minging. Half-empty coffee cups, crushed lager cans, unwashed cutlery and half-eaten yoghurts whose friendly bacteria had no doubt been battered by the unfriendly bacteria in this place.

Fredericko was a 46-year-old hippy who was popular with the kids who were hanging around. He had a constant grin on his face, smoked self-rolled fags, and wore bleached jeans which had been cut down into shorts. Shame he couldn't have used some of the bleach in the kitchen rather than on his pants.

He led me on a long, winding walk to where I would be sleeping. We set off down a dark corridor with just one electric fan that was missing its safety guard and was plugged into the wall with bare wires which buzzed dangerously. It reminded me of a previous trip to Alcatraz. Young people in surf shorts and bikinis wandered by. We continued up some dodgy stairs and across a balcony that wobbled until we finally reached my dormitory. It was a dark room with 20 or so beds in it and looked like something out of the film *Annie*. More young people came and went. *I am too old to be here*, I thought to myself. The last time I felt like this was when I finally got round to having swimming lessons at the age of 14. Most of the other kids were a lot younger than me – seven or eight. They thought I was the swimming instructor.

Fredericko stopped at a bunk bed near the window. 'This is the best bed in the hostel,' he told me proudly. I couldn't work out why, until

I met a lad from Hull who explained that if you needed to empty your bladder in the night you could use the window instead of having to walk to the toilets. Not exactly en suite, but I suppose I shouldn't moan.

The mattress was badly stained. Mine looked worse than the others due to the fact that I had daylight showing up stains that you couldn't see on the others. Someone's underpants hung on the end of the bedpost. I was going to move them then I thought they might attract the flies away from me so I left them.

I asked Christian, the show's director, how much it cost to stay here. He said £4 a night. And then Christian said goodbye and left with the rest of the crew to check in to their rented house on Rua Saint Roman.

I decided to try to get an early night. I nodded off to the sound of a kid who looked about nine years old strumming away on a guitar on another bunk bed.

WEDNESDAY 10TH FEBRUARY

I was woken by Christian pointing a camera in my face. It must have been about 7 a.m. I had slept quite well. All the beds now had people in them. Bare legs dangled from the bunks and the odd bollock was hanging out, waiting for any bed bug that was ready for a bit of breakfast in bed. I went to have a wash. The toilets were in worse condition than the kitchen.

We went for breakfast in the back of a supermarket where you pay for your food by its weight. I like this idea. They should put a twist on it and charge people by their body weight. If you're heavy you get charged slightly more, thus helping you to cut down on your food intake. I had some toast and a bit of papaya. This was the first time I'd ever eaten papaya. It was okay, but if someone told me I'd never eat papaya ever again, I wouldn't be bothered. I feel like this about most fruit. There is too much fruit in the world, and I don't like buying a lot of it, as it goes off so quickly. Maybe that's why we're told to eat five portions a day, just to get through the stuff before it turns mouldy.

First things first, I went to see if I could find a cheap hotel 'cos I didn't want to stay another night in Fredericko's hostel. But everywhere was booked up, due to it being carnival season, or at least that's what they told me. It could have been because I looked such an unwashed scruff in my shorts and slept-in T-shirt, and they just didn't want me in their hotel. Madonna and Beyoncé were in town. If Madonna got a glimpse of me in such a state she would probably take pity and adopt me to go with the rest of her collection.

Finally, Christian and Krish said I could stay with the rest of the crew at their house on Rua Saint Roman. That cheered me up.

Christian then told me I was off to meet a local man who would show me around Rio de Janeiro. His name was Celso. He was 47 years old and walked with a stick. This was quite good, as he shuffled along at a slow pace which was perfect in this heat. Within seconds of meeting him he gave me a gift. It was a condom on a string. I opened it to see a series of diagrams of two blokes putting a condom on each other. There was no need for so many drawings of men's knobs. You only need one to demonstrate how to pop it on. I asked Celso if he was gay, but he didn't answer.

Instead he took me to a health spa where he wanted to get his body waxed. Celso invited me into the small cubicle to watch. He told me a lot of men have this done in Rio to get rid of unwanted body hair, so they look better and tan better on the beach. He told me I was too hairy and should have it done too. I said no. Celso told me he has his body done every four months. I read the price list. To have hair removed from the anus would cost approximately eight English pounds. I don't know why anyone would need this doing. Who needs to get such a thorough, all-over body tan? Celso told me how he had his testicles done once and how much it hurt. Maybe this is why he walks with a stick.

After watching for a bit I decided to just get my lower back done. This is my only body hair that does seem rather long. The fact that I have to tuck it into my underpants made me realise that it was probably time to get rid of it.

It hurt – a lot more than I imagined it would. I said, 'No more . . . that's enough,' and went to get up, when Celso told me that the lady had only removed half of it.

With the waxing complete, Celso decided to celebrate by buying some new swimming trunks. He said he wanted to buy me a pair too. I said I didn't want them as I wouldn't wear them. He bought them for me anyway.

The place the crew is staying at is okay. Nothing fancy. It is quite a rough area and police are guarding the street due to a drug raid that happened a few weeks ago, so it feels pretty safe. I have a mattress with no bed and no light in the bathroom, but it's fine compared to Fredericko's hostel.

We have a cook who made some nice chicken and beans for tea.

THURSDAY 11TH FEBRUARY

Celso took me to the beach today. He asked me if I had brought my new swimming trunks. I hadn't. I did try them on last night, but the truth was I didn't like them. I didn't know how to break the news to him.

We had a long walk along the beach whilst chatting about various things – from life in Brazil to how kids these days get away with doing whatever they want. I asked about his leg problem. It was something to do with diabetes. We must have been walking for 50 minutes or so, when he suddenly announced his legs were starting to ache and he wanted to sit down. As I turned to look for a deck chair and umbrella, Celso told me how much he liked this part of the beach. It's known as the gay beach. I said, why don't we walk another five minutes or so to another part of the beach, but he insisted on staying. Everyone seemed to know him. I asked him again if he was gay. He didn't give me a straight answer.

I was feeling pretty uncomfortable and a little bit annoyed that Celso had brought me to this bit of the beach, so I decided to sit in silence as he wriggled about in the deck chair loosening his shirt. A camp friend of his then came over to say hello. He was the gayest man I had ever

ME AND CELSO.

TURN THIS PHOTO UPSIDE DOWN AND IT LOOKS THE SAME.

TRYING TO AVOID THE NUDISTS.

WEIRD INNIT?

met in my life. Every word out of his mouth was gayed up. Imagine if Kenneth Williams had a gayer brother – that was this man. He told me I should loosen up and strip off some of my clothing. I refused. Even if I had wanted to, I wouldn't now. Celso took this as his cue to remove his shorts and show off his new purchase. I wanted to leave. Celso's gay friend said I had great legs and that gay men would love me here in Brazil. He said I had 'great novelty value' but then told me I wasn't his type, as he was into black men. I had nothing to say in reply. He wouldn't give up though. He commented on my hairy legs and said I would be classed as 'a bear' in the gay community. Again, I had little to say.

I remember Ricky telling me once that if a lion could speak English we wouldn't be able to understand anything it said because the lion would have lived such a different life to us. I never understood what he meant until today.

Celso had a massage by a local man called Nelson Mandela. Celso looked like he was loving it.

I asked Celso's friend if Celso was gay. He said it was up to Celso to tell me. I turned to Celso, who now had his legs wrapped round his neck and his head wedged between Nelson Mandela's thighs, but decided that I would ask him some other time.

I left him to it and went back to the apartment.

We had chicken and beans again for tea.

FRIDAY 12TH FEBRUARY

We were up early today. 5 a.m. We were going to the Christ Redeemer. Forget body waxing and sunbathing on gay-only beaches, this is the whole reason I am here.

We set off in a van we had hired while we stayed in Rio. It came with a driver who said his name was Bin Laden. He was a miserable fella. He didn't like anyone touching the air conditioning or having too many bags on board.

We got to the Big Jesus just as the sun was coming up. Christ the Redeemer isn't as big as I'd thought it would be, but being there on our own so early in the day felt quite special. It's so high up you can look down through the clouds over the whole of Rio. God knows how they got him up here. The bloke who delivered my washer/dryer from Comet moaned about getting up to my flat on the third floor. I suppose that's why it could be a Wonder of the World.

I think the other reason that makes Christ the Redeemer one of the Wonders is the setting. I'm pretty sure if it was plonked on a roundabout in Stretford, next to the Arndale Centre, it wouldn't get a look-in.

As the sun came up so did the flying ants. Hundreds of the bloody things. Big ones too. There is no need for ants to have the ability to fly. They are useless when it comes to walking. I've watched them. They tend to cover the same piece of ground time and time again and they are even worse at flying.

We went back down to meet a woman called Dolores who loves the Big Jesus. I had a coconut on the way, which was another first for me. A drink and food all in one. It didn't look like the normal coconuts you win at fairgrounds. There was no hair on it. I don't know if that's how they grow here or if it's that Brazilians hate hair on anything and they've waxed them.

Dolores turned up in a beach buggy and took me back up to the Jesus, pointing out various landmarks as we drove, including the house where Ronnie Biggs used to live.

It was busy at Christ the Redeemer now. It wasn't half as relaxing as it had been earlier this morning. There were hundreds of tourists crammed around the bottom shouting and pushing about. Groups of 20 people being led by a guide who was trying to shout above the other guides who were leading bigger groups. Even the flying ants had sodded off because it had become so crowded. Dolores gave me some facts. It stands at 130 feet and has a chapel in the base. I told her that I like the setting but wasn't really blown away by the statue. As I was saying this, a couple from England passed by. I asked them what they thought. They weren't fans either and said they preferred the statue in Lisbon. Dolores was not happy with this comment and said they didn't know what they were talking about.

She told me that to get a really amazing view I should take a helicopter ride around the statue.

Chicken and beans was served for tea again tonight.

SATURDAY 13TH FEBRUARY

I was woken at 5.10 this morning by Christian. He said we needed to leave by 5.30 for our helicopter ride. I was really struggling. I didn't have much sleep last night. I was woken around 3 a.m. by something outside. I could hear movement in the long weeds. I got up and could see a shadow moving in the crack of the front door. I thought it might have been someone trying to break in. I couldn't ignore it so I decided to just open it and see who it was. It was a chicken. At three in the morning! What is a chicken doing awake at this hour? I don't know if having a chicken walk across your path is some sort of bad omen in Brazil. I took it as bad news anyway, as it looks like we'll be having chicken for tea again.

I grabbed a banana for breakfast and joined Bin Laden and the crew in the van. Forty minutes later I was getting onboard a helicopter. I've never been on one before. I was pretty nervous, as these things don't glide if the engines fail. I sat in the back and was given headphones to wear, and off we went. There was no safety briefing, none of the usual info you get given before take-off. There was nothing to hold on to either. Even in the back of a Ford Fiesta there is a handle on the ceiling to hold on to, but there was nothing here.

We skimmed about 20 feet above the sea along Ipanema and Copacabana beach, which worried me as it meant that even if I survived a crash I would then have to try and swim in the roughest waves I've ever seen. But once I'd got used to the sensation I started to enjoy it. It's one of the best ways to get around. We went round Christ the Redeemer four times, and it looked amazing. Dolores was right. I was getting a great view. I looked down at all the tourists crammed round the bottom like ants (mind you, they could have been ants, knowing what it's like down there).

It definitely looked more impressive from this angle. It looked taller than 130 feet. I felt I had to say how good Jesus looked. Let's face it, while I'm whizzing round his head in a helicopter at high speed, he's the last person I want to slag off. The only thing that didn't look in proportion was his chin. He looked like Jimmy Hill. I put the dodgy chin down to the fact that the sculptor may have rushed it due to all the flying ants, but once back on ground and we could all hear each other clearly enough to hold a proper conversation, Christian told me he hasn't got a big chin, it was meant to be a beard.

I really enjoyed my ride in the helicopter. Probably the best part of the trip so far.

Back at the house and my happy mood disappeared when Steve called and told me that Celso had invited me round to his place so I could find out more about Brazilian life. I said I thought it was a waste of time. I'd spent quite a lot of time with Celso over the last few days and I hadn't learnt that much from him. I still didn't even know if he was gay or not. Steve told me to stop whingeing and to go.

HELLO, MATE. WHAT'S GOING ON? HOW'S IT GOING AT THE HOSTEL?
OH, I LEFT THAT IN THE END. IT DID MY HEAD IN.
YOU LEFT IT?
YEAH, IT WAS RIDICULOUS. I MEAN I'M NOT THAT FUSSY AND THAT, BUT IT WAS MINGING. THERE WERE UNDERPANTS HANGING ON THE END OF MY BED AND THEY WEREN'T EVEN MINE.
WELL, HOW LONG DID YOU LAST IN THERE?
JUST DID A NIGHT.
LIGHTWEIGHT.
IT'S NOT LIGHTWEIGHT, HONESTLY. IT WASN'T EVEN SAFE. I SHOULDN'T HAVE BEEN THERE. I MEAN, I HAD INJECTIONS BEFORE I CAME THAT PROTECT ME FROM BEING BITTEN BY A DIRTY CHIMP, BUT I'M A BIT WORRIED THAT STOPPING THERE I WASN'T PROTECTED. SO A NIGHT WAS ENOUGH.
WELL, I'VE GOT A BIT OF GOOD NEWS FOR YOU.
GO ON.
PACK UP YOUR STUFF BECAUSE I DON'T KNOW WHAT PLACE YOU'RE STAYING IN NOW BUT I'M SURE IT'S NOTHING COMPARED TO WHERE WE'RE GOING TO SEND YOU...YOU'VE ALREADY MET CELSO, YOUR LOCAL GUIDE. LOVELY FELLA. YOU GOT ON WITH HIM, AND THAT'S A TREAT. HE HAS PERSONALLY INVITED YOU TO STAY WITH HIM IN HIS PLACE.

BUT WHAT'S...WHAT'S THE POINT OF THIS, SERIOUSLY? STEVE, DO YOU KNOW HIM? HAVE YOU EVEN SPOKEN TO HIM?
BUT HE'S ALREADY YOUR MATE. YOU DON'T JUST TURN DOWN HOSPITALITY LIKE THAT, NOT WHEN YOU'RE IN ANOTHER COUNTRY.
I WOULDN'T GO THAT FAR.
IF SOMEONE GIVES YOU A BED FOR THE NIGHT, YOU TAKE IT, MY FRIEND.
LISTEN, IF HE'S A MATE, WHY HASN'T HE TOLD ME IF HE'S GAY OR NOT? WHY'S IT SUCH A BIG ISSUE?
BUT WHAT'S THAT GOT TO DO WITH ANYTHING? THAT'S GOT NOTHING TO DO WITH IT, MATE! HE'S JUST OFFERING YOU A BED.
YEAH, BUT THAT'S WHAT WORRIES ME.
HE'S GIVING YOU A BED FOR THE NIGHT, ALRIGHT? YOU'VE ALREADY BEEN WHINGEING ABOUT HOW YOU'RE NOT HAPPY WHERE YOU'RE STAYING. HE'S OFFERED A BED FOR THE NIGHT–NOTHING WRONG WITH THAT.
BUT, HONESTLY, HE'S A RIGHT QUEEN. IT WILL BE LIKE STAYING WITH AUNTY NORA. I BET HE'S GOT ORNAMENTS ALL OVER THE PLACE. I BET EVERYTHING'S GOT A VALANCE ON IT. I BET EVERYTHING'S SORT OF FRILLY EVERYWHERE. I MEAN, IT WOULD BE NICE FOR AN HOUR...

IF YOUR AUNTY NORA INVITED ME TO SLEEP WITH HER, I'D BE ROUND THERE IN A FLASH.
WELL, WHAT AM I DOING WITH HIM? IS IT A NIGHT IN? CAN WE JUST HAVE A GAME OF CARDS OR...?
IT'S JUST A GAME OF CARDS. YOU HAVEN'T GOT TO GO OUT PARTYING.
HONESTLY?
YES.
HAS HE GOT WI-FI?
I DON'T KNOW IF HE'S GOT WI-FI. BUT THAT'S A QUESTION YOU ASK HIM. THAT'S THE FIRST QUESTION THROUGH THE DOOR. 'THANKS, MATE, HAVE YOU GOT WI-FI?' KARL, TREAT IT LIKE A B&B. YOU KNOW YOU DON'T HAVE TO BE SENSITIVE.
AIN'T THAT A GAY TERM? I'VE HEARD THAT B&B IS A GAY TERM FOR BUM AND BOLLOCKS. HONESTLY, I HEARD SOMEONE TALKING ON THE TRAIN, AND HE SAID, 'OH, I'M HAVING A BIT OF B&B TONIGHT – A BIT OF BUM AND BOLLOCKS.'
(LAUGHING) LET US KNOW HOW IT GOES...
YEAH, ALRIGHT. I'LL TALK TO YOU LATER.
ALL THE BEST, MATE.
SEE YA.

We got the Metro. It was chaos. People were pushing and shoving to get on the train worse than they do in London. It took an hour to get there. When we got off I was surprised to see the sort of area Celso lived in. He came across as a man who would have quite a fancy lifestyle. In reality, his place was a flat in a five-storey block. Old people sat outside playing dominoes. Kids played football and two toothless women stood chatting at a cola stand. It wasn't really grim, in fact it reminded me a bit of the estate I grew up on, except the old and young people seem to mix here.

'*Hiiiiiii*', shouted a camp voice. It was Celso, topless and waving a hanky between the security bars of his front window.

We made our way up the stairs, avoiding a snappy dog whose owner sat behind a locked gate staring at us.

I knocked on Celso's door. It was covered in posters for various carnival events and an advert for condoms. I wondered if these were put up for visitors to read to pass the time it took for Celso to shuffle his way to his front door. Eventually, he opened the door wearing just his silk boxer shorts and flip-flops. He had been spraying his plants and was moaning how hot it was. He seemed quieter and less confident today.

It was a tiny flat. About the size of one I used to live in, except it was cluttered, which made it feel even smaller. There was so much in the room my eyes didn't know what to focus on.

He offered me a glass of nut juice. Of all the things to get juice out of, I can't think of anything less juicy. I was still getting my head round the fact that carrot juice existed, now nut juice.

I told Celso that I found it odd that I'd only known him for a few days and yet I was welcomed into his flat. Celso explained that it is a Brazilian tradition that if you are invited to stay over it is rude to refuse. I could tell by his face that he was serious – more serious than the way he looked whilst trying on the trunks in the swimwear shop. He said I must stay in his bed. I'm normally quite good at nipping situations like this in the bud, but he kept going on about Brazilian tradition and how he would be upset if I didn't stay. So, in the end, I agreed.

I was left with Krish in the lounge while Christian went with Celso into his bedroom to interview him. I browsed through his CDs.

Dinah Washington, Dionne Warwick and Bette Midler. A lot different from the rap music that was blasting from the cars outside.

Forty-five minutes later Celso came into the living room wearing a dress, wig and make-up. I told him he reminded me of my Aunty Nora. Other than the eye make-up being a bit over the top, he looked quite good. He said I should now call him Lorna Washington. He was a drag queen. He had to go off to do a birthday party and a wedding. I asked him if this meant he was gay. He said something along the lines of 'What do you think honey?' Still not a straight answer.

Celso then told me to make myself feel at home. He told me to help myself to more nut juice. He left me his phone number, and showed me how the TV remote worked and gave me a selection of DVDs to watch, including *My Fair Lady*. It reminded me of times when my mam would go out when I was younger and give me money to get some toffees from the off-licence and tell me not to answer the door to anyone.

His cab came. I watched through the bars on his window as Lorna Washington went to work under the watchful gaze of his neighbours.

It was warm in his flat. A fan hung from the ceiling but made little difference. I sat wondering if it was part of Brazilian tradition to invite someone to stay but then fuck off out for the evening. Seems a bit odd to me. I couldn't get the DVD to work so watched a little bit of TV. I then went to the toilet where I disturbed four massive cockroaches. I can't stand those things. They move too quickly for my liking. There was also so much clutter that it made it easy for them to hide. I felt itchy. I then noticed a few bites on my legs. I think I found a new species on me that evening.

It's hard to explain the amount of clutter there was, but put it this way, it was difficult to see a space to put anything down on any surface due to stuff. I don't know why Celso kept some of the items, as I couldn't work out what some of the things were. Christian actually lost his phone in there and couldn't find it. Finally I snapped. I decided I couldn't stay any longer. I don't like being in tight spaces. The more I looked around, the more I got worked up. Plus the cockroaches didn't help. I found a dead one in the kitchen. The fact that I've heard cockroaches are one of the toughest creatures on planet earth – they can survive a nuclear attack and live for a week without a head –

KARL'S FACTS

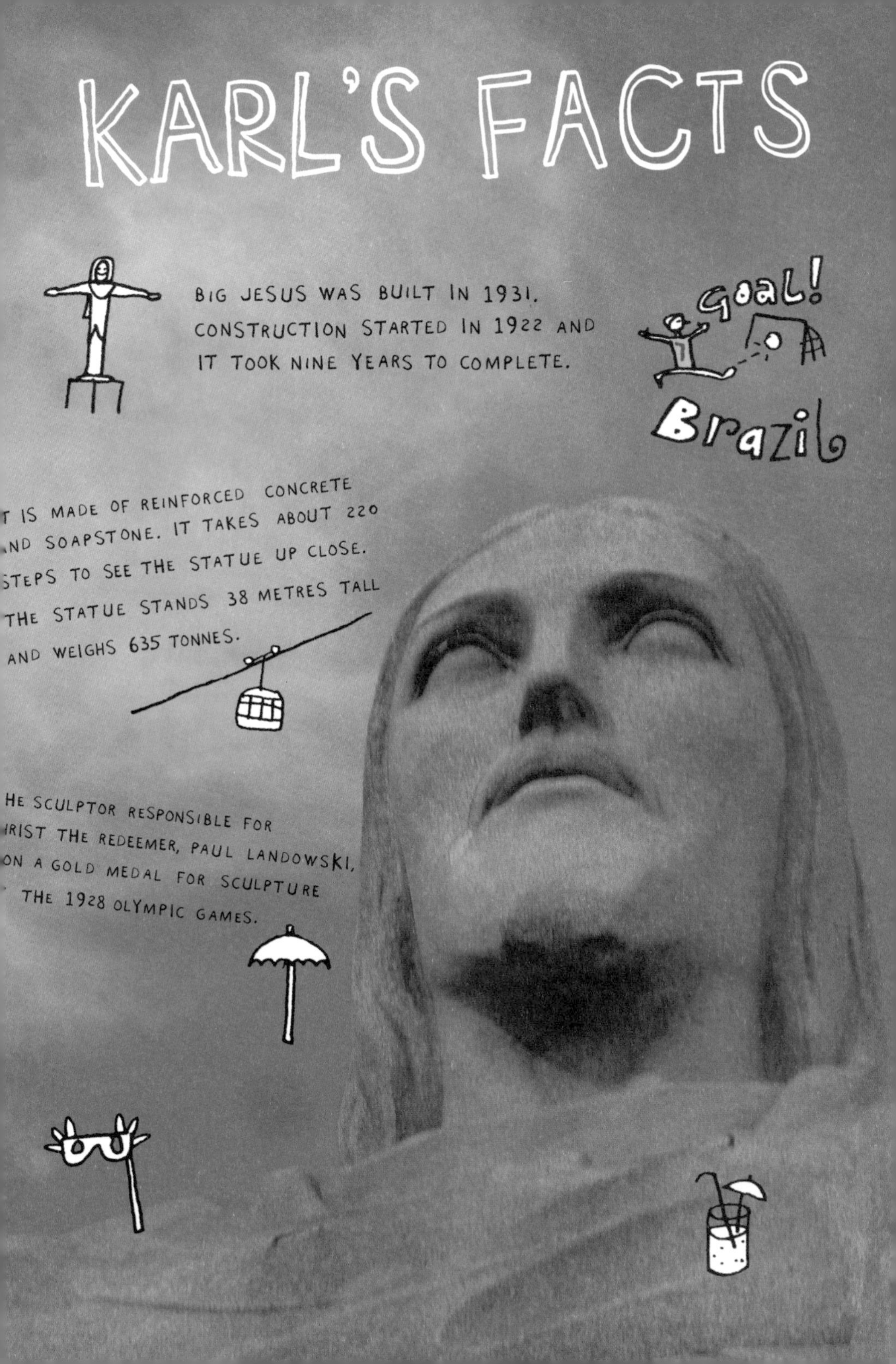

BIG JESUS WAS BUILT IN 1931. CONSTRUCTION STARTED IN 1922 AND IT TOOK NINE YEARS TO COMPLETE.

T IS MADE OF REINFORCED CONCRETE
ND SOAPSTONE. IT TAKES ABOUT 220
STEPS TO SEE THE STATUE UP CLOSE.

THE STATUE STANDS 38 METRES TALL AND WEIGHS 635 TONNES.

HE SCULPTOR RESPONSIBLE FOR
IRIST THE REDEEMER, PAUL LANDOWSKI,
ON A GOLD MEDAL FOR SCULPTURE
THE 1928 OLYMPIC GAMES.

yet this one couldn't survive in Celso's place made me realise it wasn't healthy for me to stay there.

It was 1.30 a.m. I thought it would be rude to just leave, so I called Celso and told him it was too hot and noisy to stay. He didn't sound that disappointed.

I was back in my own bed at 2.45 a.m.

SUNDAY 14TH FEBRUARY

I woke up this morning feeling guilty about leaving Celso's place. But then it occurred to me that maybe Celso had only invited me round 'cos he wanted me there for security whilst he was out working. Krish and Christian agreed that it was best that we'd left, so I didn't feel too bad.

We went to a block party today. It was the worst party I have ever been to. Aimlessly walking about as people blew whistles and made noise with air horns. I would normally avoid things like this. I remember not enjoying the Queen's Jubilee street party when I was a kid. Scruffy Sandra ate loads of the trifle me mam had made and didn't bring anything to the party. This block party was worse. There was no trifle whatsoever. People just stood around looking a bit bewildered. It was like wandering amongst the staff of an office block who are stood on the street 'cos a fire alarm has gone off. At least the noise from a fire alarm is necessary. The noise these lot were making was just noise pollution. There was a bloke walking around dressed as a pink poodle in some pants that left his arse exposed. Maybe this isn't a block party and this is an office block on fire and he's singed his arse. He got annoyed when strangers pinched it.

I saw Celso's gay friend. He was with another man. I'm not sure if it was his boyfriend as he wasn't black.

I told Krish that I'd had enough. We went back home.

I didn't really enjoy today. I had some Toblerone to cheer me up.

I said it would be nice to go to a quiet beach to get away from all the noise. Krish said he knew where a nice quiet beach was but we'd have to get up early to get there. I agreed.

We ate chicken and beans again. Christian said he would speak to our fixer about getting the cook to do something different for tomorrow.

MONDAY 15TH FEBRUARY

Got up at 5.20 this morning to go to the quiet beach. Even Ipanema and Copacabana beach would be quiet at this time of the day. Krish said it would take an hour to drive to our destination. Bin Laden seemed miserable. I don't think he likes an early start.

Unsurprisingly we were the first on the beach, apart from a man who was serving drinks under a canopy. We found a nice patch and got comfortable. I was sat enjoying the view when I was disturbed by a banging noise. I turned and saw the man under the canopy smashing ice. I also noticed he had his knob out.

I told Krish, and he didn't seem that surprised. It was a bloody nudist beach. I've never understood why people like to do this, least of all at 7.30 a.m. It wasn't that hot yet, as the sun hadn't come up properly. He still had his T-shirt on, so why couldn't he keep his shorts on? I watched, as he kept bending down to pick up more ice. It's like he was trying to wind me up. Every time he bent down his arse and balls swung in my direction. He looked like the back end of a bulldog.

More fellas turned up, chatting with their arms folded and their knobs and bollocks out. There were a few women too. Two large ladies in their late forties sat behind me. I had no idea if they were completely nude because their breasts hung that low they covered the more private areas.

A man came over and gave me a leaflet listing the rules of the beach. It had lots of useful instructions, including advice on what men should do if they had a moment of excitement. The leaflet suggested sitting down as soon as possible or entering the sea and staying there until the excitement goes away. With the women I had on view, I don't think there was any chance of any of that.

Half an hour later, the man who gave me the leaflet came back and asked me to get nude or leave. I said, 'I'll leave, thank you very much.'

ABRICÓ NATURISTS ASSOCIATION – ANA
Brazilian Federation of Naturism – FBrN

Abricó Nude Beach
Welcome to Rio de Janeiro's First Nude Beach

Resolution 64/94 Secretary of Environment Rio de Janeiro
Decision of the Tribune of Justice Rio de Janeiro 30 September 2003
City law number 4059 of may, 18th, 2005

Code of Ethics*

Naturism is a way of life in harmony with nature and characterized by the practice of nudism in a group setting with the intention of encouraging self-respect, respect for others and respect for the environment.
International Nudism Federation – INF

The following are prohibited:

1) Practicing sexual or obscene acts;
2) Acting in a disrespectful or aggressive manner toward anyone, at any time, for any reason;
3) Aggressively or passively make fellow nudists and other beach goers feel uncomfortable;
4) Playing sports outside of designate areas;
5) Satisfying biological needs in public areas;
6) Leaving trash behind when leaving the beach;
7) Using, carrying or selling any substance whatsoever which can be construed by law to be an illicit drug or other illegal object or substance;
8) Film, record or video nudists (by any means, at any distance) without the express permission of all those in focus.

* This code of ethics is the same for any other municipal beach in Rio de Janeiro with the exception of number 8). All rules will be enforced by the appropriate civil authorities, members of the Abricó Naturists Association – ANA and is applicable for all nudists and non-nudists while at this beach.

OBS:
Nude means uncovered genitals. Topless is not considered nude.

In this area everybody should be nude. Policemen, security professionals, life guards, fishermen with fishing equipment going to fish on the rocks and divers who will not stay on the beach may enter and stay dressed inside the second area while passing through or on duty. Teenagers from 13 y.o. should respect all rules.

On all other days, clothing is optional on Abricó Nude Beach until further notice. All are welcome to Abricó Nude Beach. Please follow the rules. If you see anyone breaking any of these rules, please notify any association member, the police or the lifeguards.

Abricó Nude Beach is restricted to the sand, water and rocks directly adjacent to its beach area, which starts at the signs at its entrance.

Tips

Avoid aggressive or unfriendly behavior and expressions, as well as, loud screaming, loud conversations, jam sessions and loud music. People who look for out-of-the-way nude beaches like Abricó are normally interested in enjoying quiet seclusion and communion with nature.

Avoid staring at others for whatever reason. Respect others and respect their spatial requirements.

If male beach goers should become excited and reach an erection, remain discreet about it and **avoid** exhibitionist behaviors. Remain seated or go to the water until this condition passes. Penis erection is natural but provoking or exhibiting oneself in this state is not appropriate at this beach.

Always apply sun block especially where you usually wear clothes, including the genital areas. Be discrete but do not feel embarrassed about this. Avoid handling genital parts.

Remember, on a nude beach you attract more attention and criticism if you keep your clothes on. So, take off your clothes as soon as you arrive and blend in.

Cigarette butts and straws are trash and should be taken to the orange trashcans provided on the beach or back home.

Members of the Abricó Naturists Association – ANA are always present on the beach on Saturdays, Sundays and holidays. Look for us and come say hello!

ASSOCIAÇÃO NATURISTA DE ABRICÓ
ANA

President: Pedro Ribeiro
Tel: (21) 2542 9807 / (21)9441-5652
E-mail: anabrico@anabrico.com
Site: www.anabrico.com
Newsletter Website: www.jornalolhonu.com
Brazilian Nudist Federation Website: www.fbrn.com.br
Abricó call in the beach: (21) 8639 0368

PREFEITURA
MEIO AMBIENTE

"NUDITY IS A NATURAL HUMAN STATE: NUDE IS SIMPLY NATURAL!"

I couldn't go far though. Krish and Christian and Jan (cameraman) and Freddie (soundman) had to get more pictures for the telly programme.

They were told they would have to be naked if they wished to carry on filming. So they got naked. It was the first time I felt like I got my own back on them for all the stuff they've been putting me through.

Back at the house Krish told us we were going to a favela tomorrow. They normally liked to keep everything a secret up until it happened, but Krish said he had to tell me about this, as the favelas are the roughest parts of town where drugs and guns rule and he would have to give us a Health and Safety briefing. What's going on? I didn't come to Brazil for danger. Krish was suddenly acting all serious, which was hard to handle when earlier today I'd seen him walk about a beach with his knob out.

A different cook was cooking tonight. She made spicy beef with beans.

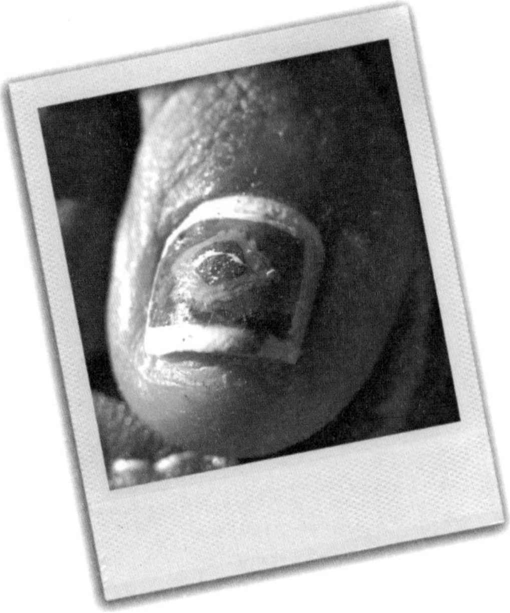

SAUDADE

TUESDAY 16TH FEBRUARY

I got up 30 minutes earlier than I needed to today as I wanted a ham toasty for breakfast and the toasty machine takes 20 minutes to warm up. I thought about how this could be my last ever meal as we were going to a favela today. In that context I suppose I shouldn't complain about having to wait for the toaster to warm up.

Over breakfast there was a lot of talk about the film *City of God*. Apparently, the favela we were going to was similar to the one that was in the film. Everyone but me had seen the movie. I seemed to remember hearing about it, but was put off 'cos I heard it had subtitles and I don't like films with subtitles. I may as well read the book.

Krish explained that we would have to sit on the back of a motorbike, as the favelas are not really suitable for vans. It's the first time Bin Laden looked happy the whole time I've been here. Easy day for him. So I got on the back of a big bike that was being ridden by a bloke called Johnny who was a local from the favela. We darted round corners and went down alleyways. As we whizzed through the streets I saw guns on every corner.

Big ones too. The crew followed behind. At certain points we were told not to film, as the gang leaders did not want to be captured on film. We had to point the cameras down to the ground so they could see we were not secretly filming.

Finally the bikes pulled up, and I was introduced to a man called Henrique. He had no weapons. He was not a gang leader. He was going to teach me a Brazilian dance called the samba.

Henrique took me to a derelict building where for two hours he taught me various moves. I showed him a few of my own moves, which he described as 'crap'. Bit harsh, I thought. The first 30 minutes seemed like fun, and I wasn't taking it too seriously, until Henrique told me I would be dancing in the Rio Carnival. Even though I'm not that well travelled I had heard of this and started to feel worried. I trained harder now. Henrique told me 4,000 people would be watching, and it was a big deal for the team I would be dancing with. They had been training all year and were hoping to impress the judges enough to go up a league in the main competition.

But the harder I tried, the more frustrated I became. There was too much to remember. In the end Henrique suggested we stop for food.

We went to a local café. The food was really, really tasty, but then I guess if your customers are coming in with grenades, machine guns and rocket launchers you wouldn't want to serve them mush.

After eating we trained some more and Henrique gave me a costume I would have to wear. It was a ridiculous thing, an Andy Pandy-style outfit with blue feathers. It made me look gormless, but Henrique told me that was the least of my worries. He told me to remember to smile. This isn't something I do a lot. I do smile, but not as much as some people. Even when I'm happy inside, my face does not always show it.

We trained for another hour or so, then stopped, as Henrique was tired due to the fact he'd been dancing at the carnival for the last three days. I was knackered after three hours. There is nothing I can do about my fitness though. There's not time, so I'll just make sure I try to get an early night and eat well.

Beef and beans again tonight. I just had beef, as I am now sick of beans.

Before I went to bed I practised my dancing in my room and then did some smiling in the bathroom mirror. It didn't look very natural to me, but then I couldn't see myself very clearly due to the fact that we had no electricity in the toilet.

WEDNESDAY 17TH FEBRUARY

Carnival day. I felt more worried about having to dance in front of a large crowd today than I did this time yesterday when I was heading into the druggy, gun-ridden favela.

We were at the carnival site for 1 p.m., but when I arrived, I was told I wouldn't be dancing until 8.45. I was already dressed in my big, feathered Andy Pandy outfit and had no other clothes with me, so I just sat in the van with Bin Laden while everyone else went to set up the camera equipment. It was a long afternoon. Bin Laden and I didn't

A SURPRISE VISIT FROM MY AUNTY NORA.

UNBELIEVABLE.
I WEAR MORE WHEN I GO TO BED.

A TRADITIONAL BRAZILIAN FUNERAL.

speak due to our language barrier. Mind you, he's such a miserable sod, it wouldn't surprise me if he had good English but just didn't want to chat to me.

I fell asleep for an hour or so until Krish and Christian woke me and said Henrique was in the parade close by. We tracked him down, and he gave me a few more moves that were easier to remember than the stuff he taught me yesterday. He then said if I forgot my moves to just use lots of energy and remember to smile a lot.

We had a Bob's Burger – Brazil's equivalent of McDonald's – and after that everything is a bit of a blur. I don't remember much about what happened from then until the start of the parade. Henrique told me where to stand and repeated his tips about 'giving off energy'. He kept reminding me to smile. Fireworks exploded, and so did my stomach. I don't know if it was my nerves or the Bob's Burger I'd eaten earlier, so I quickly used a toilet, as I didn't like the idea of getting halfway down the parade and doing a Paula Radcliffe in front of 4,000 spectators and half as many judges

I found a toilet and was charged two reals (about 60p) to use it. It was grim. I sat on the dirty toilet and saw myself in the mirror hanging on the back of the door. There I was wearing the Andy Pandy outfit and a stupid gormless hat. How did it come to this?

I didn't have time to worry though, as the owner of the loo was banging on the door. I hate being rushed on the toilet. She banged again. I got outside where the woman was pointing at the price on the door and repeating 'Two moments . . . two moments'. Sixty pence only buys two minutes of usage. Maybe I should have had the beans last night. The way them things go through you, I could have saved myself 30p.

I made my way through the crowds to the start of the parade. It was busy now. Henrique put me with an oldies' group. There was a woman wearing glasses who looked like Jim Bowen off *Bullseye*. It didn't really help me being put with the old ones though, as it just added to the pressure. I suddenly thought, if I can't keep up with this lot, that'll really knock my confidence.

And then the drums sounded and we were off. I was in the zone and gave it my best shot.

Fifty-five minutes later I crossed the finishing line. I haven't felt that knackered for years. I had a huge blister on my foot, and felt really dizzy and weak but glad it was all over.

Henrique looked pleased with me, which was good. I asked him if the class would be going up a league, but he said he wouldn't know for a few days.

THURSDAY 18TH FEBRUARY

We went home today.

I left for the airport at 1.30 p.m. and flew home via Lisbon, as there was no direct flight. I tried to look out of the plane window to see if I could see the statue that the English couple I'd met said was better than Christ the Redeemer, but it was too cloudy. I was back at home in London for 12 p.m.

I preferred Christ the Redeemer to the Pyramids. 1–0 to Brazil.

Christian just told me that Henrique's dance team missed out on promotion by 0.2 points.

CORREIO

CORREIO

CORREIO

CORREIO

CORREIO

CHAPTER THREE

THE TAJ MAHAL

'THE GATEWAY THROUGH WHICH ALL DREAMS MUST PASS.' RUDYARD KIPLING

'IT'S WEIRD HOW IT IS CLASSED AS ONE OF THE MODERN WONDERS OF THE WORLD. YOU WOULDN'T THINK SO BY THE SURROUNDINGS. IF IT WAS ON ONE OF THEM PROPERTY PROGRAMMES, THE POTENTIAL BUYERS WOULD SAY, "IF YOU COULD PICK IT UP AND PUT IT SOMEWHERE NICER WE'D BUY IT." IT REALLY SHOULDN'T HAVE BEEN BUILT HERE.' KARL PILKINGTON

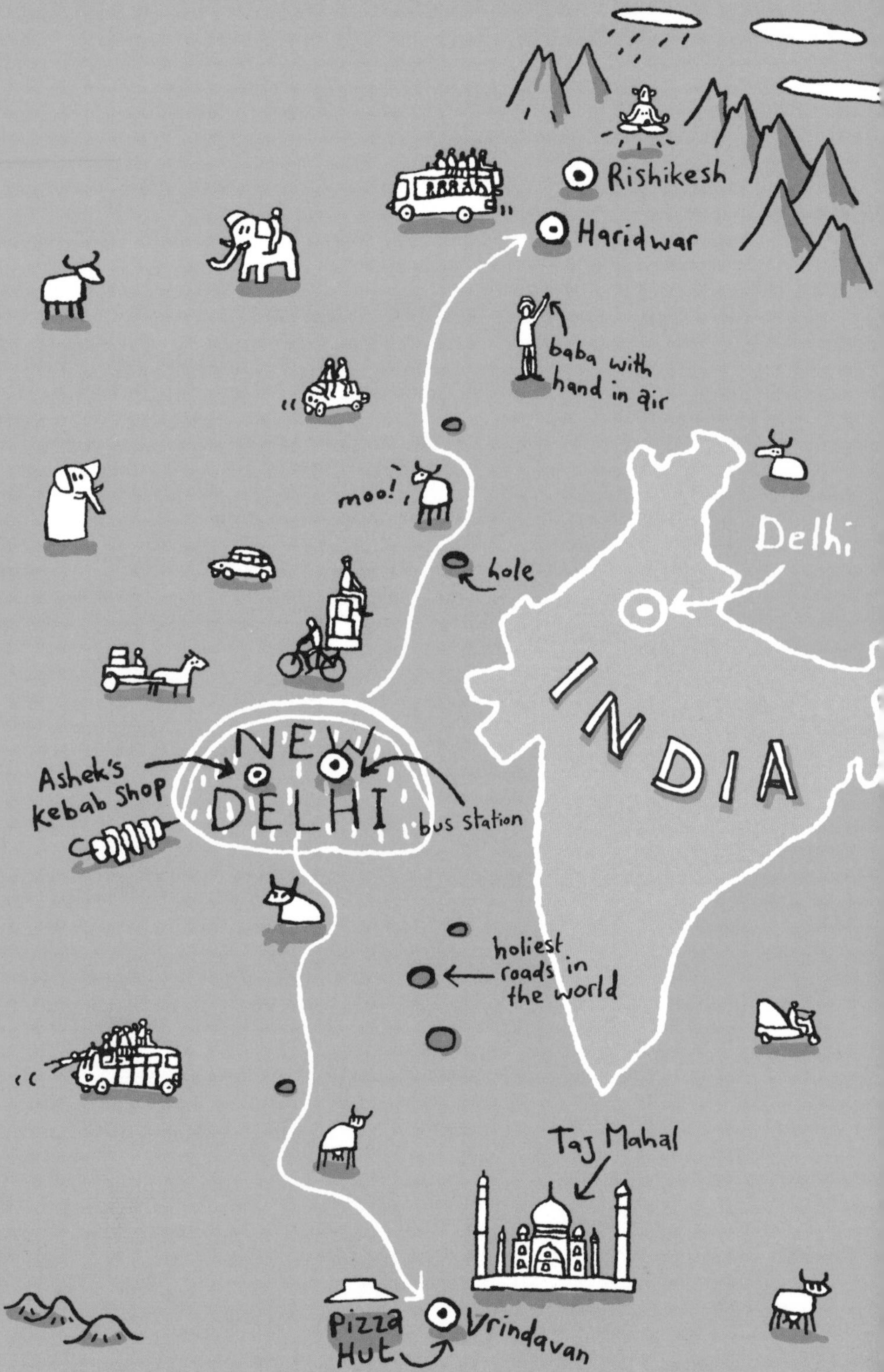

Rishikesh
Haridwar
baba with hand in air
moo!
hole
Delhi
INDIA
NEW DELHI
Ashek's kebab Shop
bus station
holiest roads in the world
Taj Mahal
Pizza Hut
Vrindavan

The Taj Mahal

THURSDAY 25TH FEBRUARY

When I was getting ready for my trip to India today, Luke the producer gave me a pack of 28 adult nappies. Not the usual going-away gift, is it? I hadn't planned on needing these in my life – well, not at least until I was well into my eighties – but I packed two of them just in case.

Everyone I talk to about India has mentioned 'Delhi Belly'. It's assumed that if you visit India you will get ill. I think it's the only place in the world that has this reputation. It must be a great place to open a restaurant. There's no comeback if a customer gets the shits from eating your food – except, well, 'Welcome to India'. It's as if it is on the menu: starter, main course, pudding, coffee and then the shits.

Luke said we might have some days where we are far from a loo, so if I'm not feeling well the adult nappy might come in handy. I don't like the idea. I worry that if I get used to the fact that I can empty my bowels anywhere I like then they might get lazy and start emptying themselves when I get back home and I'm no longer wearing a nappy.

I was given some friendly bacteria sachets to take too. They are supposed to make my stomach stronger, but I imagine the bad bacteria in India will batter this stuff in no time. In the end I packed more drugs to bung me up than clothes to wear.

FRIDAY 26TH FEBRUARY

I had a first-class seat on the flight to New Delhi. I think they call it 'New' Delhi to give the impression things have changed – a bit like them washing powder ads that say 'New and Improved'.

The flight was delayed for five hours. Reclining in the first-class lounge, it's the only time I've ever been happy to hear about a delay. But I suppose it's only delaying the inevitable. I imagine it's like having a power cut when you're due to go on the electric chair.

SATURDAY 27TH FEBRUARY

It took seven hours to get to Gandhi International Airport. I'm not sure how Gandhi would feel about having an airport named after him. It's not that special, is it? I don't know much about Gandhi other than he helped the poor, much like Bob Geldof and Lenny Henry did in the 1980s. I wonder, if Gandhi was around now, if his reputation would be as good, or if some tabloid would have found some dirt on him. Luke told me he took care of a group of poor people called 'the untouchables' – or Dalits. These people were considered the lowest of the low – shit shovellers, really. I wonder if the place was tidier back then when there were more shit shovellers? There is rubbish everywhere. I suppose when people just ate fruit and meat then everything either was eaten by animals or wasted away, but since we now have plastic bottles and crisp packets and polystyrene there are piles of it everywhere. I haven't noticed any bins anywhere yet.

We drove into Delhi in a van with a local driver. The sounds were the same as Egypt, and the road safety was similar too. Car horns beeped constantly. I'm not sure what the point of a horn is when everyone is using them at the same time. It's impossible to know if the horn is aimed at you. Large families stuffed themselves into tiny cars. Groups of four wobbled around on single mopeds wearing no helmets. The buses were crammed too. In a country with a population of over one billion, I wondered what the chances were of getting a seat on a bus in rush hour. In one of the buses we overtook I was sure even the driver was standing.

Nothing here seems finished. Roads are dug up, pavements half laid. I saw a wall that was still being built already being painted.

I passed a market where skinned chickens lay out on makeshift tables covered in flies. Not so much served as chicken 'n' chips but chicken with shits. I know I'm going to get ill – it's just a matter of how quickly.

Every time we stopped at a junction, someone would tap on the window of the van for money. I didn't have any. I gave one man whose legs were all twisted my bottle of Coke. Our driver went mad at me and told me not to give them anything.

It was interesting sat in the van looking out on all the madness, but I knew that at some point the van would pull up and I would have to step out into this crazy place.

CAMERA ON HIRE
CAMERA REPAIRES
DIGITAL CAMERA
MEMORY CARDS

Eventually we did pull up, and Luke told me to wait at a busy junction for a local lad called Ashek who would be picking me up on a rickshaw. It was like Piccadilly Circus – completely mental. It was a spot where three roads went into one. There were all sorts of modes of transport. I saw a man on an elephant. I don't understand why anyone would want one of these to get around on. There was only one man sat on the top. I wondered if local people got annoyed with people who ride elephants. Is it the same as people in London getting annoyed with owners of those big 4x4 gas-guzzlers that block up the city? Like a 4x4, these elephants must take quite a bit of fuel to feed and yet they only carry one bloke.

There were donkeys, horses, goats and pigs. A zebra crossing in India is, literally, a zebra crossing. There was a man on a pushbike carrying the biggest load I have ever seen on a bicycle. It totally covered the bike, and underneath it the owner was desperately struggling to pedal. And to make matters worse he had a man sat on top of the load. Ridiculous. If this man got on a plane, God knows what he would class as hand luggage. He wasn't alone though. Another pushbike passed us carrying a pile of flattened cardboard that must have been 15 feet high. They were like human ants – unbelievably strong. It made me feel bad about moaning about the weight of my old Sunday paper round, when all the extra supplements used to weigh my bag down.

There were hundreds of rickshaws in this area, which didn't help, as each one stopped to see if I needed a lift, and I wasn't sure if any of them were Ashek. After 40 minutes Ashek finally turned up. He said he was sorry for being late but that he hadn't been well. He looked pretty tired for a young fella. His English wasn't great, but it was better than my Indian.

Ashek drove me around, and I took in even more depressing sights. People on every street corner seemed to have an arm or a foot or a leg missing. He took me to meet his boss, who owned all the rickshaws. He said he wanted to train me to ride one. I've always been good on bikes so I was happy to give it a go. He said he would train me at a place called the dust bowl. It was a large, open area with a little bit of grass but mainly bald, dusty ground. The grass to hardened soil ratio was probably the same as the hair to skin ratio on my head.

Kids played cricket and football. Families sat around chatting while some poorer people lay around and sniffed glue.

I gave the cycling a go on the rickshaw and I thought I was quite good, but the boss said he would have to fail me because I rode too fast and didn't smile enough. Smiling has never come naturally to me, plus India isn't a place you want to smile, mainly 'cos it's best to keep your mouth shut so the flies can't get in.

Ashek invited me to his home, where he also works in the evening selling chicken kebabs. We made our way down tiny, narrow streets lined with rotting meat, guts, blood and chicken carcasses. The deeper we went, the more the fly population increased. When I was a kid, we had a fly in our house that hung around so often it became part of the family. My mam named it Harry the House Fly. She even put its name down on the form when I was doing a sponsored walk. I used to think it was happy living in our house, but I suppose India is the ultimate place for a fly. These dirty lanes were like an All You Can Eat drive-through for bluebottles.

Everywhere we walked we got plenty of attention due to the camera and sound men. The locals love to get on camera. I walked down the street feeling like the Pied Piper. At one point I must have had about 30 to 40 people surrounding me. I'd seen footage of Gandhi surrounded like this and always thought it was because he was very popular, but now I wonder if it was just because he had a camera crew with him.

We got to Ashek's place. It was tiny. I used to live in a really, really small place that was so small everything was en suite. I could have a bath, wash up and watch telly all at the same time, but this place was ridiculously small. It was one room with a shutter for an entrance and no windows. Basically, it was a small garage. At a guess I'd say it was 20 feet by 6 feet, and half of that was taken up with Ashek's kebab equipment. The living area was just a space of 6 feet by 5 feet at the back. You couldn't get more minimalist. No ornaments, no telly, no seating – just a blanket to sit on.

Why is a lad who's working all day on the rickshaw and all night selling kebabs living in this? I suppose Ashek worked all the time as there was no point having time off. He had nowhere to relax.

He told me that I'd be staying with him tonight. I looked around the

TRYING TO BLEND IN.

A COW CELEBRATING HOLI DAY.

ME RIDING ASHEK AROUND ON HIS RICKSHAW.

room and asked where would be best for me to sleep. I was feeling tired, and then it started to get very confusing:

'We don't live here,' Ashek said.
'You don't live here?'
'Yeah.'
'You do live here?'
'No, no.'
'I don't understand. What do you mean? Do you live here?'
'Yeah, I live but because today are made for you . . . okay?'
'No.'
'Okay, let me explain. We don't live here.'
'You do live here, or you don't live here?'
'I live here, yeah.'
'Right, fine.'
'But now, tonight, we do not live here.'
'Who does live here?'
'Yeah.'
'WHO?'
'Both you and me, because this is too hot for you.'
'Because it's too hot for me?'
'Yeah, yeah.'
'So we're not staying here tonight?'
'No, no, no, no. You get insulted here.'
'I wouldn't be insulted if this is where you sleep. I don't mind sleeping here. Where are we staying?'
'My friend.'
'Where does your friend live?'
'He lives near to us.'
'It's gonna be the same as this, isn't it? They all look the same.'
'No, no.'
'But now I'm putting your friend out. I don't even know who your friend is and I'm taking advantage . . .'
'You are not such a thing as that.'
'I don't mind staying here.'
'Nah, they don't mind. Only you and me here, okay?'

'I tell you what, how about this: I leave you to have a nice night's sleep? You've been working hard all day. Why don't you stay at your friend's house, and we'll stay here?'

'No, no.'

'Why? I want you to have a good night's sleep. You were shattered before. I thought you were gonna collapse on me. You turned up late, you annoyed me at the beginning, I'll be honest. I was thinking, who is this bloke? He's let me down. My first day in India, where is he? You turn up, you're a nice fella. You were ill, so I can't have a go at you. You show me how to ride a bike, you show me your business, you welcome me into your house. I want you to have a bit of goodness in your life for a change. You've been working all night, you've been sweating selling chicken, after being on the bike all day. I want you to have a good night's sleep. So go to your friend's, have a good night's sleep and let me be here, honestly. I'll be fine with that.'

'No.'

'What's this place like? Explain it to me. Is it nice?'

'This place?'

The Taj Mahal

'The place we're going to. Do I get an explanation of what it's like, or do you want it to be a surprise?'

'No, no, no.'

'We've got a bed?'

'Yeah.'

'Definitely got a bed?'

'Yeah, yeah, yeah.'

'Are you familiar with the Goldilocks story? These three bears, they're never happy. They've either got a bed that's too big or a bed that's too small, and I'm wondering whether I'm better off here, than a place I haven't seen.'

'But the other is better for you.'

'It's better for me?'

'Yeah, definitely.'

'And what is that based on? What makes you think I will be happier in this other place? Will there be a telly?'

'Yeah.'

'Toilet?'

'Yeah.'

'Let's go then.'

We got to his friend's house. He was an older man. I'd say he was in his sixties. He was pleased to put us up for the night. The place was okay. Basic but clean. Ashek wasn't lying – there was a toilet but it wasn't the usual type. It was the same style as in Egypt, so he gave me a demo on how to use it. I know it doesn't sound like a great night in, but after the day I'd had it felt quite normal, although there was nothing English to watch on the telly.

I tried to have some of my friendly bacteria powder before I went to sleep, but as soon as it hit the back of my throat I sicked it back up. It was like the Indian bacteria had already taken over control of the entrance to my throat and was letting none of this friendly stuff in.

I'm definitely going to get ill.

SUNDAY 28TH FEBRUARY

I was up early and had tea and biscuits. That makes it sound quite civilised, but Ashek's mate kept burping. I don't think it's rude to do that here. I'd have joined in but I've never been able to burp. When he wasn't burping he was coughing up phlegm. Once he started doing it, his wife joined in. I wondered if it was like yawning – once someone does it, everyone joins in. Since I've been in India I've heard more burps than mobile ringtones. I think they believe in the saying 'Better out than in'.

As we were about to leave, Ashek gave me a gown to wear. He said, cryptically, that the place I would be going to today would require me to wear this.

I was being kept in the dark again. It's the not-knowing part of these trips that's wearing me out the most.

I switched on my phone and received a text message from Steve:

TOILET

HI KARL, INDIA'S NOT ALL POVERTY AND URBAN CHAOS, MATE. TIME TO GET YOUR ARSE UP NORTH, OUT OF DELHI, TO A PLACE CALLED HARIDWAR FOR SOME EXPOSURE TO THE SPIRITUAL SIDE OF INDIA. KUMBH MELA IS THE BIGGEST RELIGIOUS FESTIVAL ON THE PLANET, ONLY 20 MILLION PILGRIMS EXPECTED. JUST ONE HURDLE – TO GET OVER THERE IT'S AN EIGHT-HOUR OVERNIGHT BUS RIDE.

I was annoyed as I really don't like crowds and I'm not into spiritual stuff.

I asked Luke how I was supposed to get there. He said I should grab a rickshaw and ask to go to the bus station. So I did. It was a motorised one. We passed plenty of cows, but in India they're not in fields – they just roam down streets and sit in the middle of roads causing traffic jams. I saw four cows in the middle of the dual carriageway. I asked the driver if seeing four cows sat down in the middle of a dual carriageway meant it was going to rain. He didn't understand.

I got dropped off near the main bus depot. As soon as I got off the rickshaw I was hit by more madness. A young lad covered in blood was cutting the heads off live chickens and throwing the headless bodies into a bin that rocked from side to side as the chicken's legs kicked for the last time. Other people seemed to be covered in blood too, or at least that's what I thought until I was dragged by a local man into his garden where there were lots of people covered in red, green and yellow paint, dancing to the sound of a drum. Before I had a chance to ask what was going on, someone poured a bucket of water over my head and then pelted me with some kind of multi-coloured powder. I looked like a Dulux colour chart.

Apparently this is an annual festival called Holi Day. I don't know what the powder was but it was burning my throat and nose. My trainers were wrecked too. I wish Luke had warned me 'cos I've only had this pair since Christmas and normally my trainers last me a full year. People were dancing to the beat while others ran around with more handfuls of

M.S. HALAL MEAT
CHICKEN SHOP

the colourful powder. I'm sure I was being picked on more than others because I had a camera crew following me. As I've already said, people love to get on camera here. It wouldn't surprise me if the lad cutting heads off chickens wasn't even a butcher. It might just have been a way to get my attention and try and get on TV.

I finally got to the bus station. It was grim. It was a dark, concrete structure that let in no daylight. The buses were little better. I've seen stock cars in better condition than these battered old buses that were parked all over the place with no indication of where they were going. I met a man who worked there. I told him where I wanted to go. Well, I wanted to go home if truth be told, but I told him I had to get to Haridwar. He led me towards a long queue but didn't stop at the back – he walked me right to the front. I don't know what he was thinking. It's not as if I didn't already stand out in the crowd. I had a camera crew following me, and for anyone who didn't notice that, I was also covered in multi-coloured paint from the Holi Festival. Even the blind would have heard me pushing my way to the front from the squelching of my trainers.

Then it all kicked off. A gang of men rushed forward to complain about my queue jumping. I couldn't blame them. I'd be angry if I was them. I said I was happy to go to the back of a queue. I was in no rush to get to a religious festival where there were due to be 20 million people anyway. It was all pretty awkward, and the bus was running late, but in truth this was no surprise. Delhi probably got its name from the word 'delay'.

This was another new low for my trip to India. As I waited, a man shuffled around my feet. I thought he was a shoe-shine man, but it was just a man with no legs dragging himself around begging. It's such a depressing place. Luke explained that the local people deal with all this disability by believing that these people were bad in their last life, so God has punished them by sending them back to live their next life with less limbs.

I eventually got my ticket and made it onto the crowded bus, where the aisle was crammed with bags. I struggled with my rucksack. As luck would have it, the man who had been the most angry in the bus queue was on the same bus. He was still red from anger. I was still red from the Holi Festival.

MONDAY 1ST MARCH

We're into March already. I always forget February is a short month. I wish the days were shorter while I was here in India, never mind the months.

We got to Haridwar in one piece, which was a surprise. The roads in India are in a right state. I thought they were speed bumps at first and then realised they were just bumps and holes.

As we got close to the festival site, there were tents as far as the eye could see. It looked similar to Glastonbury except instead of kids wearing low-slung jeans and parkas, it was full of old men with beards wearing robes and beads.

Luke told me I was staying at Lahore Hotel. I didn't have very high hopes for it, so it was a nice surprise to find that it wasn't too bad. I was put up in a smart tent overlooking the Ganges. It had electricity and a bathroom with a shower and a normal toilet. This couldn't have been better timed, as I was on my last legs and I was starting to get stomach cramps.

I had a shower and washed off all the paint from the Holi Day Festival. It was like a scene from *Psycho* as the water ran red in the shower. And then I worked my way through six cotton buds getting the paint out of my ears.

Once I was cleaned up I went to look at the Ganges. This was the first time since being in India that I'd had a little bit of calmness. Luke told me the Ganges is the holiest river in the world. I said India has the holiest roads in the world, I'll give them that.

Later we ate some curry and went to bed.

TUESDAY 2ND MARCH

The old saying 'A change is as good as a rest' came to mind this morning. India couldn't be more of a change, yet I don't feel rested. I'm also scared to relax too much as my bowels are not in good working order.

I popped a nappy into my little bag today. I didn't tell Luke because I knew that he would want to film me packing it for the TV show.

The other reason I'm finding it hard to relax is that there always seems to be something going on – something to take in. I think I've blinked less since I've been here as I don't want to miss anything, so my eyes have been open longer than normal. Maybe that's why my eyes are tired. Plus I didn't sleep well last night due to the noise outside. I woke up around 2 a.m. to some bloke on a microphone ranting on about something. Everything he said was followed by a massive cheer. It sounded like there must have been thousands of people listening to him. It was impossible to sleep. I wish I hadn't cleaned all the paint from the Holi Festival out of my ears as it had muffled things a bit.

Every day from 7 a.m. to 8 a.m. and again from 6 p.m. to 7 p.m. a chanted mantra gets played on speakers that are attached to lamp-posts. First, a man sings a version of the mantra, and then the same song is sung again by a woman. You can't escape it. It's like the time Bryan Adams was number one with '(Everything I Do) I Do It For You' and every radio station you clicked on was playing it. I'm going to be sick to death of hearing it by the end of the week. That's if Delhi Belly doesn't get me first.

Luke mentioned that a lot of people go to the Kumbh Mela festival to 'find themselves'. That's a saying I've never understood. If I did want to find myself, I don't think I'd find me at a festival with 20 million other people. I hate crowds. The other thing I worry about is what happens if I do 'find myself' and then I go home and I am all different, and Suzanne's going 'What's happened to you?' and then she doesn't like the new me that I have found. So I have just created a new problem. And then I will start to hate myself because I am not the person I thought I was. That's opening a whole can of worms. I know who I am. Bloody hell, I'm getting enough bills for Karl Pilkington so I hope I am him, 'cos if I'm not, I have no idea who I'm paying for.

I'm also worried about going to a religious festival because I'm just not that interested in it. I've never needed religion in my life. I'm not bothered that some people are into it – it's their choice – but I'm not, so what am I doing here? Even if I did get into it, I wouldn't stick at it. I don't tend to stick at anything as I get bored quite quickly. That's the reason my dad never let me keep the tortoise I found. He said they live too long and I'd lose interest. I never had gobstoppers as a kid for the same reason.

Luke gave me a newspaper to look at while we ate. It had news of Cheryl Cole's relationship problems. Weird that Cheryl Cole's love life makes it into the papers here, given all the problems there are in India. I also read about how the locals collect cow dung and clad their houses with it as a form of insulation, and then chip it off and use it to light fires with. I don't know if it's possible for houses to have 'kerb appeal' here with that going on. And I saw an advert for an Elephant Man who was due to be at the festival. He has a facial deformity but he's treated like a god as he looks a bit like the Indian god Ganesha, who has the head of an elephant and the body of a woman. I've seen quite a few ornaments of this god around India. There's also another god that has about five heads. If I see one of them as an ornament I might get it for me mam as me dad is always being heavy-handed and breaking ornaments, and the head is the first thing that breaks. At least with this one he could drop it a few times before me mam has to bin it.

There was another article about a man at the festival who has held his right arm in the air for 12 years. All the muscle has wasted away, and his nails are really long. It seems like a waste of an arm when so many people in India are missing limbs.

Then Steve called. I think he was trying to cheer me up:

ALRIGHT, MATE.
HOW YOU GETTING ON?

WELL, I'VE HAD BETTER HOLIDAYS...

IT'S NOT A HOLIDAY! I HAVE TO KEEP REMINDING YOU IT IS NOT A HOLIDAY, MY FRIEND. YOU ARE MAKING A TRAVEL PROGRAMME FOR THE TELEVISION. WE HAVEN'T JUST SENT YOU AROUND THE WORLD FOR A HOLIDAY.

NO, I KNOW, BUT THERE SHOULD BE A LITTLE BIT OF THAT. WHEN YOU SEE PEOPLE TRAVELLING AROUND, THEY'RE NORMALLY HAPPIER THAN I HAVE BEEN HERE. THAT'S ALL I'M SAYING. I HAVE HAD A LOT OF LOW MOMENTS, MORE THAN I HAVE EVER HAD, ACTUALLY.

WHAT HAVE BEEN YOUR LOW MOMENTS THIS TIME?

WELL, WHAT DO YOU WANT TO KNOW? I'VE BEEN COVERED IN A LOAD OF PAINT. I'VE SEEN DISABLED PEOPLE EVERYWHERE. I'VE HAD THE SHITS. SO WHICH ONE DO YOU WANT TO GO WITH FIRST?

WHY WERE YOU COVERED IN PAINT? DID SOME PAINT FALL ON YOU? I DON'T UNDERSTAND... DID YOU WALK UNDER A LADDER AND SOME BLOKE DROP PAINT ON YOU?

IT'S WHAT THEY DO HERE. I DON'T KNOW IF THEY HAVE A JOB-LOT OF POWDERED PAINT AROUND AND IT'S JUST THEIR WAY OF GETTING RID OF IT. THERE ARE CERTAIN THINGS IN LIFE THEY JUST HAVE TO GET SHOT OF... LIKE 'EAT 5 FRUITS A DAY'... IT'S 'COS THERE'S LOADS OF FRUIT IN THE WORLD, THEY COME UP WITH THESE THINGS.

RIGHT, I SEE. BUT THIS SOUNDS LIKE FUN. PEOPLE INVITED YOU INTO THEIR LIVES. WHY WOULDN'T THAT BE INTERESTING?

BECAUSE IT'S AWKWARD I'N'T IT? I MET A BLOKE CALLED ASHEK. LOVELY BLOKE, REALLY HARD WORKER, BUT THEN IT'S DEPRESSING 'COS HE INVITES ME ROUND AND YOU KNOW HE'S LIVING... YOU KNOW THAT FLAT I HAD, IN TOWN?

YEAH, THAT WAS A TINY LITTLE PLACE

RIGHT, IT WAS SMALLER THAN THAT.

BLIMEY. WHY DIDN'T YOU BUY HIM A MIRROR 'COS MIRRORS ARE ALWAYS SUPPOSED TO OPEN UP SPACE, AREN'T THEY?

BECAUSE HE WOULD HAVE HAD THE REFLECTION OF HIS OWN KEBAB SHOP SO IT WOULD HAVE BEEN LIKE HE COULD NEVER ESCAPE FROM WORK.

YES, BUT, KARL, I HAVE SAID TO YOU BEFORE, THE REASON WHY PEOPLE TRAVEL IS TO BROADEN THEIR MINDS. THE ONE THING ABOUT YOU IS THAT YOU'RE NOT GOOD AT EMPATHY. YOU FIND IT VERY HARD TO PUT YOURSELF IN OTHER PEOPLE'S SHOES. THIS IS IMPORTANT. THIS IS AN EYE-OPENER, A DISCOVERY FOR YOU. YOU GET TO SEE THE WORLD FOR WHAT IT IS. NOT EVERYONE HAS GOT IT CUSHY, NOT EVERYONE HAS GOT IT EASY. WHEN YOU'RE BACK IN LONDON YOU'LL BE THINKING ABOUT HIM AND REALISING THAT LIFE'S NOT SO DIFFICULT.

NO, RIGHT, LISTEN. YOU'RE PREACHING AND ALL THAT, BUT YOU'RE NOT HERE. YOU DON'T KNOW WHERE I AM. YOU DON'T KNOW WHERE I'VE BEEN. YOU ALSO SENT ME A TEXT MESSAGE SAYING GET DOWN TO THIS FESTIVAL – HAVE YOU SEEN WHAT'S THERE?

WELL, I AM JEALOUS OF YOU, MY FRIEND. THE KUMBH MELA FESTIVAL IS THE LARGEST SPIRITUAL FESTIVAL IN THE WORLD. IT ONLY HAPPENS WHERE YOU ARE EVERY TWELVE YEARS. MILLIONS OF PEOPLE WALK ACROSS INDIA TO BE THERE.
YEAH, BUT THAT'S BECAUSE THE BUSES ARE HOPELESS.
KARL, YOU ARE FASCINATED BY PEOPLE. YOU ARE FASCINATED BY DIFFERENCES. YOU'VE ALWAYS ADMITTED THAT. THERE'S PEOPLE THERE DOING EXTRAORDINARY SPIRITUAL FEATS OF ENDURANCE—BLOKES PUTTING THEIR HAND IN THE AIR FOR YEARS, PEOPLE WHO LIE ON BEDS OF NAILS. THEY'RE FASCINATING. SURELY YOU WANT TO GET INSIDE THEIR MINDS? SURELY YOU WANT TO UNDERSTAND WHAT MAKES THEM TICK? WE'RE NOT TRYING TO CONVERT YOU, WE'RE TRYING TO GET YOU OUT THERE TO EXPLORE AND TO MEET PEOPLE. THIS IS AN EXTRAORDINARY OPPORTUNITY.
WHAT IF I TELL YOU THIS THOUGH, THE BLOKE YOU'RE TALKING ABOUT, RIGHT, WITH THE HAND IN THE AIR, RIGHT. I SAW SOME PICTURES OF HIM TODAY IN THE PAPER, AND IN ONE PICTURE IT WAS HIS LEFT HAND, AND IN ANOTHER PICTURE IT WAS HIS RIGHT. HOW'S THAT HAPPENED? WHAT'S GOING ON THERE?
GO AND FIND HIM AND ASK HIM. YOU DON'T KNOW WHAT THE RULES ARE. THEY MAY BE ALLOWED TO SWITCH HANDS EVERY TEN MINUTES. I DON'T KNOW. MAYBE IN ONE OF THEM HE WAS JUST PUTTING HIS HAND UP TO ASK A QUESTION AT A LOCAL MEETING, AND IN THE OTHER ONE HE WAS DOING HIS SPIRITUAL THING. WE DON'T KNOW, BUT THESE ARE THINGS YOU CAN ASK...
PHONE CUTS OFF
HELLO?
HELLO.
Bombay

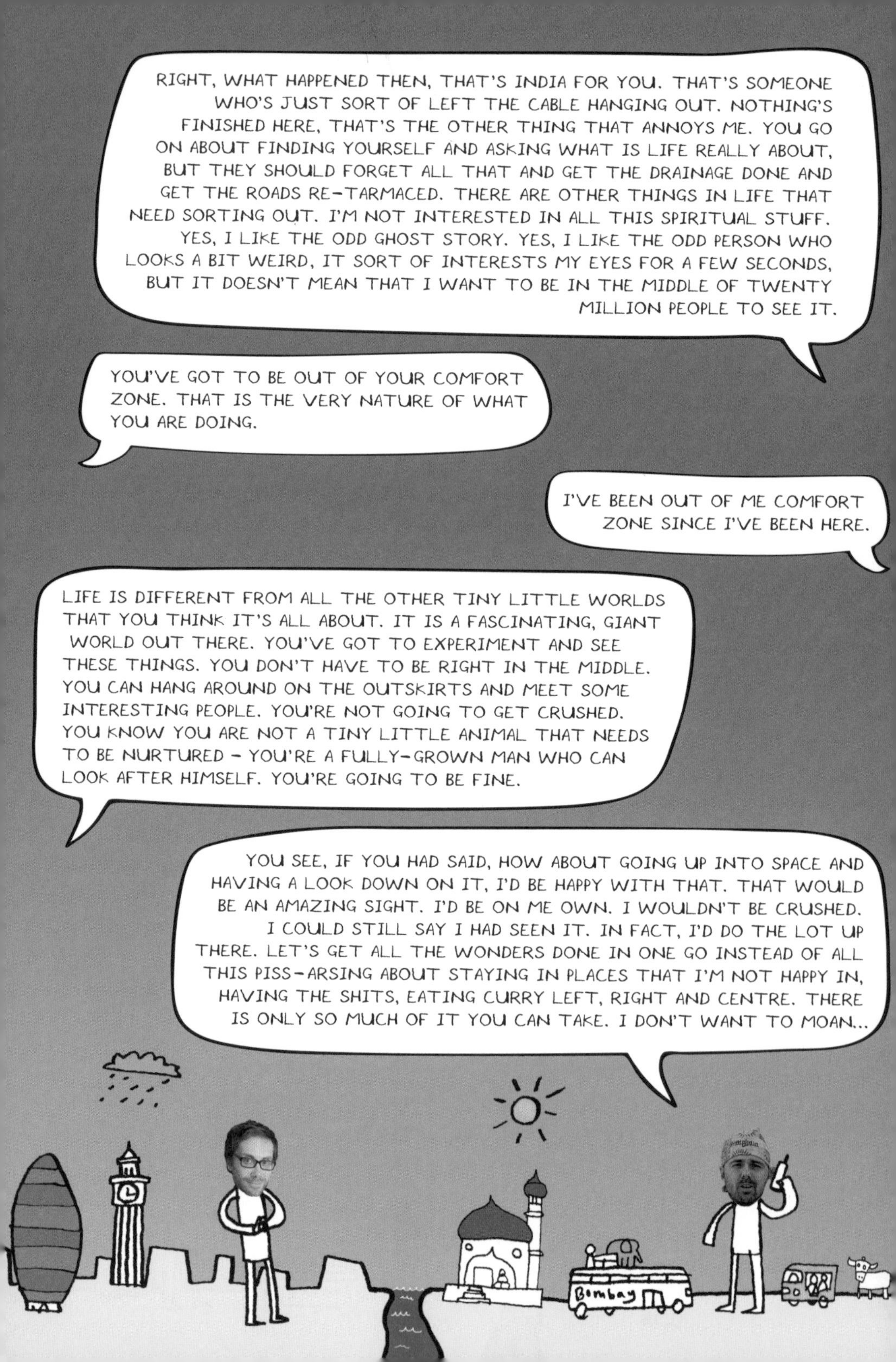
RIGHT, WHAT HAPPENED THEN, THAT'S INDIA FOR YOU. THAT'S SOMEONE WHO'S JUST SORT OF LEFT THE CABLE HANGING OUT. NOTHING'S FINISHED HERE, THAT'S THE OTHER THING THAT ANNOYS ME. YOU GO ON ABOUT FINDING YOURSELF AND ASKING WHAT IS LIFE REALLY ABOUT, BUT THEY SHOULD FORGET ALL THAT AND GET THE DRAINAGE DONE AND GET THE ROADS RE-TARMACED. THERE ARE OTHER THINGS IN LIFE THAT NEED SORTING OUT. I'M NOT INTERESTED IN ALL THIS SPIRITUAL STUFF. YES, I LIKE THE ODD GHOST STORY. YES, I LIKE THE ODD PERSON WHO LOOKS A BIT WEIRD, IT SORT OF INTERESTS MY EYES FOR A FEW SECONDS, BUT IT DOESN'T MEAN THAT I WANT TO BE IN THE MIDDLE OF TWENTY MILLION PEOPLE TO SEE IT.
YOU'VE GOT TO BE OUT OF YOUR COMFORT ZONE. THAT IS THE VERY NATURE OF WHAT YOU ARE DOING.
I'VE BEEN OUT OF ME COMFORT ZONE SINCE I'VE BEEN HERE.
LIFE IS DIFFERENT FROM ALL THE OTHER TINY LITTLE WORLDS THAT YOU THINK IT'S ALL ABOUT. IT IS A FASCINATING, GIANT WORLD OUT THERE. YOU'VE GOT TO EXPERIMENT AND SEE THESE THINGS. YOU DON'T HAVE TO BE RIGHT IN THE MIDDLE. YOU CAN HANG AROUND ON THE OUTSKIRTS AND MEET SOME INTERESTING PEOPLE. YOU'RE NOT GOING TO GET CRUSHED. YOU KNOW YOU ARE NOT A TINY LITTLE ANIMAL THAT NEEDS TO BE NURTURED – YOU'RE A FULLY-GROWN MAN WHO CAN LOOK AFTER HIMSELF. YOU'RE GOING TO BE FINE.
YOU SEE, IF YOU HAD SAID, HOW ABOUT GOING UP INTO SPACE AND HAVING A LOOK DOWN ON IT, I'D BE HAPPY WITH THAT. THAT WOULD BE AN AMAZING SIGHT. I'D BE ON ME OWN. I WOULDN'T BE CRUSHED. I COULD STILL SAY I HAD SEEN IT. IN FACT, I'D DO THE LOT UP THERE. LET'S GET ALL THE WONDERS DONE IN ONE GO INSTEAD OF ALL THIS PISS-ARSING ABOUT STAYING IN PLACES THAT I'M NOT HAPPY IN, HAVING THE SHITS, EATING CURRY LEFT, RIGHT AND CENTRE. THERE IS ONLY SO MUCH OF IT YOU CAN TAKE. I DON'T WANT TO MOAN...
Bombay

YOU DON'T WANT TO MOAN, YOU DON'T WANT TO MOAN!

BUT I DON'T UNDERSTAND WHY YOU THINK I HAVE GOT TO 'FIND MYSELF'. WHERE'S THAT COME FROM? YOU'VE NEVER SAID THAT TO ME SINCE I'VE KNOWN YOU.

I'M NOT SAYING THAT. I'M NOT SAYING THAT YOU HAVE TO 'FIND YOURSELF'. YOU COULD TRY AND FIND YOURSELF AND HAVE A LOOK FOR ME WHILE YOU'RE THERE. IT'S UP TO YOU, I DON'T MIND. I AM SAYING, JUST GO AND EXPERIENCE IT. YOU DON'T HAVE TO HAVE A RELIGIOUS EPIPHANY, YOU DON'T HAVE TO FIND SPIRITUALITY OR GOD, YOU DON'T HAVE TO BECOME HINDU – JUST GO.

BUT THAT'S LIKE GOING TO A BROTHEL AND GOING, 'DON'T MIND ME, I'M JUST GOING TO STAND OVER HERE AND WATCH.' EITHER YOU GET INVOLVED OR YOU SHOULDN'T BE THERE, AND THAT'S HOW I FEEL. I SHOULDN'T BE THERE. I'VE GOT NO AIM IN LIFE TO SUDDENLY FIND MYSELF OR ... OR THIS SPIRITUALITY STUFF YOU KEEP ON HARPING ON ABOUT. IT'S NOT ME, AND WHAT HAPPENS IF YOU CHANGE ME AND YOU CHANGE ME A LOT, AND THEN WE DON'T GET ON? WHAT THEN? YOU'VE LOST A MATE.

WE'RE NOT GETTING ON RIGHT NOW SO WHAT'S THE PROBLEM? MAYBE YOU WILL BE A CALMER AND NICER BLOKE BY THE END OF IT. MAYBE YOU WILL BE SOMEONE WHO IS NOT WHINGEING ALL THE TIME! BLOODY HELL, MATE, YOU'VE BEEN TO EGYPT NOW. YOU'VE BEEN TO RIO ... I THOUGHT YOU WOULD START TO SEE HOW THINGS ARE DIFFERENT AROUND THE WORLD.

YEAH.

IT'S A BEAUTIFUL, WEIRD AND EXTRAORDINARY PLACE.

WEDNESDAY 3RD MARCH

I was told that when I go to the Kumbh Mela Festival I'm not to wear any leather otherwise I won't be allowed in. It's the cow thing again. I still don't know who came up with the cow rule.

I saw lots of babas at the festival today. These are people who walk about with next to nothing on and have ash all over their bodies. I was blessed by quite a few of them. The interpreter told me I had to give each one of them 100 rupees (£1) if I took a blessing. It could be an expensive place to be if you had a cold and kept sneezing.

I did some yoga with a baba. He laughed because I couldn't stretch as well as he could. It was hardly surprising really as he was stark bollock naked apart from a pair of shades, while I was wearing combat pants with the pockets stuffed full of toffees I'd taken from the first-class lounge at the airport. The guide said if I gave him some more money he would show me more. I don't know what more there was to see from this fella. The way he was bending upside down in my face I could have checked his prostate gland. Instead I asked if he knew the one-armed baba or the Elephant Man. He pointed me in the right direction and I wandered off.

As I walked, another baba who looked like Bill Oddie tried to get me to smoke some drugs, but I turned him down. The interpreter said I might have disrespected him by doing this. I asked Bill Oddie if he knew the one-armed baba. He said he did. It felt a bit like a big council estate where everyone knows each other, but only by their nickname. On the estate I grew up on there was Scruffy Sandra, Jimmy the Hat, John the Screw, Fred the Veg, Shorts Man, Miss Piggy and Tattoo Stan (he was my uncle).

We found Elephant Man. To be honest, I couldn't tell if he was happy as his face didn't have any sort of expression. He also had what looked like little tumours all over his body. It sounds strange to say it, but he didn't look that weird to me. I don't know why, maybe it's 'cos I've seen a lot of extraordinary things while I've been in India. The other thing was, he wasn't wearing much. I think he probably would've looked weirder if he had been wearing a pair of jeans and a shirt and tie. I don't know if that makes sense, but it does to me.

GANESH LOOKY-LIKEY.

A BABA AT WORK.

ONE-ARMED BABA.

I asked how old he was as it was impossible to tell. I've always thought about that when I've watched the *Elephant Man* film. He could've got on a bus and taken the OAP seat, or bought fags underage. The baba said he was around 45/46. He said he was happy with his condition. He was looked at as a god and was proud to be part of this clan. And he said he wouldn't have an operation to sort it out.

I think the man he was sat with felt left out and wanted some attention. I say this 'cos he suddenly got up and wrapped his knob and bollocks around his walking stick and then jumped up and down. It looked unbelievably painful. I asked what he was playing at. Our interpreter said something about how sex is not important to him and he lets people know this by wrecking his knob and bollocks. I asked if he had to have the walking stick because he was pulling that trick day-in day-out, but the interpreter didn't want to ask.

It was definitely one of the strangest moments of my life – sat in India with a man with the head of an elephant while his mate twisted his tackle around a stick. There you go, Steve. I've broadened my mind.

I eventually met the one-armed man I had seen in the paper. He was surrounded by lots of hangers-on. It seemed like he was the main baba to be with. I sat down and gave him 200 rupees, and he blessed me and gave me some ash to eat. I know it sounds odd, but after having curry three times a day, eating ash was a refreshing change. I asked why he'd decided to do this endurance thing with his arm. The translator told me it's not a new thing – there are some babas that do it with one leg up, both hands up, both legs up. They never stand on their feet. Apparently doing it is a way to get closer to connecting with the gods and to focus on what life is about.

I asked a few questions the translator didn't want to ask the baba. I asked if the baba was right-handed before he did this. I wanted to know how much he gave up for his beliefs. I then asked if he could remember the last thing he did with his arm before he gave it up. Again the translator didn't want to ask. I told him I thought it was a good question as it must have been quite a significant moment in his life. Eventually the translator asked and then told me that the baba didn't want to answer. In fact, he said that we should leave. I really hope I didn't upset him.

I thought about the one-armed man on the way back to the tent. We all dedicate our lives to something. I've been with Suzanne for 17 years. That's dedication. I don't know if the one-armed man is married – I should have asked that. And how would he help around the house? Other than the ironing, most chores would be impossible. Suzanne wouldn't be happy if I said, 'You'll have to change the sheets on your own from now on as I'm gonna stick me arm in the air for the rest of my life.' It's just a great excuse to be lazy, really. I noticed in every picture that the baba's sat down. It's not like he's running about having to make his other arm do extra work to pull his weight. He's just sat there doing nothing.

Bit daft, really.

THURSDAY 4TH MARCH

I met a guru in an ashram today. He was an old, friendly fella. He was called Swami Ji. We talked to each other about our beliefs. He told me how our hearts should control our actions, but too many people let their brains rule their lives. I said that I'm like that. The only time my heart tells me anything is when it gets heartburn, and it's telling me I've had too much pie. Pastry does that to me.

I think he liked me. We had a good laugh together, and even though we had totally different lives we agreed on a lot of the rules by which we lived. We meditated, and I had a go on his rubber dinghy, and then I swam in the Ganges. I wasn't planning on getting in, but I liked the way he listened to my point of view after I had listened to his, so I felt that I should do something for him. Maybe that was my heart talking.

India is finally starting to feel quite normal.

I'm staying in his ashram tonight and have to be up early as we are making our way over to Agra to finally see the Taj – that, after all, is the whole reason for being here. But I don't know if my memories of India will be of a building. They'll be of the weirdness of the place.

I checked my phone before I went to bed. Ricky had left a message for me:

> ALRIGHT, MATE, HOW'S IT GOING? JUST HAVING A CUP OF TEA. JUST CATCHING UP ON SKY PLUS. JUST GOT BACK FROM NEW YORK – FLEW OVERNIGHT, FIRST CLASS, BA, DON'T GET BETTER THAN THAT. SLEPT ALL THE WAY AFTER A FEW GLASSES OF CHAMPAGNE. THOSE FLAT BEDS ARE AMAZING, AREN'T THEY? YEAH. SPEAK TO YOU LATER. BYE. MUST GET ON WITH IT.

I hate to think how much it cost me to listen to that.

KARL'S FACTS

THE TAJ MAHAL TOOK 20,000 WORKERS 22 YEARS TO BUILD.

MORE THAN 1,000 ELEPHANTS WERE USED TO TRANSPORT THE BUILDING MATERIALS.

THE TAJ IS PINKISH IN THE MORNING, MILKY-WHITE IN THE EVENING AND GOLDEN IN THE MOONLIGHT. LOCALS BELIEVE THAT THIS WAS SUPPOSED TO DEPICT THE CHANGING MOODS OF WOMEN.

FRIDAY 5TH MARCH

I was woken early and had breakfast with the guru. We had some spicy Rice Krispies and a spicy biscuit with some really sweet, milky tea. Not the way I normally like it, but I drank it anyway as I didn't want to offend him. I suppose that is my heart telling me how to act instead of my head again. My arse may get involved later though.

And so we set off to see the Taj. I was expecting it to be a full day of travelling, until we pulled over and Luke asked me to come and meet a Hare Krishna. He gave me a tour of his cow sanctuary. These cows were spoilt rotten. It's all to do with the Hare Krishna god being a fan of cows. I helped wash one, and then they sang a song to it and blessed it. It didn't look very happy. It looked embarrassed, if anything.

They then got me to help make some dung cakes. These are the same cowpats I had seen in the newspaper that the locals use to clad their homes with, and then chip off to help fires burn for longer. They told me to get both hands into the big fresh pile of dung and to make a pancake by slamming it on the ground and then patting it flat. Odd how they made a point of saying how the dung was 'fresh', as if that makes it more acceptable to stick your hands in. It's the first time I've heard the word 'fresh' used while in India.

I made two dung cakes, and they got me to sign my name in them.

Before I left, they took me to the gift shop. I was the only one in there, which was no great surprise given that all the products were made from cow poo and piss. Hardly Bodyshop, is it? In this day and age, when every product has to list all its contents on the label, a shop like this is never going to be big business. They packaged them up well, but as the saying goes, 'You can't polish a turd'. And believe me, this place has tried.

They were selling face creams, soaps, cures for baldness and obesity, soap and a special urine 'antiseptic aftershave for men'. The man rubbed some of the baldness cure cream onto my head. It was definitely a hairdressing 'first'. Back home I ask my barber to do a number two, but normally it stands for the shaver guard size – not literally a number two.

As I write this, I'm back in the van on the way to Agra. It seems like a more mental place than Delhi. I think the choice of names in India really sums the place up. I've already said Delhi sounds like 'delay', and now I think about it, India sounds like 'In Dire' and Agra like 'Aggro'. It can't be a coincidence.

I will have to stop writing now as the roads are bad and I feel sick. It's difficult to know if it is car sickness or the smell of cow shit on my head that's causing it.

SATURDAY 6TH MARCH

I really didn't sleep well at all last night. I felt really ill. Woke up in the night being sick, and I also had a dodgy belly. The toilet is too far from the sink which is not what you need in India as both are often required at the same time when it's coming out of both ends. I've spent more time sat on the loo in this hotel room than anywhere else. To me, it's a loo with an en suite bedroom.

To be honest, I wasn't really in the mood to see the Taj Mahal, what with the Delhi Belly and everything, but we had to go as we only had permission to film in there for today.

Luke told me it is a mausoleum that took 22 years to build. The Mughal Emperor Shahjahan had it built for his wife, who died giving birth to their fourteenth son. It was supposed to stand as the perfect symbol of love.

It seems to me like it was something the man had always wanted to build but his wife didn't let him, so when she died he used it as an excuse to build his dream. My uncle always wanted a plasma telly, but his wife didn't want him wasting money on one. Soon as she died he got one.

We went to get a closer look. It's weird how it is classed as one of the modern Wonders of the World. You wouldn't think so by the surroundings. If it was on one of them property programmes, the potential buyers would say, 'If you could pick it up and put it somewhere nicer, we'd buy it.' It really shouldn't have been built here.

There were hundreds of people outside: half of them selling postcards, plates, key rings and snow domes; the others were tourists.

As soon as we got in we were greeted by another queue. This time it was to get on the Princess Diana bench. This is where Diana had her photo taken when she was having her problems with Charlie. Everyone said this is why she looked so miserable, but to be honest I think it was nothing to do with him. I just think she was sick of being in India. It does have that effect on you. If you're having a low moment in your life, India isn't a great place to come to try and get over it. I'd have suggested Center Parcs to her over this place.

The Taj Mahal

There was a woman sat on the bench who was trying to re-enact the famous Diana shot. A man with a camera directed her. 'You look too happy. Look sadder.'

I was shown around by a guide called Remish. He was better than most guides. We chatted as we walked, which made a change from just being talked at for an hour. He told me how the building was perfectly symmetrical. Again this seemed an odd idea for a structure that was

built to show true love. I wondered if the man had some sort of OCD.

Remish showed me some optical illusions. When I moved backwards and then forwards while looking at the Taj from an archway, it gave the illusion that it was moving with me. There was also a marble effect that messed with your eyes and gave the impression the marble was cut at angles when it was actually flat. All of which was very clever, but I didn't really understand why the Mughal emperor would put optical illusions onto his wife's tomb. It would be like having a Suduko carved into your loved one's gravestone.

The more I saw, the more impressed I became with the workmanship. Maybe I liked it for the wrong reasons, but it really was amazing.

The Taj Mahal

We decided to lose the crowds and catch a view of the Taj from a boat on the Humana River. It was much quieter on this side of the building. In fact, it was probably the most relaxed I'd been since arriving in India. No car horns, no begging, no shouting, no mantras. It was almost perfect. I say 'almost', as I noticed a plume of smoke coming from the edge of the river just next to the Taj. I asked Remish what it was, and he told me it was where they were burning dead bodies.

Like I've said, you're never far away from something mad when you're in India.

GET YOUR PHOTOS
COLOUR & B/W FILMS
By COMPUTERISED MACHINE
MUGHNI & SONS.
MIRINDA

ROYAL ENFIELD

ROYAL ENFIELD

ENFIELD

ROYAL ENFIELD

CHAPTER FOUR

CHICHEN ITZA

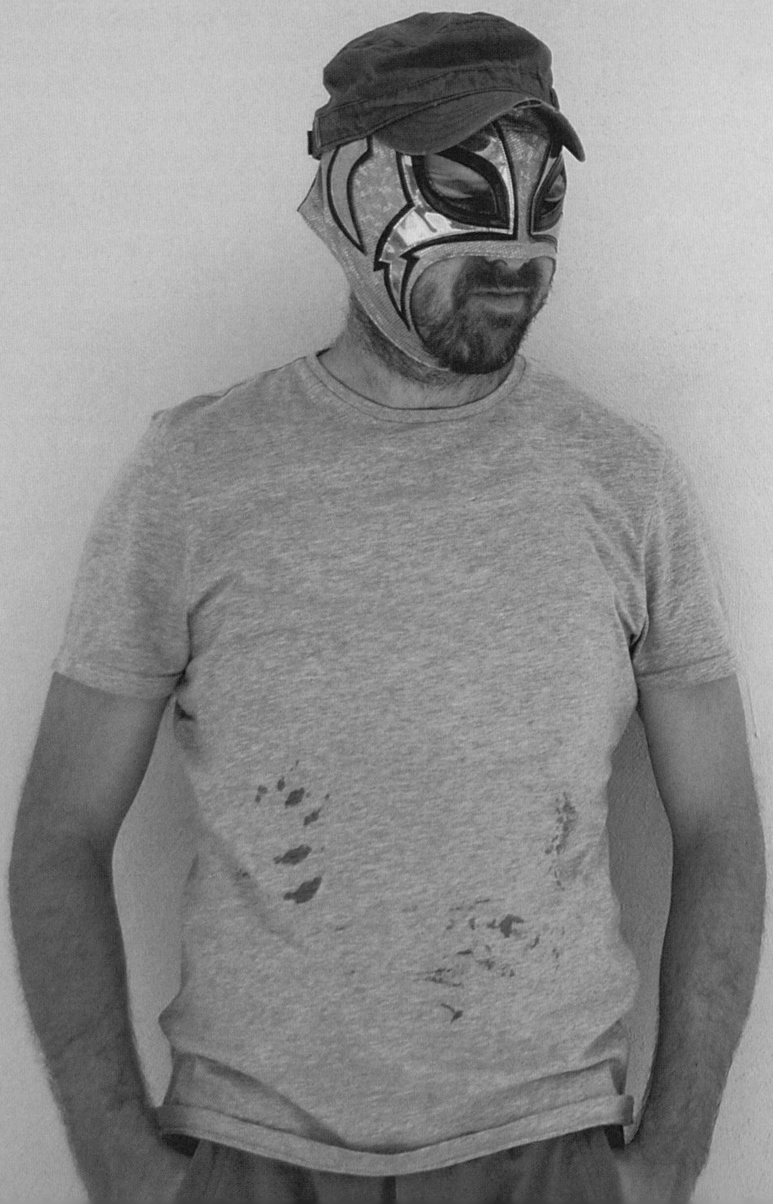

'THE MOST FAMOUS, SPECTACULAR AND, CONSEQUENTLY MOST FREQUENTLY VISITED OF MEXICO'S MAYAN SITES.' 1,000 PLACES TO SEE BEFORE YOU DIE

'IT'S AN ODD ONE, THE CHICHEN ITZA. IT WAS BUILT BY THE ORIGINAL MAYANS AS A PLACE FOR SACRIFICE AND RIPPING OUT PEOPLE'S HEARTS AND CUTTING HEADS OFF. NOT EXACTLY ALTON TOWERS, IS IT?' KARL PILKINGTON

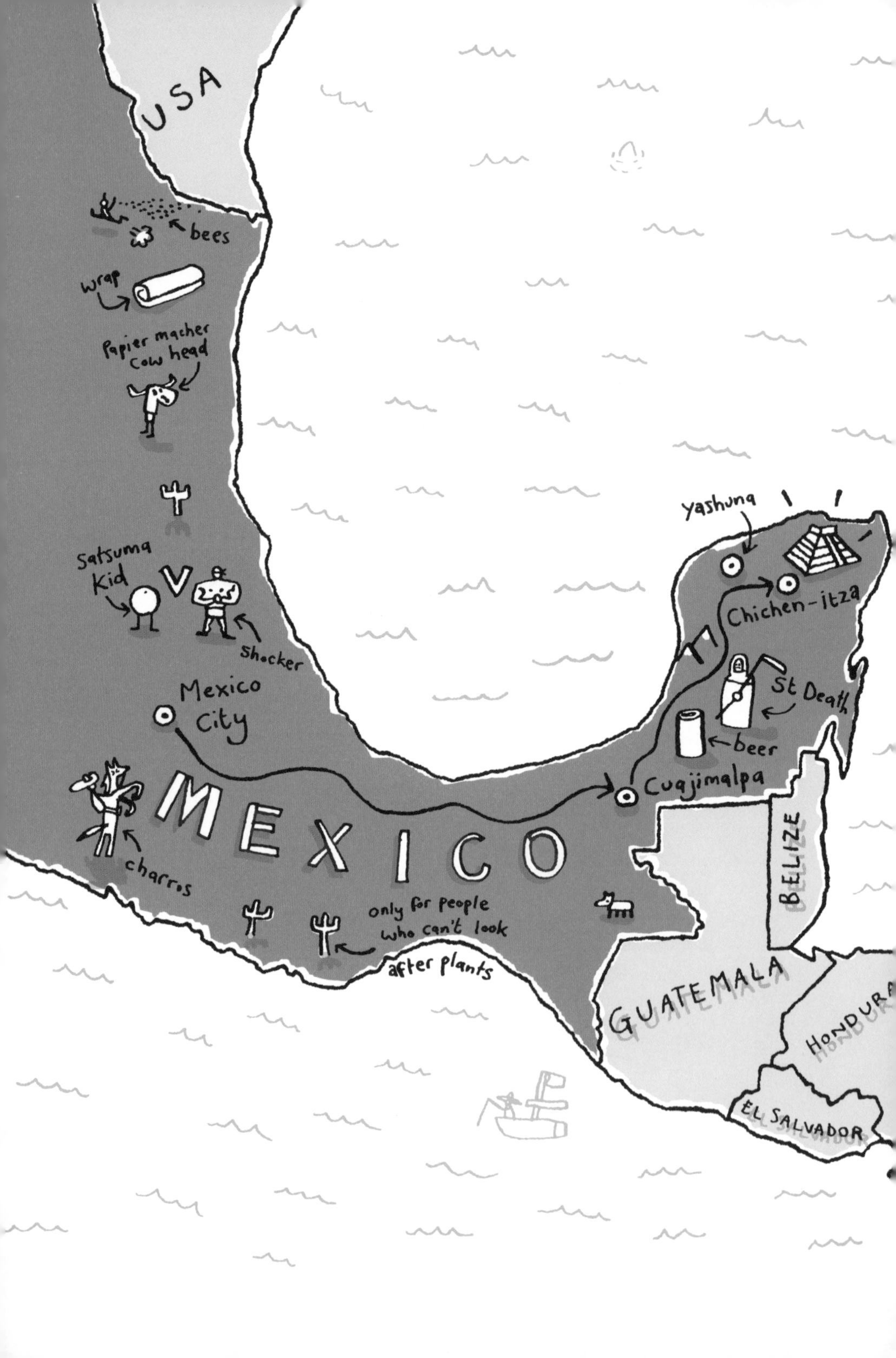

USA
bees
wrap
Papier macher cow head
Satsuma Kid
V
Shocker
Mexico City
MEXICO
charros
only for people who can't look after plants
Cuqjimalpa
beer
St Death
Chichen-itza
Yashuna
BELIZE
GUATEMALA
HONDURA
EL SALVADOR

THURSDAY 1ST APRIL

I'm quite lucky really. It's only just hit me that not many people get to go and see the things I'm seeing and get paid for the privilege. I looked at a world map in a bookshop the other day to see where I've already been. It wasn't that long ago when I was telling Ricky that he was daft for having a world map in his house. I remember saying, 'Why do you need that? It's not the sort of map you'd ever need in your glove compartment in the car, is it?' Mind you, they do maps of the universe now. At what point do you take that with you when you leave the house? It's not as if astronauts would even buy it as I've heard the universe is forever expanding so the book's out of date before the ink's even dried.

I got my stuff together today. Jamie the producer came and chatted while I packed. I told him I had no idea about Mexico. The only thing I could think of was Chiquito, that Mexican restaurant you normally find in those shopping centres off motorways. They have wraps and spicy dips, which I quite like, but liking the food doesn't mean you'll like the country. I like curry, but India was the worst place I'd ever been to.

Jamie told me that Mexico is quite a lawless place. I don't know if that's a bad thing. If I lived in a place where there were no laws I don't know if I'd do anything too differently. I think most people who do illegal stuff are doing it 'cos they know it's wrong. They do it for the buzz. I nicked stuff as a kid, but it was stuff I didn't really need. I nicked from my local newsagent – things like rulers and pens, and a protractor. I didn't even know how to use it, but I knew I shouldn't have been taking it. If they'd been free, I wouldn't have been interested.

Now Jamie has told me this lawless stuff, I'm guessing Mexico will be like the game *Grand Theft Auto* I used to play on my PlayStation. You could just drive around running people over or shooting and blowing things up, but you soon get bored with it. I think you need to feel like you have a purpose in life.

The only other thing I'm aware of in Mexico is cactus. Odd things, they are. I'd never buy one. They're for people who can't look after nice plants. They're not that nice to look at. The only place I ever see them is in doctors' and dentists' waiting rooms. My auntie has a few but she's put them in her porch as some sort of security round her windows. She uses them as natural barbed wire.

FRIDAY 2ND APRIL

Good Friday. Our flight today was with a Mexican airline and I'm not a fan of flying with foreign airlines as all the announcements were in Mexican before English, which worried me. In an emergency everyone would be well out of the aircraft before I even knew what was happening. I suppose this is a good reason to learn a language.

It was a long flight, about 12 hours. I'm not very good at sitting in a chair for any length of time – it's one of the reasons I could never go on *Mastermind*. I suffer with Restless Legs Syndrome. My legs aren't happy unless they are walking somewhere or moving about. People who don't have it can't understand it. I sometimes go to bed and leave my legs hanging out the side with my feet on the ground as this takes away the odd sensation. I'm the only person I know who has to go to bed before my legs do.

What didn't help was the plane having a big screen at the front that kept informing us of how long there was to go before landing. I don't like knowing stuff like that. I had to turn the word count off my laptop when I was writing my other books as it does my head in knowing I have to write 40,000 or so words. There's a saying that goes 'Why use 100 words when you can say it in 10?' I'll tell you why – I have a word count to meet.

I was picked up at the airport by a bloke called Edgar. He couldn't pick me up right outside the airport as he was not an official taxi driver.

He called me to say he was on the other side of the dual carriageway. I had to cross the busy roads while getting directions off him on the phone and dragging my suitcase. It was like playing *Frogger*. He was holding a sign that said 'Karlos Piklington'. I couldn't be bothered correcting him. People in England always get it wrong – Pillington, Pilockton, Pillickington and Dilkington – so I could hardly have a go at him.

SAINT DEATH. A FEW YEARS OLDER THAN THE POPE.

ME AND EDGAR THE CAB DRIVER.

THIS IS JACK. HE LOOKS FRIENDLY BUT HE'S A KILLER.

Edgar's cab was quite battered. He had a dog but not a dog that I would have expected a man like Edgar to have. It was a Chihuahua called Jack. It was hyperactive. If it wasn't jumping all over me and trying to have it away with my arm, it was coughing up hairballs. The problem with Chihuahuas is they have bulbous eyes so it looked like it was choking even when it wasn't. Edgar explained that it had been given to his mam as a gift, but she gave it to Edgar to look after. We were given me mam's mam's dog when she died. It was a poodle-style thing that had been spoilt rotten. It never really settled with us as we didn't have time to spoil it. It ended up looking a bit of a mess after crawling under our car and getting covered in oil. It also got hit by a car and ended up running sideways like a crab. It used to howl whenever the *Coronation Street* theme tune was coming from the telly as it must have reminded it of me mam's mam, who was a big fan. Me dad had it put down one Christmas. *Coronation Street* had been on almost continually over the festive period and the howling was doing his head in.

Edgar chatted a lot, like most cabbies, except his opening gambit wasn't about football or politics. He just wanted to know if my girlfriend had a nice arse. I told him there was plenty of it. He laughed. Talk of Suzanne's arse broke the ice, which was good. I might have to bring it up again with other people I meet if the conversion becomes a struggle.

Edgar then put his stereo on and said he would play me some traditional Mexican music. It sounded quite upbeat and reminded me of the music my mam used to have blaring out of the caravan in Wales from our 8-track player. I asked what the song was about, and he told me it was about drug dealers in Mexico. He explained the lyrics – something about a car that is found in the middle of the road with the doors open and the passengers have had their heads cut off and blood is oozing out of the car. I don't know how the story ends as his dog was coughing up hairballs again and I couldn't really hear what Edgar was saying.

After a few miles Edgar pulled his car over and told me he wanted to show me Santa Muerte. In English this translates to 'Saint Death'. It was a glass box about the size of the small kiosks you get outside Tube stations selling chocolate, crisps and fags. There were no crisps in this

THE STALL DIDN'T HAVE ANY MONSTER MUNCH.

JESUS AND HIS DISCIPLES.

FUN FOR ALL THE FAMILY.

box, but there were fags along with a skeleton dressed in robes surrounded by booze. The poorer people and criminals of Mexico who are not very religious but not quite atheists either worship Saint Death. I've never thought about it before but I suppose bad people might need someone to pray to, too. As we looked at the skeleton, a car with tinted windows pulled over for a few seconds. The men in it bowed their heads before skidding off again.

We drove on to an Easter festival that Edgar said it would be worthwhile my having a look at. Easter seems to be a big deal in Mexico. I saw people acting out some Bible story on stage watched by hundreds of people. I heard choking, but it wasn't Edgar's dog this time. It was coming from a man who was being hanged. The thing is, Mexico loves violence so much it could just be something to keep the crowd interested before the Jesus bit happens. Kids aged two and three were sat on their dads' shoulders so they could see the hanging being acted out.

I wandered off around the market where I found a woman selling dead crickets. Ricky used to buy them to give to his pet salamander, but it was locals who were knocking these ones back. I'm not sure how long a bag of crickets should last – I don't know what the recommended daily allowance is – but one old man whom I'd expect to see sucking on Werther's Originals couldn't get enough of them. They were quite cheap so maybe it's the low cost that attracts people to them. Or should that be locust? Oh, never mind.

They were stacked high on a metal tray with half a lime placed on the side as a garnish. Flies circled. Maybe they were a pudding for anyone who was after a second course.

I'm not very good with strange food. I don't like the stuff that chef Heston Blumenthal knocks up, like bacon-and-egg ice cream. I don't want to be challenged when eating, I just want to get rid of hunger.

Jamie the producer kept asking me to try a cricket. He said he wasn't going to let me leave without eating one. So I did. It didn't taste bad but it wasn't great either. I'd heard street food was a big thing here in Mexico but I didn't think it meant the creatures that lived on the street.

I carried on watching the Easter parade. I'm not a big fan of Easter, though I did have a chocolate egg before I left that was a gift from

Suzanne's mam. She knows I'm a fan of chocolate more than a fan of religion, but I am a fan of chocolate. I think that's how most people are with Easter. It's a religious event that's been created to get fat, greedy people interested. I don't know why we celebrate with an egg. Bit odd that it's all about Jesus being crucified and giving up his life, and then years later we give him respect for what he did by eating a chocolate egg . . . with a small bag of Smarties inside. Are Kinder Eggs sold all year round for really religious people who never forget?

I stood on a busy corner and waited for something to happen. Twenty minutes later a crowd came walking up the street. In the middle was a man who was dressed like – and looked like – Jesus, carrying a massive cross while being lightly whipped. Jamie told me that every year there is a long list of people who want to play Jesus. It is a real privilege to get the part. I never wanted to play him in the school nativity play, which is just as well as I was never offered it. I got to be a shepherd and say the line 'We've travelled from afar' and then I played the drum during the song 'Little Donkey', even though I wasn't supposed to, as the drum was actually there for 'We Three Kings', but I couldn't help myself. Still, it was more than me mate Carl Grimshaw got to do; his job was to hit a triangle as the star appeared in the sky. This is the problem with overcrowded inner-city schools – there aren't enough parts for everyone in the nativity story. I'm surprised Mrs Mathews didn't change the carol to 'We Six Kings' just to get more kids involved.

I was walking alongside Jesus when he started to struggle carrying the big oak cross up the steep hill. I could imagine that this is how it really was all them years ago, if you took away the taco and candyfloss stalls. Jesus dropped the cross. I thought it was all part of the act until I saw the equivalent of a St John's Ambulance man getting out a tube of Savlon to rub on Jesus's leg, which ruined the illusion a bit. And all this was happening as a man dressed as a guard played the recorder, an instrument I thought was only played by four-year-olds. All in all it was really doing my head in.

They eventually got to a field where the crosses were erected, and Jesus and two other fellas were sacrificed. Not for real – though Jamie did say they used to put real nails through their hands and feet but stopped in the late 1980s, maybe thanks to the invention of Unibond No More Nails.

Before we left, one of the other blokes who was on a cross (not sure who he was playing the part of as I don't know the story well enough) was taken down and put into an ambulance. Not exactly a happy family day out, this one. A chocolate egg would lighten the mood a bit.

We got to the hotel quite late and I fell straight into bed.

Woke up in the night to use the toilet (don't think the cricket I ate agreed with me) to find that it wouldn't flush. The ballcock had lodged the water inlet so the cistern wasn't filling. I fixed it. It's not exactly the sort of problem Michael Palin has to deal with is it? I noticed a sign stating that toilet paper should be put in the bin and NOT DOWN THE TOILET. I think we should do this at home. We would get fewer criminals nicking people's identities if they had to rummage through bin bags full of used toilet tissue.

SATURDAY 3RD APRIL

I woke up this morning to find that Ricky had sent me a text.

CALL ME.
NEED TO GO OVER THE RULES OF MEXICAN WRESTLING WITH YOU.

I called him.

DID YOU GET MY TEXT?

I GOT SOMETHING ABOUT WRESTLING.

YEAH. DID YOU PACK ANY SHORTS OR SWIMMING TRUNKS OR ANYTHING? MAYBE A LEOTARD?

NO, I DIDN'T PACK ANYTHING LIKE THAT. NO.

THAT WAS A LONG SHOT, WASN'T IT? BUT, LISTEN, YOU'LL BE ALL RIGHT. I'VE ARRANGED FOR YOU TO DO A BIT OF WRESTLING.

WRESTLING?

YEAH.

WHAT DOES THAT HAVE TO DO WITH THE SEVEN WONDERS? I'M HERE TO SEE A WONDER.

YEAH, WELL, THE GENERAL PUBLIC WILL COUNT IT AS A WONDER, SEEING YOU IN A BOSTON CRAB BEING FLUNG AROUND. IT'S AN HONOUR. IT'S HUGE IN MEXICO. WRESTLERS ARE LIKE SUPERSTARS. THEY'RE HEROES, AND THEY'VE GOT OUTFITS AND NICKNAMES. WHAT I WOULD LIKE TO SEE MAYBE IS YOU IN A FLESH-COLOURED BODY STOCKING AND LIKE A SPIDERMAN MASK, BUT IT'S COMPLETELY ORANGE. IF YOU GET A STRETCHY ONE, IT'LL FIT YOUR PERFECTLY SPHERICAL HEAD. OR MAYBE JUST STICK YOU IN A HOLLOWED-OUT PUMPKIN OR SOMETHING AND THEN YOU CAN BE THE SATSUMA KID OR THE TANGERINE DREAM, OR WE CAN JUST GET THE BLOKE WHO CALLS YOU OUT TO GO, 'AND HERE'S KARL PILKINGTON. HE'S GOT A HEAD LIKE A FUCKING ORANGE.'

SOUND ALL RIGHT?

IS IT LIKE OLD-FASHIONED WRESTLING WHERE NOT MUCH HAPPENS AND YOU SORT OF JUST PUSH EACH OTHER AROUND?

YEAH. I'M SURE ONCE THEY TEACH YOU A FEW MOVES AND HOW TO LAND WITHOUT BREAKING ANYTHING IMPORTANT, IT'LL BE FINE. OH, AND EXPLAIN TO THEM THE SAFEST THING FOR YOU IS TO LAND ON YOUR HEAD. TELL THEM THAT YOU'RE NOT LIKE OTHER MEN, AND THAT AS LONG AS THEY AIM FOR THE LITTLE, ROUND, REALLY HARD, HOLLOW BIT ON THE TOP THAT YOU PROBABLY WON'T SUSTAIN ANY MAJOR INJURIES. IMAGINE IF SOME FELLA, RIGHT, PICKED YOU UP AND THREW YOU ACROSS THE RING, AND YOU GOT UP AND STARTED QUOTING OSCAR WILDE, PICTURE THAT. IF THEY LITERALLY KNOCKED SOME SENSE INTO YOU. JUST GO AND ENJOY IT.

WELL, I'VE HAD ENOUGH PRACTICE. I MEAN, YOU'VE HAD ME IN A HEADLOCK NOW AND AGAIN.

AND THEY PROBABLY WON'T BE AS HEAVY AS ME.

BUT THEY ARE WRESTLERS. THERE'S NO MORE SURPRISES HERE, IS THERE? IT'S NOT NAKED SUMO OR ANYTHING?

NO. THAT'S WHEN YOU GO TO JAPAN.

ALL RIGHT.

ENJOY YOURSELF.

I haven't seen wrestling since the 1980s. I used to watch it with me dad on Saturday afternoons – Big Daddy and Giant Haystacks and the rest. It was a good thing to watch as a kid as it was never that violent. It was just two sweaty, old, overweight men pushing and shoving each other until one of them wanted to stop to get something to eat. There doesn't seem to be any sport for fat people since they stopped it.

By about 1983 people were embarrassed to say that they watched it. That's probably why some wrestlers started wearing masks; they were embarrassed to be involved with it.

Mexican wrestling was different. Ricky was right. They do dress like superheroes.

I met Sandy, the woman who ran the wrestling arena. She took me through some photos of the wrestlers she looked after. She had all shapes and sizes. Something for everyone. El Porky, a little, chubby fella who looked like Russell Grant; midgets; big women; and sexy women.

I texted Suzanne to let her know I was about to do some wrestling. She just said to be careful but then went on to ask how to set the DVD player up as it wasn't plugged into the telly. It's not the greatest encouragement, is it? It's not the sort of message Rocky got from Adrian before a big fight. I didn't bother replying.

Sandy took me to meet the wrestler I'd be training with. His name was Shocker. He was built like a brick shithouse. He looked bigger because he did that thing all people with muscles do of tucking his T-shirt into his jeans. I asked Sandy if I could get one of the midget fighters but she said none of them was around today.

I explained to Shocker that he would have to be careful with me as I did my back in when I was a kid by trying to kick my height and landing on my arse, my wrist is also weak from a crash I had, and I've got a trapped nerve in my leg. He didn't really seem to be listening, which was a worry. He gave me an outfit to wear. I looked a mess. I decided to name myself Shocking.

I did some weights and about 45 minutes in the ring with Shocker and two other fellas. I felt so sick. I'd eaten some marshmallows earlier – not the greatest pre-fitness food – so that combined with being thrown around was not a good idea.

Shocker was a year older than me, but I felt a lot older. I had to stop

THE PROFESSIONAL'S NAME IS SHOCKER.
I'M SHOCKING.
I DON'T BELIEVE IN FIGHTING
TILL THE END.
HARDLY L.A. FITNESS, IS IT?
WE'RE PLAYING TWISTER HERE.
I'M WINNING.

as I felt exhausted and really dizzy. I was trying to get out of the ring when one of the other two wrestlers grabbed me and sat on me whilst wrapping my legs around my neck. I felt helpless, like a deer that was slowly being eaten by an anaconda. The only memory I have was how the wrestler's balls that were thrust into my face left a saltiness on my lips. At first I assumed it was from the tacos, and then I realised I'd not eaten any today.

I stayed in and watched Shocker fight tonight. He was with two other wrestlers, the Blue Panther and El Porky. They won. The crowd seemed to love El Porky. It must annoy Shocker when he trains so hard and eats so well to then have to fight with a bloke whose main exercise is to the fridge and back.

Off to bed now 'cos I'm knackered. The Mexican altitude makes everything tougher and more tiring. I reckon I could have beaten Shocker if I was on my own turf.

SUNDAY 4TH APRIL

I had about four hours sleep then was woken by police sirens. They have a selection of sirens to choose from. One goes *waaa . . . waaa*, then there's *woo woo* and *woooooooooooo* and *daaa daaa*. The copper seemed to decide to go through the choice of sirens at four in the morning outside my room. He was like one of them people on the Tube in London who decides to use their commute to see what other ringtones they've got on their mobile.

I had breakfast downstairs while having to listen to a loud American woman who kept asking why the French bloke who ran the hotel sounded French rather than Mexican. I could see she was annoying him, but he just smiled. She was doing my head in. Where is a noisy police siren when you want one?

Then Steve called.

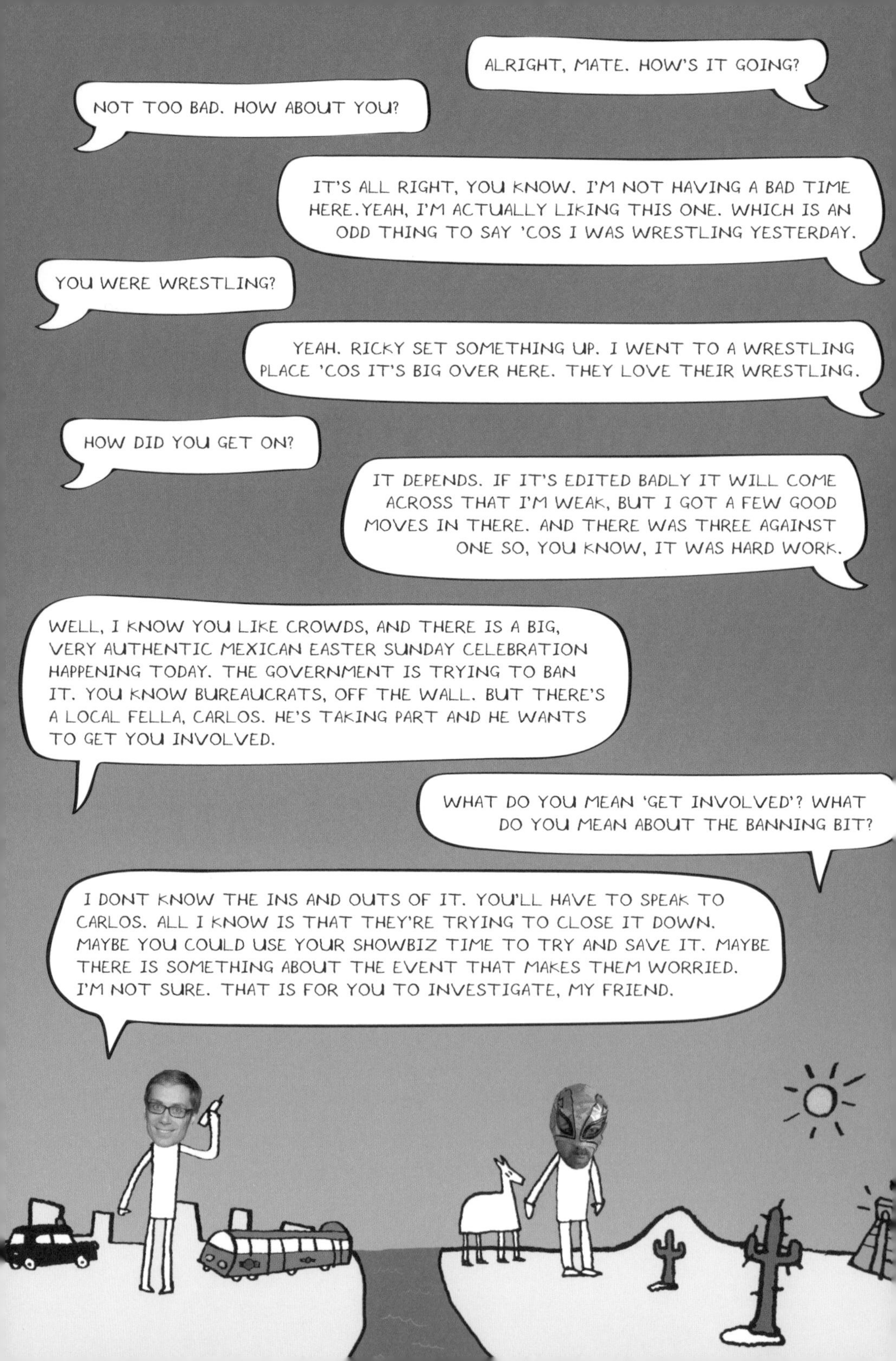
ALRIGHT, MATE. HOW'S IT GOING?
NOT TOO BAD. HOW ABOUT YOU?
IT'S ALL RIGHT, YOU KNOW. I'M NOT HAVING A BAD TIME HERE.YEAH, I'M ACTUALLY LIKING THIS ONE. WHICH IS AN ODD THING TO SAY 'COS I WAS WRESTLING YESTERDAY.
YOU WERE WRESTLING?
YEAH. RICKY SET SOMETHING UP. I WENT TO A WRESTLING PLACE 'COS IT'S BIG OVER HERE. THEY LOVE THEIR WRESTLING.
HOW DID YOU GET ON?
IT DEPENDS. IF IT'S EDITED BADLY IT WILL COME ACROSS THAT I'M WEAK, BUT I GOT A FEW GOOD MOVES IN THERE. AND THERE WAS THREE AGAINST ONE SO, YOU KNOW, IT WAS HARD WORK.
WELL, I KNOW YOU LIKE CROWDS, AND THERE IS A BIG, VERY AUTHENTIC MEXICAN EASTER SUNDAY CELEBRATION HAPPENING TODAY. THE GOVERNMENT IS TRYING TO BAN IT. YOU KNOW BUREAUCRATS, OFF THE WALL. BUT THERE'S A LOCAL FELLA, CARLOS. HE'S TAKING PART AND HE WANTS TO GET YOU INVOLVED.
WHAT DO YOU MEAN 'GET INVOLVED'? WHAT DO YOU MEAN ABOUT THE BANNING BIT?
I DONT KNOW THE INS AND OUTS OF IT. YOU'LL HAVE TO SPEAK TO CARLOS. ALL I KNOW IS THAT THEY'RE TRYING TO CLOSE IT DOWN. MAYBE YOU COULD USE YOUR SHOWBIZ TIME TO TRY AND SAVE IT. MAYBE THERE IS SOMETHING ABOUT THE EVENT THAT MAKES THEM WORRIED. I'M NOT SURE. THAT IS FOR YOU TO INVESTIGATE, MY FRIEND.

BUT I'VE BEEN HERE FOR A COUPLE OF DAYS AND I'VE SEEN THAT THEY'RE NOT REALLY BOTHERED ABOUT THE HEALTH AND SAFETY OF ANYTHING. SO IF THEY'RE ACTUALLY WORRIED ABOUT THE HEALTH AND SAFETY OF SOMETHING IT MUST BE PRETTY MENTAL.
WELL, YOU'RE MEETING CARLOS AT SOME PLACE CALLED THE RAMBO CHICKEN SO MAYBE THAT'S GOT SOMETHING TO DO WITH IT.
THE RAMBO CHICKEN? THERE'S A CHICKEN NAMED RAMBO?
I DON'T KNOW THE INS AND OUTS OF IT. I HAVEN'T BEEN THERE. I'M ENVIOUS OF YOU, AS ALWAYS.
I'M MEETING HIM AT A CHICKEN CALLED...IS THAT WHAT ...IS THE WONDER CALLED CHICKEN EATS YA? IS THAT WHAT THAT'S NAMED AFTER? IS THAT WHAT THIS IS ALL ABOUT? A TOUGH CHICKEN?
IT COULD JUST BE AN INCREDIBLY VIOLENT CHICKEN. I DON'T KNOW, MY FRIEND. I AM JUST A MESSENGER FROM CARLOS.
ALL RIGHT THEN. I'LL GO AND SEE HIM.
CHEERS, MATE. AND IT'S NICE TO SEE YOU FINALLY EMBRACING THIS.
NO, HONESTLY, I AM. I HAVEN'T BEEN MOANING THAT MUCH AT ALL ON THIS ONE. I THINK YOU WILL BE PROUD OF ME.
GOOD, MATE. I'M ALREADY PROUD OF YOU.

Carlos was a decent enough lad. He took me round the food market. I saw loads of chicken heads laid out on a tray. It looked like the kids' game Guess Who? I eat chicken – big fan of it – so I should be happy to eat its head, but these ones didn't look happy. At least when you see a fish head they don't have an upset expression on their face, but the chickens looked proper dead with their eyes rolled into their heads and beaks open. Carlos said Mexicans just boil them and they're ready to eat. I wonder if someone has got chicken heads mixed up with chicken eggs.

Before we left the market I tried donkey meat. This was the worst meat I have ever had. It's dark, chewy, fatty, smelly meat. I've heard the dodo died out due to it not tasting nice, in which case I think the donkey will be next.

Carlos then took me to his neighbourhood. People were out on the streets. Small papier-mâché bulls were being painted. Carlos told me that local people attach fireworks to these model cows, stick them on their heads and then run into a crowd. Mexico is like MTV's *Jackass*. As we were walking down the street I saw the man who was making the fireworks. I'm not sure if he saw me as he only had one eye. At home he'd be retired now after an accident at work like that. Here in Mexico they say, 'Carry on working. You have another one.' He was working out of two carrier bags. One contained paper that he was using to make the tube, the other bag was full of gunpowder.

We carried on to Carlos's home, where I met his parents. While we were having a drink there was a massive explosion. It reminded me about what Steve had said about the event being banned. Carlos said it has already been banned in many areas of Mexico due to deaths. Jamie the producer came in from outside acting all weird. I asked him what was going on, but he wouldn't say. He then asked if I wanted to get involved and run down the street with a bull on my head while fireworks went off. I said the cyclops firework-maker had put me off going anywhere near this event. I asked Carlos if he would be doing it. It turned out that Carlos normally stays in on this day as it can be quite dangerous on the streets. His mam and dad went on to say how they normally go away for the weekend but stayed this time as they knew I was coming.

Outside, I saw a crowd of about 300 people and a papier-mâché cow covered in fireworks. People were throwing buckets of liquid over themselves. I thought it might have been petrol just to add a bit more danger to the whole thing, but Carlos told me it was water so they can't catch fire. The fuses were lit, and the crowd ran. I hid behind a wall until the fireworks stopped then I told Jamie the producer that I wasn't hanging around. But as I walked down the road I heard people shouting. I turned to see I was being chased by what seemed like the whole neighbourhood. I legged it. Carlos caught up with me, and we ran into a house that belonged to his cousin. He said we should go up to the roof where we would be safe.

What the hell has this got to do with Easter?

We stayed on the roof for a good two hours, dodging fireworks. Finally, there seemed to be a quiet spell – I suppose the one-eyed firework-maker couldn't keep up with the demand – so we ventured out to a local place for something to eat. It was my kind of place – mainly old people. There was a live band playing nice, happy-sounding music. It was all in Mexican but it sounded good. But then who knows, it could have been about someone having their head cut off like the stuff Edgar told me. I sat and watched old people dancing while munching through some biscuits that were on the table until an old woman came over and dragged me up. I thought she might have lost her husband recently so I felt I had a duty to give her a dance, but then I saw her five minutes later with another bald-headed fella. I think she was just old and her eyesight had gone a bit and she thought I was him. I really don't know how people get to be old in this mental town.

MONDAY 5TH APRIL

I caught sight of a few local newspapers today. They all had gruesome pictures on the cover. There was a big photo of a car accident with dead bodies and a picture of an old man who had shot himself in the head. Back home a headline like 'Shocking images inside' normally end up being just of Charlotte Church on a beach with a spot on her arse. I suppose if you're seeing bloody images like this every day they're bound to become less shocking and make you more immune to violence.

The papers were also carring an image of the Chichen Itza with Elton John's face next to it. He's playing a gig there soon.

That's where we were heading too.

We flew to Cancun today to get closer to Chichen Itza. On the way to the hotel we stopped off at a graveyard. I often have a walk round graveyards when Suzanne and me go away for the weekend. We like looking at how long the people lived for. This graveyard looked a lot different to any I'd seen before. It was really colourful. The graves were painted in blues, pinks, yellows and reds. They looked more like the beach huts you get in Kent. And the whole family seems to get buried together – some of these graves were bigger than the flat I used to live in. I like this. Why does a graveyard have to be so morbid? Andreas, who has been with us during filming, told me that they have a thing in Mexico called the 'Day of the Dead'. It's a massive celebration of death where everyone has a day off to remember friends or family, and in Mexico with all this violence I'm guessing there is a lot of remembering to do. I like the Day of the Dead idea. We have a day dedicated to eating pancakes so why not have a day for the dead? I don't know why we don't like talking about death in Britain. I wanted to do a TV programme on death, but everyone I met to talk about it said they don't think people want to hear about it. It's about time we did something to make people less worried about it.

I suppose that Grim Reaper image we use to depict death doesn't help. He's a morbid-looking fella, isn't he? Just 'cos he's the bringer of bad news, why does he have to look so fed up? My postman brings me nothing but bad news in the form of bills, but I can't shut him up. Perhaps the Grim Reaper has just been in the job for too long. Getting rid of the hoodie would be a good start.

I like the hotel, it's quite fancy. The towels in the bathroom are laid out to look like a family of swans. I wonder if they do other animals for different days. I'll keep an eye on it.

TUESDAY 6TH APRIL

I met a man called Eugene today who took me to meet some charros. Charros are Mexican cowboys who do horse shows. I wasn't looking forward to it. I never played at being a cowboy even when I was younger. I was given a cowboy outfit when I was about five, but that was only because the shop had run out of Batman costumes. I didn't even wear jeans until I was about 17 'cos I didn't think they were comfy. And for me a horse is too much hassle anyway. They take over your life and cost a fortune. A girl who lived next door but one to us had a horse but couldn't afford to look after it properly. She didn't even have a stable for it, so they just kept it in their house. I saw it in their lounge one day when I was going door-to-door selling plants to make some money.

The other reason I never got into horses was 'cos my dad didn't rate John Wayne as an actor so I didn't get to see many westerns on the TV. Oh, and then there's that time I came off a horse at a local fête and was dragged along being kicked in the head. That's probably the main reason why I'm not a fan.

Eugene took me to a market before going to the ranch. He bought me lunch, rabbit in a spicy sauce. He had the rabbit's head. He said it was the best part as you get the brain. I didn't bother fighting him for it.

When we got to the ranch, I met the main men, who were brothers. They wore the proper cowboy kit and showed me some of their skills, from lassoing to doing a skid on a horse. They were really good. The first shock of the day was not from horses though, but from a swarm of bees that flew over us. It looked like a black cloud. It took my breath away. I quite like a bee on its own, but en masse they're quite frightening. Eugene said he hoped they weren't African bees as they could kill us. He said if one African bee stings you, they leave a smell that makes the other bees attack. He said even if you jumped in water they would wait for you to emerge and then get you. I'd never heard of this. I'm going to look it up on the internet once I'm back home.

Once the swarm had gone, I was given a horse called Espanner. It was so well trained it almost second-guessed what I wanted it to do. Eugene gave me a small whip to speed the horse up, but whenever it got a glimpse of the whip it bolted. I wanted to give the whip back to Eugene

WHY THE LONG FACE?
SUZANNE WARNED ME ABOUT BROKEBACK MOUNTAIN.
ONE TOO MANY TEQUILAS.

but every time I tried the horse saw it and bolted. This is what I don't like about horses. They're too big and they have a mind of their own.

After an hour or so of trotting and learning a few tricks Eugene said the charros would like to celebrate all my progress by drinking some tequila. I've never been a fan of the stuff but I said okay as I didn't want to be rude. The charros turned up with a huge bottle of the stuff and poured me a big one – with a worm in it! I've seen booze with insects and creatures in it before but I've always avoided it. I've seen scorpions and snakes shoved into bottles but I just thought it was a way of ripping off the customer, as they're getting less tequila due to all the space taken up by having a huge lizard in there. They do it in Thai restaurants in London. You ask for a drink, and it comes in a glass with loads of seaweed and pebbles in it like a scene from *Finding Nemo*.

Eugene said I was lucky to get the worm and that I should try it as it is very tasty. I said I'd eat half if he had half. Before I'd finished saying that he had eaten his half. Now I was left with half a worm, which in a way is worse than a full one. As I put it close to my mouth I gagged and with my hand shaking so much I ended up dropping the worm.

'I'm not bothered about it being on the floor. That isn't a problem. It's just a bit of soil. I can eat that,' I said.

Eugene said, 'We can wash it.'

Great. 'Do you chew or do you just swallow?' I asked.

Eugene said, 'Of course you chew. And you try to figure out the flavour and everything.'

I said, 'I don't know what a worm should taste like. I don't know if it's off. Do you know what I mean? There's no reference point. I swear it's still moving. It's just pissed up. Look at me hand shaking. I can't hold it still.'

Eugene said, 'You can't imagine how expensive a couple of hundred grammes of this is at a restaurant. In the most expensive area of Mexico City for this kind of worm they are, like, I don't know, £50 at least.'

'For worms?'

'For worms. And they are very good.'

'And that's a romantic night out, is it?'

'It might be. They are known to be an aphrodisiac.'

I decided. 'Right, here we go. Just do it. It's like me neck knows what's happening. It's going "no, I'm not letting it in". Did you see that then? I was almost sick. Something came up. A couple of crickets from the other day probably. Come to say hello, it's a mate of his. Why can't I do this? Errr. I can't do it. I can't. Have I got to chew it? It's still in there . . .'

I finally swallowed.

'Oh, there you go.'

Eugene then tried to get me to ride a bull.

I refused.

He asked again.

I asked to see the bull first.

I saw the bull.

I refused.

I don't know why, with all these horses about, anyone would need to ride a bull around here. One of the brothers started to do a hand signal at me. Eugene said it was a signal that suggested I was scared. I told him I had worked that out myself. It wasn't difficult. He was basically mimicking an arsehole opening and shutting.

I said he could make all the hand signals he wanted.

The charro then went and got his son, who looked about two or three years old, and sat him on the bull. I doubt this kid could even ride a bike, yet here they were sticking it on a bull with no helmet or kneepads just to try and make me look like a chicken. I told them they could stick their younger baby on it if they wanted as I wouldn't be getting on it.

I headed back to the van as I wasn't going to be pressurised into riding a bloody bull. Everyone was shouting me back, but I took no notice and kept walking. Then I heard buzzing. I looked up to see about 300 bees crawling and flying all over the place. I legged it.

Nowhere is bloody safe here.

WEDNESDAY 7TH APRIL

Woke with a sore arse after all the horse-riding and also from the spicy rabbit I ate yesterday.

I just noticed the cleaner has made a swan again out of the bath towel, but it seems she didn't have time to do them properly today. The baby swan just looks like a flannel. And I've left all my soap and shampoo in the other hotel, which is well annoying as it was all new for this trip. I had to use the free stuff, which isn't very good for me as I've got sensitive skin.

We didn't do much today. Just sat on the balcony and had a walk around the local shops. I didn't buy anything. Suzanne expected a gift when I got back from Egypt, Brazil and India, but I never saw anything she'd like. And now, I figure, I don't really need to get her anything as she has probably stopped expecting stuff.

As I write this I have just discovered a basket of chocolate in the hotel room. I decide to try a Mexican Milky Bar. I wish I hadn't. The chocolate seems off to me. It's like the heat has melted it and then someone has frozen it again. I'm not prepared to pay for that so I've wrapped it up again, put it back in the basket and covered it with a bag of M&Ms.

THURSDAY 8TH APRIL

I met some Mayan people today. They are the ones who built the Wonder years ago. They lived in the middle of nowhere in huts made of straw and bamboo shoots.

One of them was a guy called Luis who didn't live in the village anymore but had family who did. As I arrived, his uncle was about to set off to get some honey. We decided to go with him. I just thought we'd be nipping to a local shop until I saw a big pole with an axe strapped to the end. We would be getting the honey from a wasps' nest.

Everything they eat has to be caught or killed as there was no local shop. Luis showed me a few plants they get food from and a tree that supplied a type of gum that could be used to clean your teeth with.

As I walked with Luis and his uncle, a local man who was leaning on his wall next to his hut watched us. He had the happiest face I'd seen in years. There was a younger lad playing with a piece of rubber who looked like he didn't know what day it was. But when you live in a place like this I don't think days of the week matter.

I asked Jamie about it. 'It can't be good for you, this, can it? This sort of remoteness. He hasn't even been to Mexico City. Brain numbing, innit?'

Jamie said, 'What do you think you'd do if you lived here?'

'I don't know. I wouldn't hang around here. I think I'd have to keep walking. You're all right up until about the age of six, because you've got a slide and swing, but after that it's a lot of hanging around. It's like waiting for a bus that's never coming. And I don't know how I would react to that. Hanging around just waiting all day. Cleaning your teeth with that stuff.'

'If you were the chief of this village what changes would you make?'

I said I'd bring in a shop.

'What kind of shop?'

'Just a hardware shop to make life easier. Sell toothpaste. That's a start, innit? I don't know. Maybe bring some more people in. That would be good.'

'How would you get them in?'

'Maybe have an open day sort of thing. Get people here. Chat about stuff. But the thing is, if you're doing nothing all day what do you chat about? It's like them old people you see sat at restaurant tables that are with each other all day. Nothing to talk about other than what flavour ice cream they're going to have for pudding. You need to stimulate your mind, don't you? I don't know how you can do that here. Yeah, you can plant stuff, but you have to wait ages for something to happen.'

Jamie asked me what kind of stuff I'd bring in.

'Like a film, to show them what else goes on?'

'Which film?'

'Just stuff, *Die Hard*? You know, Bruce Willis. Action stuff.'

'Which *Die Hard* would you show first?'

'Probably 2. Is that the one with the plane?'

Jamie said it was.

MEETING THE CAST OF THE MAYAN VERSION OF *HIGH SCHOOL MUSICAL.*

THE MAYAN VERSION OF PASS THE PARCEL ISN'T AS MUCH FUN.

I SAID THIS WAS NO WAY TO WAKE GRANDMA.

The smiling man was still looking on. So Jamie asked me If I wanted to go and chat to him.

'I don't know. What would he have to tell me? Interesting though, i'n't he? Look at him. Don't you think he's got a good face? Luis, what would they talk about? I was just thinking if I lived here, part of like living somewhere is talking to your neighbours. A bit of gossip.'

Luis said, 'Oh, they talk about what has happened in the day. What they found in the cornfield, in the jungle.'

'Doesn't that get a bit samey? "Oh, I found another chicken." "Yeah, I know. We found one yesterday and the day before." Do you know what I mean? Are there any surprises?'

Luis said, 'Sometimes they find gold in this area. We're part of the ancient city, and if you're out walking you can find a bowl with some simple coins in it. Gold.'

'Gold?'

'Yes, because when they had money the ancient people put it in a bowl underground for safekeeping. And they are lucky. If you find something from the ancient times this is good for you. And some relics, for example. Relics, little things inside the vegetation. Well, those things are new for them, and they feel more happy.'

'Is he on a lunch break? What's he doing? 'Cos he hasn't done much in the last ten minutes.'

Luis spoke to the man in Mayan. He answered.

Luis said, 'He says he is just watching us. Watching us. Because this is new for them.'

'What? Having us here?'

'Yeah. Watching people from different places is new for them.'

We walked towards the wasps' nest. I heard it before I saw it. It sounded like there were thousands of wasps in it, but Luis said there would only be a few hundred. I was still worried. I said I'd like to get the wasps' nest for his uncle so I stood on an old wall made of rocks and stretched as high as I could to hack away at the branch that held the nest. It was about the size of a basketball. Just as I got close to unhooking the nest, the wall beneath me collapsed, and I went arse over tit while trying to keep hold of the 20-foot stick with the axe on the end. Luis's uncle took over. He climbed the tree and got really close before

KARL'S FACTS

CHICHEN ITZA MEANS: 'WELL AT THE MOUTH OF THE ITZA'.

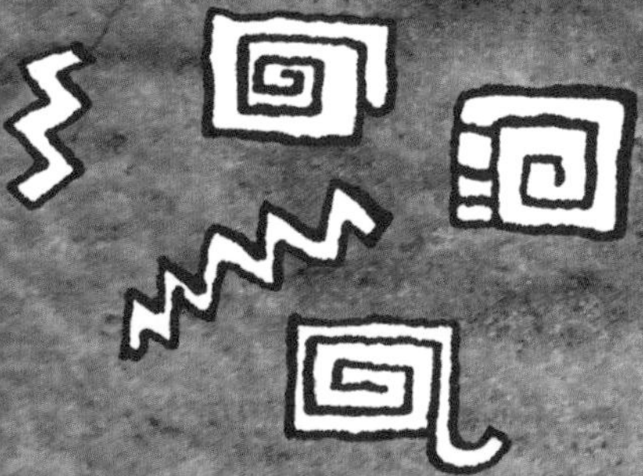

THE BUILDINGS OF CHICHEN ITZA ARE CONNECTED BY A NETWORK OF PAVED ROAD CALLED *SACBEOB*. ARCHAEOLOGISTS HAVE FOUND ALMOST 100 *SACBEOB* CRISS-CROSSING THE SITE.

THE MAYANS OFFERED UP HUMAN SACRIFICES TO THE GODS. IN SOME MAYAN RITUALS PEOPLE WERE KILLED BY HAVING THEIR ARMS AND LEGS HELD WHILE A PRIEST CUT THE PERSON'S CHEST OPEN AND TORE OUT HIS HEART AS AN OFFERING.

dropping the nest. He told me not to worry as wasps always fly upwards. He sounded certain, but I don't like taking things for granted. It would only take 10 or 20 mental wasps to decide they were sick of people ripping their nests down and I'd be done for. I told him about the film *My Girl* with Macaulay Culkin, who dies from bee stings after messing with a nest, but neither of them had seen it. Maybe that would be a better film to start with, rather than *Die Hard 2*.

Luis's uncle picked up the nest and, as they predicted, all the wasps had left. He gave me some of the wasp honey to eat. It was tasty. We then took the nest back to their hut where the family totally stripped it. There was Luis's uncle, two big women, a grandma and about five kids all in the one hut. They made me eat some wasp larva in a tortilla wrap. What am I doing? I didn't want to eat insects before I came to Mexico, now I'm eating them before they are even bloody born.

In return I gave them a packet of Monster Munch and a chunky Kit-Kat. They seemed to enjoy them. I think they got the better end of the deal.

Later Luis said he wanted to take me for a swim in a cenote. This is a massive hole, about 150 feet deep and full of natural water. I'm not a fan of swimming but thought at least if I went I wouldn't have to hang around being forced to eat cockroach sorbet or whatever else they'd found under a rock.

I enjoyed today.

FRIDAY 9TH APRIL

I was up early this morning to see the Wonder. Jamie wanted me to see it without having tourists everywhere. Problem was I still couldn't see it, as we got there so early it was still pitch black.

We wandered around in the dark for 30 minutes trying to find the Chichen Itza and eventually found it once the sun came up. I may as well have had a lie-in. I didn't have a guide today as Jamie and Barney decided I'd get all the information I needed by listening to an audio guide on some headphones.

It's an odd one, the Chichen Itza. It was a place built by the original Mayan people and was known for sacrifices (Elton John sang a song called 'Sacrifice' – maybe that's why he's playing here) and ripping out people's hearts and cutting heads off. Not exactly Alton Towers, is it? So it's an odd thing to make into a tourist attraction. May as well start doing tours around Fred West's house if this is what people want.

Considering that the Mayans live in huts made from bamboo and straw these days it seems a bit over the top that they built such a big, strong structure as a place to cut off heads.

The Chichen Itza is just a pyramid with four sides, with stairs on each side leading to some kind of bungalow on the top. Thinking about it, all those stairs defeat the idea of the bungalow on the top.

I tried to imagine what it would be like on the day of sacrifice. I suppose years ago it would have attracted big crowds 'cos there was

nothing else to do.The audio guide didn't talk much about how the head-cutting was done, but I imagined crowds gathered at the bottom and the head being cut off at the top and rolling down one of the sets of stairs. It must've been a bit of a gamble for a spectator picking a staircase and waiting. It would have been better if they had gone for a Helter Skelter-type design so no matter where you stood, everyone would see a rolling head.

The crowds of tourists started to enter around 8 a.m. I noticed tour guides getting groups of people to clap in front of the pyramid. It creates an odd echo, which I put down as coincidence, but the guide said the pyramid was designed to make this sound as it's like the cry of the quetzal, a sacred Mayan bird.

Unfortunately the clapping didn't stop from that point on. No wonder Elton John played here. It's probably the only place he can perform that

'Circle of Life' song that was in the *Lion King* film and get applause.

I wandered away from the tourists and found another cenote like the one I swam in yesterday. The audio guide said this would have been the Mayans' main source of water. Some say these holes where made by meteorites that hit earth millions of years ago. Apparantly the cenote was another place they sacrificed people.

I was looking into it when I noticed I was surrounded by lizards. Big ones. I gave one of them a bit of one of my Hobnobs. It seemed to love it. It ended up eating two to itself.

I realized then that I had swapped lives with a lizard on this latest trip. Here it was eating my Hobnobs and there I'd been eating crickets, worms and wasp eggs. It's odd to think the Mayans have probably never tried a Hobnob, yet this lizard had.

Back at the hotel, I found that the cleaner had left my Milky Bar out on the dressing table. I felt like a kid who'd been caught nicking again. Great, I thought, she found that but she didn't make me a proper flannel swan.

I told Jamie they might get charged about £2 for some chocolate. He said Sky should be able to cover the cost.

SATURDAY 10TH APRIL

We went home today. We had to fly into Dallas to get a connecting flight. While I was killing time in the airport, I decided to get some perfume for Suzanne from Duty Free. I soon wished I hadn't bothered. It was a right pain in the arse. Due to security, I had to put the small perfume box into another box that was about four times bigger and then check in the box, as I was not allowed to take any liquid onto the plane. I almost missed my connecting flight. The other annoying thing about that bloody box was that Suzanne looked disappointed when she opened it – I think she thought it was a bigger and better present judging by the outer box.

Checked online. African bees can kill a man.

$ 15.00
SABROSOS
Nachos

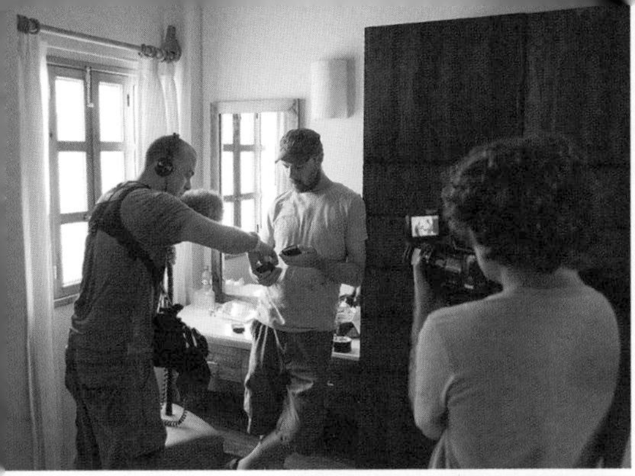

CHAPTER FIVE

THE GREAT WALL

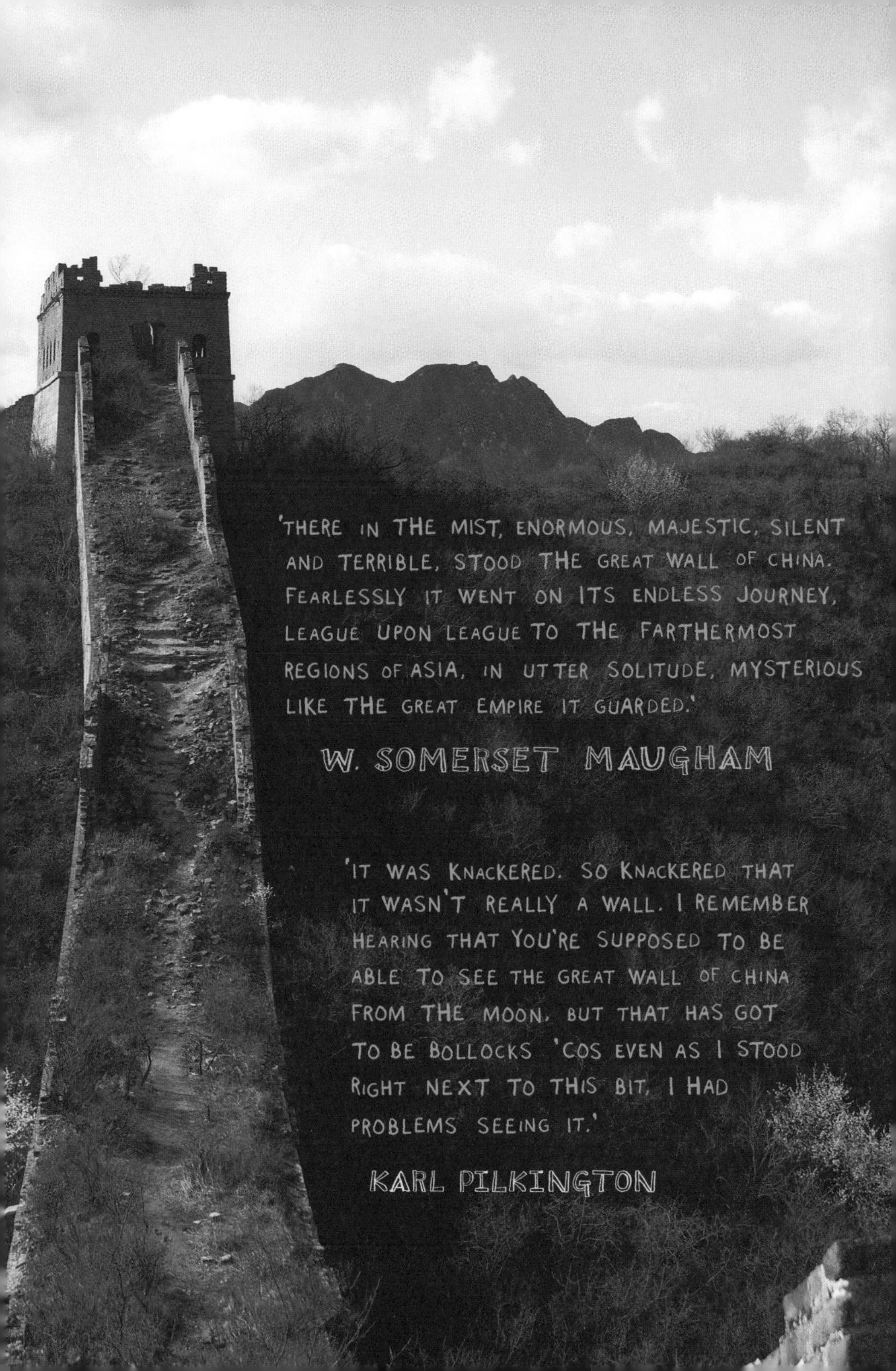
'THERE IN THE MIST, ENORMOUS, MAJESTIC, SILENT AND TERRIBLE, STOOD THE GREAT WALL OF CHINA. FEARLESSLY IT WENT ON ITS ENDLESS JOURNEY, LEAGUE UPON LEAGUE TO THE FARTHERMOST REGIONS OF ASIA, IN UTTER SOLITUDE, MYSTERIOUS LIKE THE GREAT EMPIRE IT GUARDED.'
W. SOMERSET MAUGHAM
'IT WAS KNACKERED. SO KNACKERED THAT IT WASN'T REALLY A WALL. I REMEMBER HEARING THAT YOU'RE SUPPOSED TO BE ABLE TO SEE THE GREAT WALL OF CHINA FROM THE MOON, BUT THAT HAS GOT TO BE BOLLOCKS 'COS EVEN AS I STOOD RIGHT NEXT TO THIS BIT, I HAD PROBLEMS SEEING IT.'
KARL PILKINGTON

CHINA
Badaling
The "Great" Wall
Hou Hai Lake
Xi Zha Ziba Dao He
Beijing
Shanhaiguan
Cricket fight
Redcapital Hotel
you want toad?
YELLOW SEA
snake
toad?
worm?
Wang Fu Jing food market
karl
fortune teller
sin paper
One of these with a door would be good!
by train
coffin
national sport
Zheng Zhou
Denfeng
FIRE!
Massage
man landing on head

The Great Wall

SATURDAY 17TH APRIL

The odd thing with China is, they like to go out of their way to do things differently. Even something simple like reading a book they mess with. They read books from top to bottom and then back to the top again. It looks like they're agreeing with everything they're reading. Their food looks different too. I used to walk through Chinatown on the way to work and the food I'd often see hanging in the restaurant windows was bright red chickens. I don't know if they did something odd to the chickens, or if they had just been sat in the window for so long that they had got a tan.

I like to have Chinese food maybe once a month but the idea of having it every day for a week doesn't excite me that much. China is also the country that seems to eat anything that moves. When I was growing up, there were always rumours of the Chinese eating dogs. When Small Terrance took over the local chippy and sold Chinese as well as fish and chips, people on the estate started to blame him for their missing pets.

Ricky and Steve think I should eat anything the locals eat, but I don't see the point of this in the long run. If the locals eat toads, and I try it and find that I really like it, I won't be able to find any butchers that sell toad back in London, so what's the point of getting a taste for it in the first place?

I also associate crazy inventions and technology with China. I have a book that is full of odd Chinese inventions. I remember seeing a hat with a toilet-roll holder on the top, and a picture of small mops on cats' feet so when they wander around the kitchen waiting to be fed they can clean the floor at the same time.

The Great Wall of China is the reason I'm visiting the country. I can't say I'm looking forward to seeing it. I always have a problem liking things that I'm told I should like. This has been the problem with most of the Wonders I have seen so far. The fact that this one is called the 'Great' Wall of China annoys me. I'll decide if it's great or not. It might end up being the 'All Right Wall of China' to me.

I'm expecting the Chinese to be really polite. I don't know why. I don't know if I read it somewhere, or I was told, or I've just come to that conclusion based on the fact that all the Chinese people I have met in my life so far have been polite. Which makes me wonder even more about the Wall being 'Great'. Even if it was rubbish, I have a feeling the Chinese would be too polite to say so. I suppose I'll find out, soon enough.

SATURDAY 24TH / SUNDAY 25TH APRIL

It was a really long flight. Out of the plane window I saw the sun, then the moon, and then the sun again. But I am glad to have seen the sun so much, because it doesn't look like I will be seeing much of it while I'm here, due to all the pollution. When we landed the sky was a murky, foggy grey. It was really cold as well. I had to get me coat out. I thought China was full of sweatshops but I don't know how in these temperatures.

We left the airport and got dropped off in town. Krish the producer said I should try and find my hotel by asking local people for directions. Great. I asked about 15 people, and not one of them spoke English. I showed the name of the place where I was staying on a piece of paper to an old man, and he grabbed my arm and walked with me. I thought he knew where the hotel was, but he just took me to a small seat, sat me down and then pummelled my back. He was a massager. He must have been about 80 years old but he was still pretty heavy-handed. I've never been touched by such an old man. But then again, was he really old? I've always thought that the Chinese don't age very well, that they look healthy and good-looking until about the age of 35, and then they just look old. I told Ricky once I thought that they maybe aged overnight like a pear, but he didn't understand what I was going on about.

This bloke who was massaging my back might only have been about 38. You decide.

Normally, a massage would be given with the sound of panpipes or a CD of whale noises, but in Beijing all I could hear was throats being cleared and spitting. It mustn't be rude to spit here, as everyone seems to do it. Finally, I found a young girl who translated what was on my piece of paper to a rickshaw driver.

The hotel I'm staying in seems nice enough, although my room is

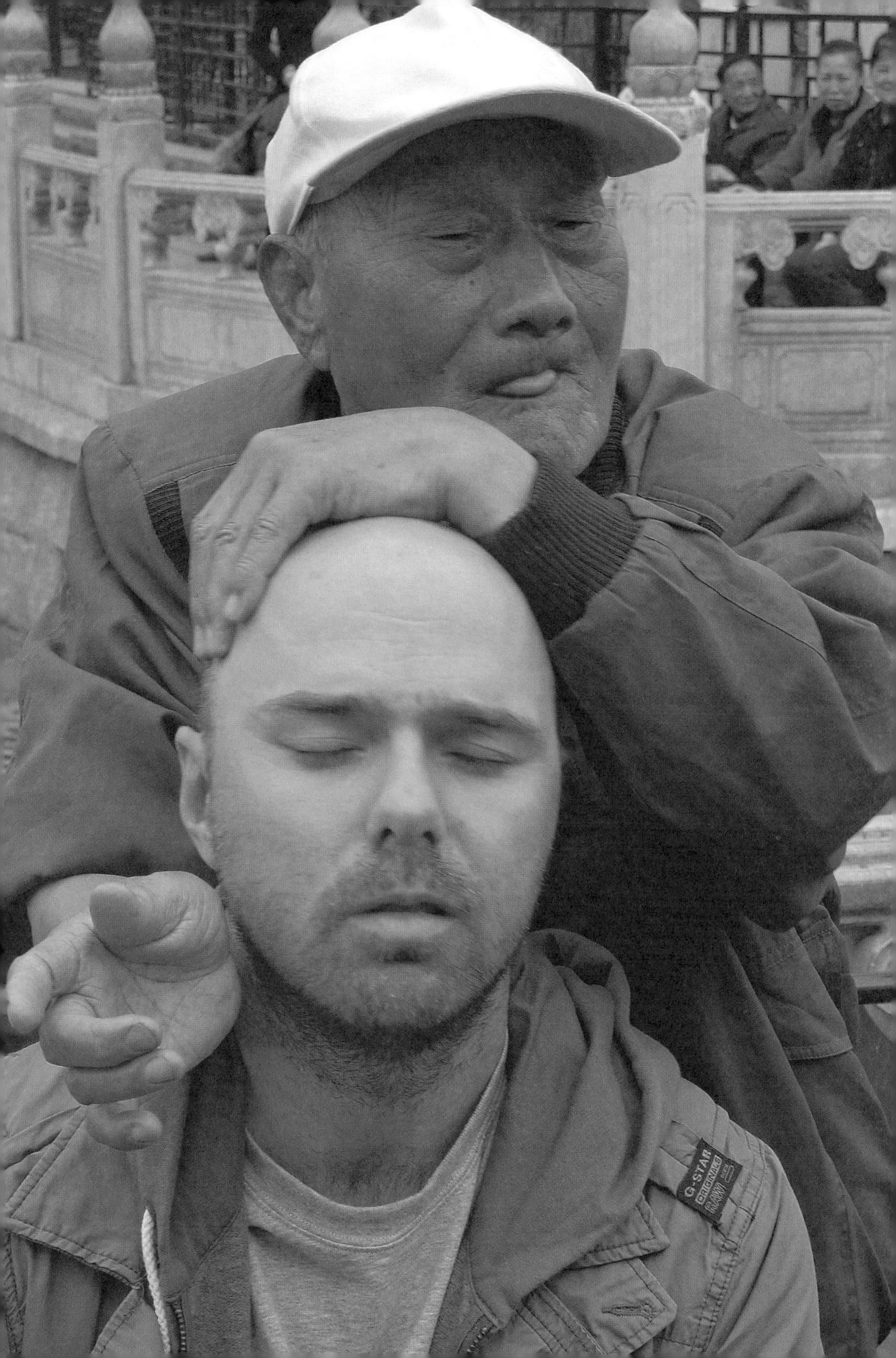
G-STAR

pretty small. I have a kettle and teabags, and next to that I have two goldfish in a bowl. I'm not sure if they're for company or for a snack. There is also a budgie hanging outside the window. I think I'll be happy here. I ate a packet of my Monster Munch that I had brought with me, and then we wandered off to an old local market. The smell was similar to Chinatown in Manchester and London – that sort of sweet and sour smell. The first thing I saw was a man on a street corner crouching next to a few washing-up bowls full of large catfish and eels. As I was looking at the fish, he pulled out three carrier bags. One was full of toads. At first I thought they were dead, as there wasn't much movement, but then one of the 80 or so toads tried to escape. The man grabbed it when it jumped and cut its head off. He then continued his way through the rest of them. It was a complete toad massacre, all because one had tried to get away. One by one, he took the head off, stripped the skin off the body, put the meat into one bag and the skin in the other. The toads went from hopping in carrier bag number one to being dead and stripped in bags two and three in a matter of seconds. I didn't find it easy to watch, but he was impressively fast and seemed to know what he was doing. The scissors cut through the toad's neck in one easy cut. They were just a basic pair of scissors similar to the ones I've got at home, the sort you use to cut string and wrapping paper, Sellotape . . . and toads' heads. He was an expert at toad stripping. He seemed pleased to show us his skill. He could probably do it blindfolded, like those soldiers you see putting together a machine gun.

As we watched, a few policemen turned up, and Krish thought we had better move on, as we were not supposed to be filming around there. They like to protect how China is perceived, and there was a chance that they could take the tape from the camera off us. We went to a newer part of the market. The stalls and layout looked more similar to the markets I see at home, until I got a closer look. They were selling insects. Rows and rows of bugs on sticks. They had big black scorpions, snakes, worms and locusts all laid out like they were queuing to get on Noah's Ark. People had told me about street food in China, but I didn't think it meant making food out of stuff that normally crawls the street. Most of the bugs had been dipped in some sort of oil to make them look more tempting to the eye while the lizard looked like someone

had just found it crushed under a breezeblock and stuck a stick up its arse. Seeing all this makes me wonder if the old woman in the nursery rhyme who swallowed a cat to catch the bird to catch the spider was Chinese. That sounds like a normal diet round here.

Our van driver stopped off to eat some duck foetus eggs. They looked rank. I said before I came here that the Chinese eat anything that moves; I've now found out that they'll eat stuff before it's even had a chance to move. Why they can't just wait for it to be born and eat it as a duck I don't know. They might as well eat duck sperm to save even more time. I've heard that they also eat 100-year-old eggs but I don't know how anything gets to be that old here without someone eating it. We went back to the hotel. I ate one of my five Twix bars and another packet of Monster Munch. I should've brought more.

MONDAY 26TH APRIL

I didn't sleep very well because the buzzer for the front door of the hotel is next to my room. It sounds like a car alarm. Roadworks also started really early, which seemed to irritate the budgie, so then it tweeted for half an hour. I don't know how it isn't dead. It's freezing out there. I checked my phone. My mam had emailed to ask if I was okay and wanted to know if I would be seeing the Terracotta Army, as she had seen it on the telly and it looked good. Talking about the Terracotta Army reminded her that me dad had painted her gnomes, so she'd attached a photo to her email. Suzanne had also texted to say good-night. The time difference is going to make it tough to have a chat with anyone at home. Seven hours' time difference.

Just as I nodded off, Krish woke me up to tell me that Steve had left a message on my phone. I hadn't been listening to voicemail, as it's too expensive, but Krish said I needed to hear it to find out what plans I had for today.

HELLO, KARL, MATE. IT'S STEPHEN HERE. LISTEN, I'VE GOT A LITTLE TREAT ARRANGED FOR YOU TODAY. I KNOW THAT YOU'RE FASCINATED BY THE STRANGE, THE WEIRD, THE ESOTERIC, AND OBVIOUSLY ONE OF THE BIG PARTS OF CHINESE CULTURE IS FORTUNE-TELLING. SO WE'VE ARRANGED FOR YOU TO GO AND SEE A FORTUNE-TELLER, TO GET SOME PREDICTIONS ABOUT YOUR FUTURE, MY FRIEND. ENJOY.

I wasn't happy about this. I don't want to know what the rest of my life is going to be like. Even if what he says is nonsense I think it will play on my mind and stop me getting on with my life. The best thing about life is the surprises, and we're getting fewer and fewer surprises these days. Even the simple thing of waking up in the morning and opening the curtains to see what the weather is like is a nice surprise, but now *Countryfile* with John Craven has taken that away with its five-day forecast. In truth, the only thing that would have been handy about knowing my future is that we wouldn't have booked into this hotel, as we'd have known about the bloody roadworks outside. In the morning I got up and had a hard-boiled egg and some odd bread, and then headed over to the fortune-teller.

The place didn't look very mystical. It was on a dual carriageway with a 'wash while you wait' car wash on one side and a block of flats on the other. It turned out that the fortune-teller didn't speak a word of English, so we had to use a translator. After asking the date and time of my birth he got straight on with the fortune-telling.

The translator said, 'The south side of your house is quite low. Is that right?'

'Err, low, yeah, I'm on the ground floor. It's low. Yeah, I'll give him that.'

Mr Sow, the fortune-teller talked in Chinese.

The translator said, 'You will have to pay attention to your health because you have some kind of heart problem.'

'Oh, here we go . . . What sort of heart problem?'

The translator said, 'Something to do with your heart, blood vessels, so you really need to take care of that.'

'It's weird, because my dad had a problem with his heart, and they say it runs in the family.'

The translator said, 'You be very careful if you do have a problem. It's probably something to do with your heart.'

'Is it going to kill me then? Is this what he's telling you? That the problem with the heart is going to finish me off?'

'Ninety per cent.'

'Ninety per cent!'

'But maybe we can change it.'

'All right, that sounds better.'

The translator said, 'Do a lot of good things. Try to raise the goodness in your life.'

'Wha–? I've got to look at the good things in my life? Do a lot of good things, like helping people? I do loads of that. I do loads of good. Tell him I do Tools for Africa – four quid a month, Help the Aged – I think they get a fiver, deaf kids, and the latest one was Red Cross, so that's four charities each costing on average five quid a month so that's 20 quid a month I'm giving to charity.'

The translator talked in Chinese to Mr Sow, then said, 'Well done. Otherwise you would be even worse. You would be more ill than you are now.'

After he told me this news he asked me to write down three sins. After quite a bit of thinking, I went with the following:

SIN 1 I AM SORRY ABOUT NICKING MARS BARS FROM THE NEWSAGENT'S THAT I DELIVERED PAPERS FOR. I HELPED MYSELF TO ONE EVERY DAY, SEVEN DAYS A WEEK, FOR OVER TWO YEARS (MAYBE THIS IS WHY I'M GONNA HAVE A HEART ATTACK).

SIN 2 I AM SORRY FOR OPENING THE POST THAT WAS ADDRESSED TO BRUCE (THE MAN WHO USED TO OWN OUR FLAT) INSTEAD OF FORWARDING IT ON.

SIN 3 I AM SORRY FOR PUTTING PUTTY IN CARL GRIMSHAW'S HAIR WHEN I WAS A KID. IT ALL GOT TANGLED UP, AND HE HAD TO HAVE HIS HEAD SHAVED. HIS MAM WENT MAD AT ME BECAUSE HE HAD A FUNNY-SHAPED HEAD AND THIS MADE IT STAND OUT EVEN MORE.

Mr Sow then told me he would burn one of the sins and I must take the other two and dispose of one on a mountain and the other in the sea. He and his workers then did a small ceremony for me, which involved standing with a joss stick in the freezing cold while people danced around me setting fire to paper. All this standing about in the cold can't be good for a man with a heart problem. Later, we went to a local place for something to eat. I played it safe and had some noodles but ate another Twix when I got back to my room.

TUESDAY 27TH APRIL

I woke up at 4.30 a.m. I still have jet lag. I looked out of the window to see that even the budgie was asleep . . . or dead.

To kill some time I picked up a book in my room with quotes from a man called Mao Tse-Tung. He was a Chinese statesman. He once said: 'We think too small, like the frog at the bottom of the well. He thinks the sky is only as big as the top of the well. If he surfaced, he would have an entirely different view.'

It made me think about how I was a bit like that frog before I started to travel the world for this programme. Having said that, I'm not sure it's even worth the frog coming out of its well to see more of the sky anyway, as it's pretty grim here with all the pollution, plus the fact that it ain't safe for a frog in China 'cos someone would come along and

THE FORTUNE TELLER, OR MISFORTUNE TELLER IN MY CASE.

MY SINS ARE ABOUT TO GO UP IN SMOKE.

HOW ABOUT BUILDING A FEW GREAT WALLS IN THE TOILETS?

I BOUGHT THESE THEN WISHED I HADN'T. WITH ALL THE POLLUTION IN BEIJING YOU CAN'T ACTUALLY SEE THE SUN.

grab it, cut its head off and eat it. So, all in all, it wasn't good advice from Mao Tse-Tung. I had a hard-boiled egg for breakfast again. The crew were filming on the street today, getting pictures of traffic and local people. As they worked, I realised I needed the loo. I popped into one that was close by and was greeted by two blokes squatting on their haunches. The cubicles didn't have doors on them.

One of the men gave me a wink. At first I thought he may have just been straining then I noticed it was one of the chefs from where we ate last night. The other fella was busy nattering on his mobile, probably taking an order for a takeaway. I nipped out and told Krish about my dilemma. I have always struggled with these hole-in-the-ground toilets. It's not so much the hole in the ground, more the fact that there is no door. It's odd to think they built the Great Wall of China but can't be bothered to get a bit of MDF, stick some hinges on it and make a door. There were no sinks or toilet paper either. I wonder if I can find one of them toilet-roll hats I saw in my invention book. I went to an indoor market while they carried on filming. The place was filled with replica goods being sold at low prices: clothing, DVDs, mobile phones, watches and shoes. I bought a mobile-phone holder, a coat and a DVD to watch, as there are no English-speaking channels on the telly. I was going to get something to eat but even this place, which is specifically aimed at tourists, still offered up odd food. Blood cake was everywhere. Big blocks of the stuff. A block of blood should not have the word 'cake' after it. It doesn't kid me into wanting some. They may as well say 'Shite Gâteau'. I drove back in the bus with everyone else. The driver broke wind twice. He didn't seem embarrassed about it. When I got back the others told me the coat looked nice enough but probably isn't very waterproof.

I had some more noodles at the place on the corner and was told by Krish that I would be seeing the Wall tomorrow.

I watched the DVD I bought before I went to bed. It was a pirate copy so the quality was really poor, but the film wasn't very good anyway – it had been recorded with a camcorder in a cinema. I saw a bloke get up and leave the cinema about 35 minutes in, so even he thought it wasn't very good.

They're probably right about that coat not being waterproof.

WEDNESDAY 28TH APRIL

I was up early again so I managed to talk to Suzanne before she went to bed. I told her that I was off to see the Wall. I told her that I can't be doing with the Wonder part of these trips, but she said it should be the icing on the cake. But the thing with me is, I don't really enjoy the icing on a cake. I often pull off the icing and leave it. The icing is just there to get your attention, but I wouldn't say it's the best bit. And that's how I feel about the Wonders – they're the reason I'm going everywhere, but they're never my favourite bit. I've never liked wedding cake due to the amount of icing, but then imagine a wedding cake without it; just a dark, stodgy, horrible dry sponge. The icing covers up the mess, and that's how I feel about most of the Wonders. They use them to get people to visit a place that you probably wouldn't think about visiting. Maybe blood cake would look better with icing though.

We had the usual hard-boiled egg for breakfast and made our way over to the tour buses. Ricky and Steve had arranged for me to get a lift on a tour bus so I could learn a few things about the Wall before seeing it.

There must have been about 50 coaches parked up ready to head over to the Great Wall. After asking around I found the right bus. It was a full bus. About 50 people. About 50 Chinese people. The tour guide got on. He was also Chinese. He turned on the microphone and started his tour in Chinese. Brilliant.

I didn't have a clue what was being said so I just tried to enjoy the trip.

The passengers all looked really old, but maybe I'm just right about them not ageing well. The average age seemed to be about 70. I don't understand why so many old Chinese people have not seen the Wall at some point in their life already, which makes me think it can't be very good. If they're late in their life and haven't bothered to make the journey to see it before now, what does that tell you?

In a way it's just as well I can't understand the Chinese tour guide as I wouldn't have been able to hear him anyway due to the amount of coughing and clearing of throats on the bus. Coughing and clearing of throats must have the same effect as yawning as everyone was doing it. I was sat next to an old woman who looked like butter wouldn't melt in her mouth . . . mainly due to the fact that she'd cough it up with the

THE GREAT WALL BY GOLF BUGGY.

ME ON A BUS.

COME TO THE GREAT WALL! IT'S GREAT!

VAN DRIVER WHO EATS ANYTHING. HE'S NOT SMOKING THAT FAG. HE'S EATING IT. HIS HAT ISN'T A NOVELTY HAT, IT'S WHAT'S LEFT OVER FROM BREAKFAST.

rest of her phlegm before it had a chance to melt. Every minute she'd clear her throat and then spit into a carrier bag she had with her. I couldn't wait to get to the Wall. With all this spit flying around I suppose I'll find out if this coat I have bought is waterproof or not. Eventually we pulled up in a huge car park next to some market stalls selling novelty Chinese hats, woolly hats, scarves, fridge magnets and plates. I bought a woolly hat as it was freezing and then joined the massive queue to get in.

Once I was through the entrance I could see the Wall for miles, like a long snake making its way across the mountains. It was pretty impressive. I wanted to stop for a few minutes to take it all in, but the guide shouted at me to move along. I told Krish that we may as well go it alone now, as we were not going to gain anything by staying with a guide who only spoke Chinese. He agreed.

We managed to find a bit of the Wall that wasn't too busy. I looked at it. It looked quite new. I was trying to understand what all the fuss was about, but it wasn't easy when I knew nothing about the Wall. Krish gave me a guide to China that had a chapter on the Great Wall. It said it was heavily restored in both the 1950s and 1980s. Surely it can't count as a Wonder if it's not original? If when I went to see the Taj Mahal in India I got there to find a new house built there with a double garage and a gravel driveway, they couldn't still sell it as the Taj Mahal, so why is the Wall getting away with it? Bloody hell, is everything fake in China? The coat I bought, the DVD and now the Wall.

I said I'd had enough and wanted to leave. I had another message on my phone.

HELLO MATE, STEVE MERCHANT HERE. HOW YOU DOIN'? I HEARD THAT YOU WENT TO SEE THE GREAT WALL OF CHINA TODAY, OR 'THE WALL' AS IT'S KNOWN IN CHINA. I'M SURE YOU ENJOYED IT. OBVIOUSLY, IT'S AMAZING. I KNOW YOU LIKE A BIT OF D.I.Y. SO I IMAGINE YOU LOVE TO SEE HOW A NICE WALL HAS BEEN MADE, AND RICKY AND I WANT YOU TO SEE MORE OF IT. IN FACT, WE WERE HAVING A CHAT AND WE'D LIKE YOU TO SEE ALL OF THE GREAT WALL. LITERALLY ALL OF IT. WE WANT YOU TO TRAVEL THE ENTIRE LENGTH OF THE WALL. SO, ENJOY IT! SEE YA!

I didn't want to see any more of the Wall, but Krish said it would be worthwhile as I'd get to see other parts of China along the way.

We're staying at a different place tonight. It's a house in the middle of nowhere. It looked quite new at first but on closer inspection it was falling apart. The front door wouldn't close, and it is really cold, and my room smells damp. There's a few teabags but no milk.

THURSDAY 29TH APRIL

I saw an old, original part of the Wall today high up in the mountains. It was knackered. So knackered that it wasn't really a wall. I remember hearing that you're supposed to be able to see the Great Wall of China from the moon, but that has got to be bollocks 'cos even as I stood right next to this bit, I had problems seeing it.

I don't know what would make me happy. I didn't like the brand new Wall, and this old bit isn't impressing me either. I'm harder to please than Goldilocks. Still, the journey wasn't a complete waste of time, as I got rid of one of my sins on the mountaintop.

We drove on to a small village where we decided to get out and take a wander. I passed a house with a man doing some D.I.Y. I couldn't work out what he was making, but I guessed that it wouldn't be a toilet door. I asked Krish if I had time to nip in and get a closer look. It turned out the man was making a coffin. Huge thing, it was. I asked who it was for. He said it was for the woman who lives in the house. At that point the woman came to the door. She told me that it is normal practice to have a coffin made for you at your house. She was 69. After what the fortune-teller told me maybe I should get this fella's number.

I'm not sure I like the idea of having the coffin made in my own front garden. Every day when you leave the house, there it is. It's probably the only time I wouldn't want a handyman to complete the job in the estimated time. Plus, the flat I live in has not got the space to have something like that just sat there, and if I popped it outside I would have to get a parking permit for it.

As the man worked away on the coffin, the woman looked on, inspecting it as if she was having her porch painted. She said, 'Once this is done, I'll feel much happier. Because I'll know it has been done. And I will know what sort of coffin I'll be in when I die. I will be much happier.'

She told me that her husband died 20 years ago at the age of 50 and his coffin wasn't ready. They don't normally plan to have the coffin made until they are around 70, so he ended up being buried in the one that was prepared for her mam.

We left them to it and carried on walking. I saw another coffin outside another house. This one was finished and painted black, and it was pushed up against the wall ready for whoever needs it. If we did this, my mam would have filled hers with clutter in no time. Wherever there's a space, she fills it with something. Saying that, it wouldn't be so bad if they got rid of the lid and used it as a big windowbox or something, and popped some flowers in until it was needed.

While I'd been checking out the coffins Krish had arranged for me to have some lunch at a local's house. In return I chopped some wood for their fire. There was a woman and her husband with a small kid. The gran also lived with them. The kid wore some pants with the arse cut out. These are popular here, as kids are potty-trained before they

KARL'S FACTS

DURING ITS CONSTRUCTION, THE GREAT WALL WAS CALLED 'THE LONGEST CEMETERY ON EARTH' BECAUSE MORE THAN ONE MILLION PEOPLE DIED BUILDING IT.

ACCORDING TO LEGEND, A HELPFUL DRAGON TRACED OUT THE COURSE OF THE GREAT WALL FOR THE WORKFORCE. THE BUILDERS SUBSEQUENTLY FOLLOWED THE TRACKS OF THE DRAGON.

THE CHINESE INVENTED THE WHEELBARROW AND USED IT EXTENSIVELY IN BUILDING THE GREAT WALL.

THE LENGTH OF ALL CHINESE DEFENCE WALLS BUILT OVER THE LAST 2,000 YEARS IS APPROXIMATELY 31,070 MILES.
THE EARTH'S CIRCUMFERENCE IS 24,854 MILES.

learn how to remove pants. Something else I learned about young kids in China was that parents like their children to have flat heads at the back. I never got the full story. I must look online when I get home.

As I was chopping the wood, I turned to see the woman of the house throwing something around in the air and then bashing it on the floor. It was a toad. Ten minutes later it was cooked in a bowl with some pork and salad. I took some pork and salad, and commented on how nice it was, but the gran kept pointing to the bowl of toad. I said I was okay with the pork, at which point she basically wrestled with me and forced a piece into my mouth. That isn't normal, is it? Hardly the sort of thing you see on *Come Dine with Me*. I yelled at her, which I suppose is a bit rude, but I didn't like being force-fed toad. I told her that the baby needs help being fed, not me. I grabbed some and forced it in her face. She didn't seem too happy about it either. I wouldn't be surprised if no one eats toad in China, and it's just something Ricky and Steve sorted out to wind me up.

I left the village and saw more of the Wall that afternoon. As I got higher up, my phone picked up a message. It was from Steve.

HELLO, MATE, IT'S STEPHEN HERE. HOPE YOU'RE DOING WELL. JUST WANT TO LEAVE YOU A QUICK MESSAGE. WE'VE SORTED SOMETHING OUT FOR YOU – ONE OF THE GREAT ELEMENTS OF CHINESE CULTURE AND POPULAR OF COURSE IN THE UK IN THE 1970S. WE'VE ARRANGED FOR YOU TO SEE SOME KUNG FU. YEAH, ENJOY IT! SEE YA.

Great.

FRIDAY 30TH APRIL

Saw more of the bloody Wall today on the way to the kung fu school. I don't have much more to say about it. Krish tried to sell it to me by

功德無量
重興大法王寺

saying it's impressive because it's so long, but so is the M6, and that's older than a lot of this Wall.

We got to the Shaolin School where they teach kung fu. It's not something I've ever been into – kung fu, or any martial art for that matter. I've always thought it just made fights longer than they need to be. Any kung fu film where you see a fight can go on for ages. I bet most of the time people who have a fight in China forget what the argument was about by the time they've finished fighting. There can only be one winner so why not just get it done sooner? To me it's like people who have it away all night. I had some neighbours like that once; they'd be at it all night. Why? Get the job done and get to sleep.

When we arrived at the Shaolin School there were kids everywhere doing kung fu. All in sync and all wearing the same uniform. It was nothing like PE lessons at my school. Most of that lesson used to be spent in Lost Property trying to find shorts that fitted me. No one remembered their own kit. It was more like Trinny and Susannah than a PE lesson.

A man called Leo introduced himself and said he would give me a guide around the place. He was a teacher and kung fu expert who explained why the art is such a big deal in China and how training methods can produce extraordinary skills and abilities.

First he took me up into the hills, where there were four students who demonstrated some of their skills. One smashed a wooden pole over another's back, another broke a metal bar on his head, and one bent a sharp spear using the ground and his neck. I didn't see the point of some of these tricks. I told Leo the only one I thought that might come in handy was smashing the metal bar, as I'm always banging my head, but he told me the spear to the throat was useful too, as the throat is one of the most sensitive parts of the body and this activity makes it stronger. At that moment Leo went and poked me in my throat with two fingers. I didn't even see it coming. It took my breath away for a moment. He was fast. I wouldn't be surprised if he'd checked my prostate gland at the same time.

The youngest of the students was a ten-year-old lad with a runny nose who did a forward roll and bounced off his head. This kid didn't smile much. I don't think he liked being at this school. Leo said the lad practised landing on his head every day and it would help strengthen his neck. At the moment it just looks like it's helping clear the snot out of his nose.

Leo kept telling me that a healthy body makes a healthy mind. I told him this is not always the case. 'Look at Stephen Hawking', I said. I don't think he knew who he was though. Before Leo left he said he wanted to give me some training tomorrow morning and would meet me at 4 a.m. I told him it was a daft time to get up. I said I would meet him at 5.30 a.m. He was adamant that we meet at 4 a.m., so in the end I had to agree. I'm staying in another hotel tonight. It isn't very nice. There are spit stains all over the carpet. I tried to get an early night but couldn't due to a kid outside who went up and down the corridor on a tricycle, so I got up and ate my last Twix.

The Great Wall

SATURDAY 1ST MAY

I was woken at 4.05 this morning by violent banging on my door. It was Leo. He told me I was late, handed me my outfit and stormed off.

He had relaxed a bit by the time I got in the van, but not as much as the driver, who broke wind twice during a 15-minute journey. It's amazing how acceptable spitting and farting seem to be. I don't know what you would have to do to be classed as rude in this country.

Leo worked me hard. I had a run, did some serious leg stretches, then he had me doing a toad hop up some stairs and throwing needles into a tree. He put his hand through some bricks (maybe that's why the Great Wall is such a mess?). I also tried to attack him when he seemed off guard. Each time he had me on the floor. I liked Leo and I have bruises to remember him by. I was aching

WARM-UP EXERCISES AT THE SHAOLIN SCHOOL.

IT'S MURDER GETTING THESE SHOES OFF.

AN AMAZED CROWD LOOKS ON.

a lot, so Krish said that the Chinese are into massage stuff and I should take advantage of having one as it would do me good after the workout I'd been having.

On the way to the massage we stopped off at a little café. It was a bit rank, but there was nothing else around and we were hungry, as we'd been up since 4 a.m. Loads of plates were brought to the table. I tucked in. Then Emma the translator walked in and told me I'd been eating dog. If the camera had been rolling I'd have thought I had been set up, but it wasn't, and everyone else looked at their plate to see if they had eaten it too. They hadn't. Just me. Just my luck. It didn't taste that good. I just thought it was cheap beef. Even food that I have at home tastes different here, so I didn't really question what it was.

Oh, well. Isn't there a saying that goes 'You can't keep an old dog down'? Guess I'll find out in the next few hours. Over at the massage place, I entered a really warm room that seemed to have way too much furniture in it for its size. I was greeted by a woman who asked me to remove my trousers and gave me some shorts. She rubbed my legs and feet, which was lovely. And then she set fire to them. Mental.

She dipped some rags into some type of oil and then placed them on my legs and set fire to them. I've no idea what good it does. I should be able to relax when having a massage but instead I was yelling me head off while looking for a fire extinguisher. She didn't stop though. You'd have thought that, even though she couldn't understand English, me yelling my head off would indicate that I wasn't happy. Like I've said, the Chinese mess with everything for the worse.

I was pissed off with Krish for putting me through that and then got even more wound up when I picked up a message from Ricky.

OH, COME ON, MATE, ALWAYS BE IN CONTACT. YOU NEVER ANSWER YOUR PHONE. I'VE CALLED A FEW TIMES NOW. YOU'RE NOT ON HOLIDAY. YOU'VE STILL GOT OTHER BUSINESS TO ATTEND TO. YOU KNOW THE RULES – GIVE US A CALL, ALWAYS BE IN CONTACT, ALWAYS BE AVAILABLE FOR WORK. THIS IS BAD, SON.

How can he still be so annoying when he's so far away?

I called him when I got to the next hotel.

HOW'S IT GOING?
WHY HAVEN'T YOU CALLED? DID YOU GET MY MESSAGE?
YEAH, I GOT YOUR MESSAGE, BUT I'VE BEEN IN THE MIDDLE OF NOWHERE, HAVEN'T I, LOOKING AT THE WALL.
NOT REALLY IN THE MIDDLE OF NOWHERE. THERE'S A BILLION PEOPLE IN THE PLACE YOU'RE IN, SO I DON'T THINK YOU COULD EVER BE IN THE MIDDLE OF NOWHERE.
WELL, WHEN YOU SEE IT YOU'LL SEE HOW LONELY I'VE BEEN. I'VE BEEN IN THE MIDDLE OF NOWHERE LOOKING AT A WALL. IT'S REALLY WEIRD HERE.
WHY?
JUST... EVERYTHING. EVERYTHING THAT HAPPENS HERE, IT'S JUST WEIRD. IT FEELS WEIRD. THE ATMOSPHERE'S WEIRD. EATING TOAD WAS WEIRD.
YOU DIDN'T EAT TOAD?
I HAD A LITTLE BIT OF TOAD.
I THOUGHT THAT WAS A MYTH. I DIDN'T REALISE THEY REALLY DID EAT TOAD THERE. I THOUGHT YOU JUST MADE THAT UP.
A WOMAN FORCED ME TO HAVE A BIT OF TOAD. I WAS WORRIED ABOUT GETTING A TASTE FOR IT. THAT WON'T BE HAPPENING. WHAT ELSE HAVE I BEEN UP TO? TOILETS. DO YOU KNOW HOW WHEN I GO INTO A PUBLIC TOILET I NIP IN WITH A COIN AND OPEN THE DOOR? WELL, YOU COULDN'T DO THAT HERE, 'COS THERE'S NO DOORS ON THE TOILETS.

I WAS WALKING DOWN THE ROAD THE OTHER DAY, AND THEY WERE FILMING SOME STUFF ON THIS STREET, TRAFFIC AND STUFF. I SAY, 'I'M JUST NIPPING IN HERE.' WALKED IN, WAS GREETED BY TWO FELLAS SQUATTING.
WHAT DID THEY SAY?
WELL, TO THEM IT'S NORMAL, SO THEY JUST SORT OF GAVE ME THE NOD. I WANDERED IN, AND STRAIGHT AWAY... WHEN YOU OPEN THE DOOR YOU DON'T TURN A CORNER OR ANYTHING, YOU WALK IN, AND THEY WERE JUST SAT THERE. THEY WERE CHEFS FROM THE PLACE ON THE CORNER, SO THAT'S REASSURING.
OH, NO. UNBELIEVABLE.
HONEST TO GOD, ONE OF THEM WAS ON THE PHONE TAKING AN ORDER. I'VE NEVER SEEN ANYTHING LIKE IT. I DON'T THINK I COULD EVER GET USED TO THAT. YOU NEED TO HAVE YOUR OWN SPACE WHEN YOU'RE DOING THAT. AND THEY'RE JUST THERE, ONE'S ON THE PHONE, THE OTHER ONE'S JUST SORT OF LOOKING AROUND.
THAT'S UNBELIEVABLE.
ARE YOU IMPRESSED WITH THE WALL?
IT'S NICELY DONE, BUT THEN AGAIN IT SHOULD LOOK ALL RIGHT – THE BIT I SAW THEY DID UP IN THE EIGHTIES.
THE OLDEST BITS ARE HUNDREDS OF YEARS OLD. WHAT DID THEY DO, JUST WALLPAPER AND PLASTER OVER IT? WHAT D'YOU MEAN THEY DID IT UP?

THEY DID IT UP AND MADE IT NICE, AND IT'S JUST LIKE ANY WALL THAT YOU'D SEE ANYWHERE. THERE'S NOTHING SPECIAL ABOUT IT. IT'S THE CHINA WALL BECAUSE IT'S IN CHINA. IT'S NOT GREAT. I DON'T KNOW WHY THEY USE THE WORD 'GREAT' IN IT.
WERE THERE LOADS OF PEOPLE ON BICYCLES?
NOT THAT MANY. BUT THEN THE FEW I'VE SPOKEN TO HAVE HAD OLD RELATIONS WHO'VE BEEN, LIKE, KNOCKED OVER ... ONE FELLA LOST A LEG, FROM BEING ON A BIKE. SO I THINK THEY MUST HAVE CUT DOWN ON THE NINE MILLION BICYCLES. I SAW ONE GET CRUSHED BY A VAN, SO THERE'S DEFINITELY NOT NINE MILLION. IT'S AT LEAST ONE LESS.
I DON'T THINK YOU SHOULD GET ALL YOUR INFORMATION ABOUT CHINA FROM KATIE MELUA SONGS EITHER. I DON'T KNOW IF THAT ONE'S OFFICIAL.
WELL, I KNEW NOTHING ABOUT THIS PLACE BEFORE I CAME HERE. PEOPLE HAVE BEEN SAYING 'OH, WELL, WHAT DID YOU THINK? WHAT DID YOU EXPECT?' I KNEW NOTHING. I WAS THINKING ABOUT THE PHILIP BAILEY SONG 'CHINESE WALL'. HE CERTAINLY DIDN'T SAY IT WAS BUILT IN THE 1980S. I THINK THAT SONG'S OLDER THAN THE WALL ... HONESTLY, I'VE HAD ENOUGH. I WANT TO COME HOME NOW.
I DON'T KNOW WHAT PEOPLE WATCHING SKY ARE GONNA DO WITH THE INFORMATION ON CHINESE PEOPLE HAVING A SHIT WITH NO DOOR WHILE TAKING AN ORDER FOR FOOD. BUT, YOU KNOW, IT'S THE TRUTH.
IT IS THE TRUTH.
ALL I'M TAKING FROM THIS IS, THE NEXT TIME I ORDER A TAKEAWAY I'M GONNA ASK THE FELLA 'WHAT ARE YOU DOING NOW?' I'M NEVER GONNA ORDER A NUMBER TWO, I TELL YOU THAT.
OR A KING POO CHICKEN.

SUNDAY 2ND MAY

Such a gloomy day today. We went to see the end of the Wall. It runs straight into the sea. There weren't many tourists about. It reminded me of an old seaside town in Britain. There was a man selling hot dogs, a woman selling postcards and a man hiring out little, battery-powered go-karts. I counted 24 people, and that's including the hot-dog seller. You'd expect more at a Wonder of the World, wouldn't you? I didn't mind though. It was the best thing about this part of the Wall.

I had a go on a battery-powered go-kart and left. On the way back, we passed a truck on the motorway full of dogs. It must have had about 100 dogs in it, all of which I presumed will be eaten.

I've never really understood the problem with eating dog. After all, it's just a meat and should just be like eating pig, cow, sheep or chicken, but people look at it differently. There are times when I think having another meat would be handy, as there are seven days in a week but only four main meats, which means that by mid-week I have to start eating things I've already eaten. Why don't we like the idea of eating dog?

We followed the truck to see where it was going. We ended up at a dog farm. It looked like any other farm. I wandered in where there was a big Alsatian wandering about. 'Free Range' dogs, I thought, until I met the bloke who ran the place who said it was his pet dog. I then saw the dogs that are there to buy as food. They were

mainly St Bernards. He said these big dogs can easily feed a big family. St Bernards are the ones you normally see as rescue dogs with a drum of brandy round their neck. The Chinese probably look at this as a meal with a free drink. The man who ran the dog farm then got out a brochure with the different dogs that people eat.

I decided to have a word with him through our translator. 'It's weird, because you've got a dog yourself. It's odd to see big dogs trapped in small spaces. Yet your dog runs free. I didn't think you'd be a dog lover, really.'

The translator said, 'My pet is different from all those dogs, because he's specially for guarding the gate.'

'Right. Yeah. And how's business? Is it busy? Lot of people want to eat dog here?'

The translator replied, 'A lot of different people come to buy the dogs. Big ones and small ones, because I have all kinds of dogs.'

'What's your dog's name?'

'Fluffy.'

'You wouldn't sell this one then?'

'I've trained him already, so I wouldn't sell.'

'So what happens now? If I wanted to buy one of these dogs, would I buy it and take it away, or do you kill them and prepare them for somebody to sell as food?'

The translator said, 'We only do the farming here. We don't kill the dogs. So, if somebody wanted to buy one, they would take it away and kill it.'

I asked him if it was one of his favourite meats.

'China has a long history of dog eating.'

'Do you enjoy it? I had it and I thought it was like beef. I couldn't tell the difference.'

'Dog meat tastes very different from beef. We have a minority of North Koreans. They love eating dog.'

I asked him if it was a poor man's food.

'You eat it no matter if you're poor or rich. But my pet, my Fluffy I would never eat him. If he died, I could never eat him.'

'See that's the bit I don't understand really. Surely, when it's your own dog, you know where it's been and how it's lived. So, I think that would make it easier for me to eat it than eating a dog that I know nothing about. And what about cat? Do people eat cat here?'

'Cats – normally we use them as pets and I can never remember anybody eating cats.'

'I don't understand that really. To me it's just the same. If you're eating dog I don't see the problem in eating a cat. If anything it's easier 'cos they're not as friendly, cats . . . they sort of come and go as they please.'

The translator explained. 'Because cats are quite small, and there's not much meat on them, but in Guangdong Province people do eat cats as well.'

Of course they do.

MONDAY 3RD MAY

When I got home I checked online about the thing I heard about babies having square heads. Apparently, sometimes a book is tied round the back of the baby's head to help flatten it. Parents do this because a flat head is a sign of beauty. I also read that it stops babies rolling about when they're in a cot.

Bizarre.

berghaus

福

维

心碰头
CARE OF HEAD
通往洗手间
Go To WC
EXIT
去往地面南出口
TO THE SOUTH EXIT

CHAPTER SIX

PETRA

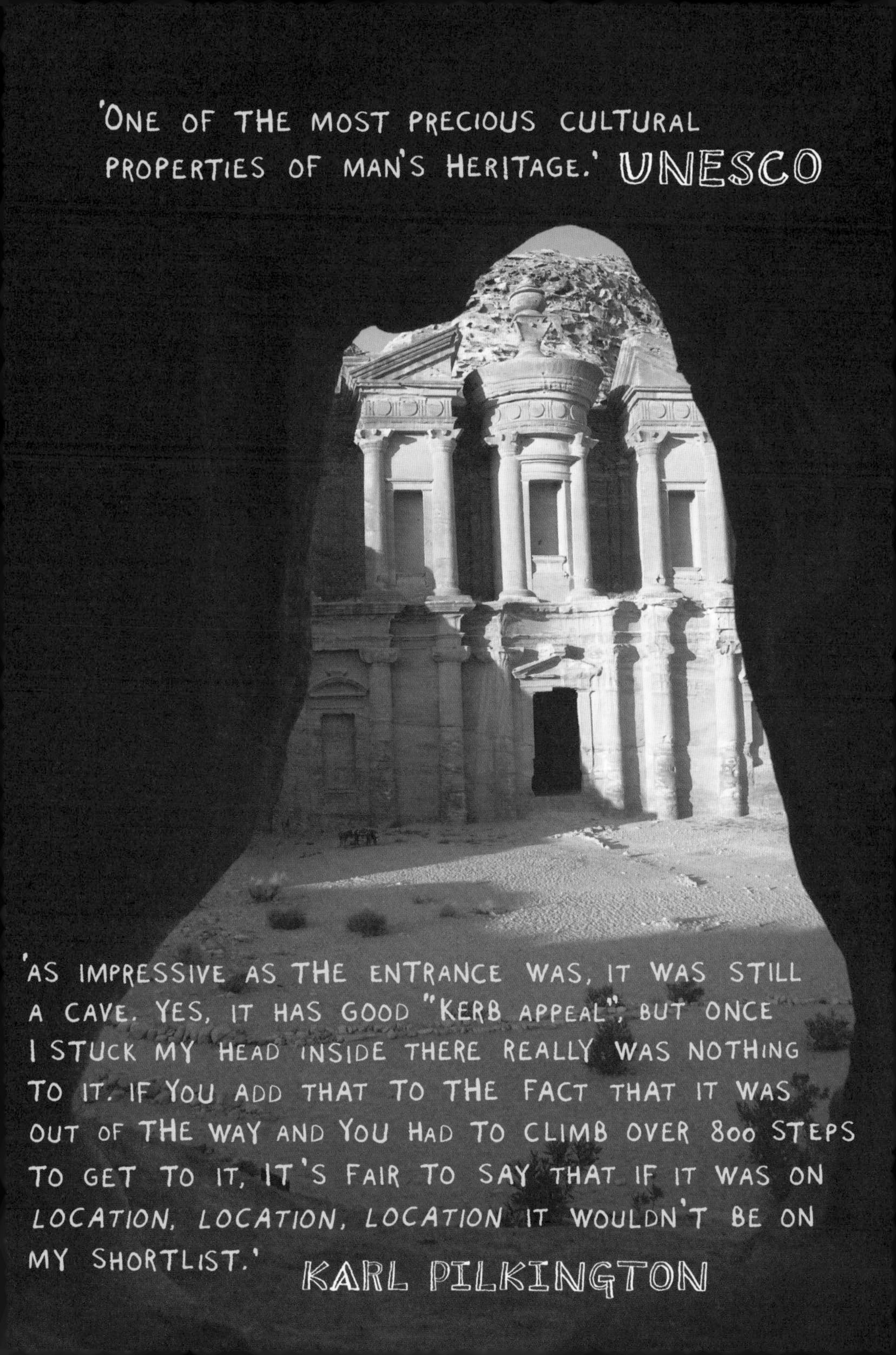

'One of the most precious cultural properties of man's heritage.' UNESCO

'As impressive as the entrance was, it was still a cave. Yes, it has good "kerb appeal", but once I stuck my head inside there really was nothing to it. If you add that to the fact that it was out of the way and you had to climb over 800 steps to get to it, it's fair to say that if it was on *Location, Location, Location* it wouldn't be on my shortlist.' KARL PILKINGTON

LEBANON
Damascus
SYRIA
Tel Aviv
WEST BANK
ISRAEL
Jerusalem
Bethlehem
Ammam
Wadi Musa
Dead Sea
JORDAN*
* the country
the building cut into stone
Wadi Rum
SAUDI ARABIA

SATURDAY 22ND MAY

I was told this morning by Luke and Ben, the director and producer, that we would be travelling right through Israel, on through Palestine and finally into Jordan. I wasn't happy about this. When I told me Dad I was going there he said that he wasn't going to tell me mam 'cos she would only worry. Every time I hear about Israel on the news it's normally something bad. It's never a light-hearted news story. It's never a story about a man who's grown the world's biggest melon, is it? Its problems are normally related to religion, and seeing as I'm not into religion in the slightest, I don't understand the situation in Israel and it's too complicated to learn overnight, I'd rather leave it. It's the same reason I've never bothered learning chess. The problem I have with all this religion stuff is that I can't relate to it. I think most people got into 'cos it gave them something to do on a Sunday, but since all the shops are now open it isn't required as much.

Steve said I may as well visit the place, as there is so much history in Israel it would be a shame not to stop off and see some of it while I'm in that neck of the woods. I suppose he thought I must have some interest in history as it was him and Ricky who called up my school twenty years after I had left and asked for my exam results, which I had never collected. They found that all I had achieved was a grade E in GCSE history.

One of my wisdom teeth is playing up. My dentist said it is known to happen with some people when they're stressed. My teeth seem to know I'm stressed before I do. Maybe that's why they're called wisdom teeth.

We got to Israel really late. The only place that was open was a 24-hour breakfast cafe. I've never agreed with these places as they just encourage people to get up late. Breakfast should be a treat for those of us who have to get up early. I had some pancakes and eggs.

I finally got to bed at 3 a.m. It would have been slightly earlier, but Luke told me that Ricky had requested that I have a shave before we start filming.

SUNDAY 23RD MAY

I was woken up at 7 a.m. by Luke and Ben.

I asked them what I was doing today that is so important that I had to have a shave. Luke told me it's got nothing to do with any of today's activities, it's just 'cos Ricky said my head looks rounder on the telly once it's shaved.

Luke changed the subject and said he had to give me a safety briefing. It wasn't the best time, considering my brain wasn't properly awake. It reminded of the time a policeman came round to our house when I was a kid and got me out of bed at 3.30 a.m. It was about a car that had been stolen and for some reason I was linked to it. I swear the policeman came round at this time because he knew I was too sleepy to make up any lies. My brain wasn't awake then, and it wasn't awake when Luke kicked off the safety briefing:

'Right, there's a high level of risk to your personal safety in Israel and the occupied Palestinian territories. The prolonged, on-going conflict is punctuated by occasional ceasefires. When no long-term resolution has been reached, regular military incursions including rocket fire and airstrikes take place, and the fall-out is indiscriminate. The situation remains unstable and extremely unpredictable, so, just on a general level, you got to be wary of that when you go out the door . . .'

That's not the sort of stuff I'm good at taking in when I'm wide awake, so it was never going to go in at 7 a.m. I've never understood how people can listen to Radio 4 in the morning, due to the level of concentration needed.

Anyway, I didn't have much option so I had a shower and got in the van. Luke didn't tell me where we were going. After a little while I noticed that the van had driven into some sort of training camp. I hopped out and met a man named Ronan. We were having friendly chit chat about my time in Israel when a car screeched up, and two or three men – it might have even been four – jumped out and pushed me to the ground. They threw a bag over my head and tied my arms behind my back. I was then dragged off and dumped in the back of a car, where they sat on my back and tightened up the plastic ties on my wrists. I could feel the ties cutting into my skin. As the car drove off, my head started banging against the wheel arch while a man yelled at me in some language I didn't understand. At which point my wisdom tooth starting aching again.

I've always thought I was good at dealing with bad situations. A tramp in Manchester once tried to nick my trainers off me in Piccadilly Gardens. I acted like I was mad and he gave up. But in the back of this car in the middle of Israel I couldn't even do that, because of the language barrier. I was helpless.

Finally, I was dragged from the vehicle and taken inside somewhere and shoved into a seat where someone continued to yell at me – this time in English.

'Who is your manager? What is their phone number?'

I told them it was Richard Yee, at the TV company back in London. I didn't know his phone number though. Who knows phone numbers these days? There is no need to remember numbers now they're all programmed into your phone. I don't even know my own home number off by heart as I never really call it. Having said that, I don't even use it when I'm at home. It's got to the point that I don't even answer it when it rings, as it's normally a woman who thinks it's her doctor's number. There's about five messages on the answer machine from her telling me her throat is still sore and the rash hasn't gone away. Maybe that's how Dr Shipman started.

After about what felt like twenty minutes (but was apparently only five) the bag was removed from my head. Luke and Ben were in the room with Jan the cameraman and Freddie the soundman. In my panic I'd completely forgotten we were making a telly programme.

The terrorist man told me that I have a lot to learn. I should always carry a document explaining who I am and what I am filming, along with the phone number of my manager. I had nothing on me. I didn't even take a note of which hotel I was staying in.

He then gave me a phone and asked me what I would do with it if I were in trouble. I told him I'd call my girlfriend as I don't know anybody else's number off by heart. He asked me to tell him what I would say to her.

'I wouldn't want to panic her straight away so I'd say, "How is everything?" and then say, "Right, listen . . . a bit of a problem . . . I was taken away." She's probably sat there going, "What do you mean?" And I'll go, "Shhh, quiet. I'm on low battery . . ."'

'Where are you? Where are you?' The terrorist was pretending to be Suzanne now, which was a bit weird.

'Shhh, don't shout, because they can hear me. I'm in a bush.'

'In a bush? Why? Where? What country?'

'Well, you know where I am . . .'

'Where?'

'You see, you never listen to me, you see! You keep going on about your hair cuts . . .'

'Where are you, where are you?'

'I'm in Israel.'

'Where are you?'

'Stop talking!'

'I'm coming. I'm coming over.'

I tried a different tack

'Can you call Richard?'

'Richard?'

'Yes, Richard!'

'Richard, right. What's his phone number?'

The terrorist had me again.

'You're right. I'm useless.'

I was shaking for a good half hour afterwards. Normally if I get the shakes like this it's 'cos I need a Mars Bar or a Twix for a sugar hit – I think I might even have a touch of diabetes. But today it was 'cos of the stress. Even though my brain knew it was all just a test, the rest of my body didn't.

The main man at the security camp told me I needed to have contact information for people back in London with me at all times, and that I needed a code word that could be used to warn the team back in London that there was a real situation.

I told Luke to tell London that I'll use the words 'Congress Tart' as my emergency code. Congress Tarts were my favourite cakes when I lived in Manchester, but I can never find them in London. For some reason the name is still rattling around me head so it may as well be used for something. I hope Luke tells London 'cos I'm starting to take this seriously now.

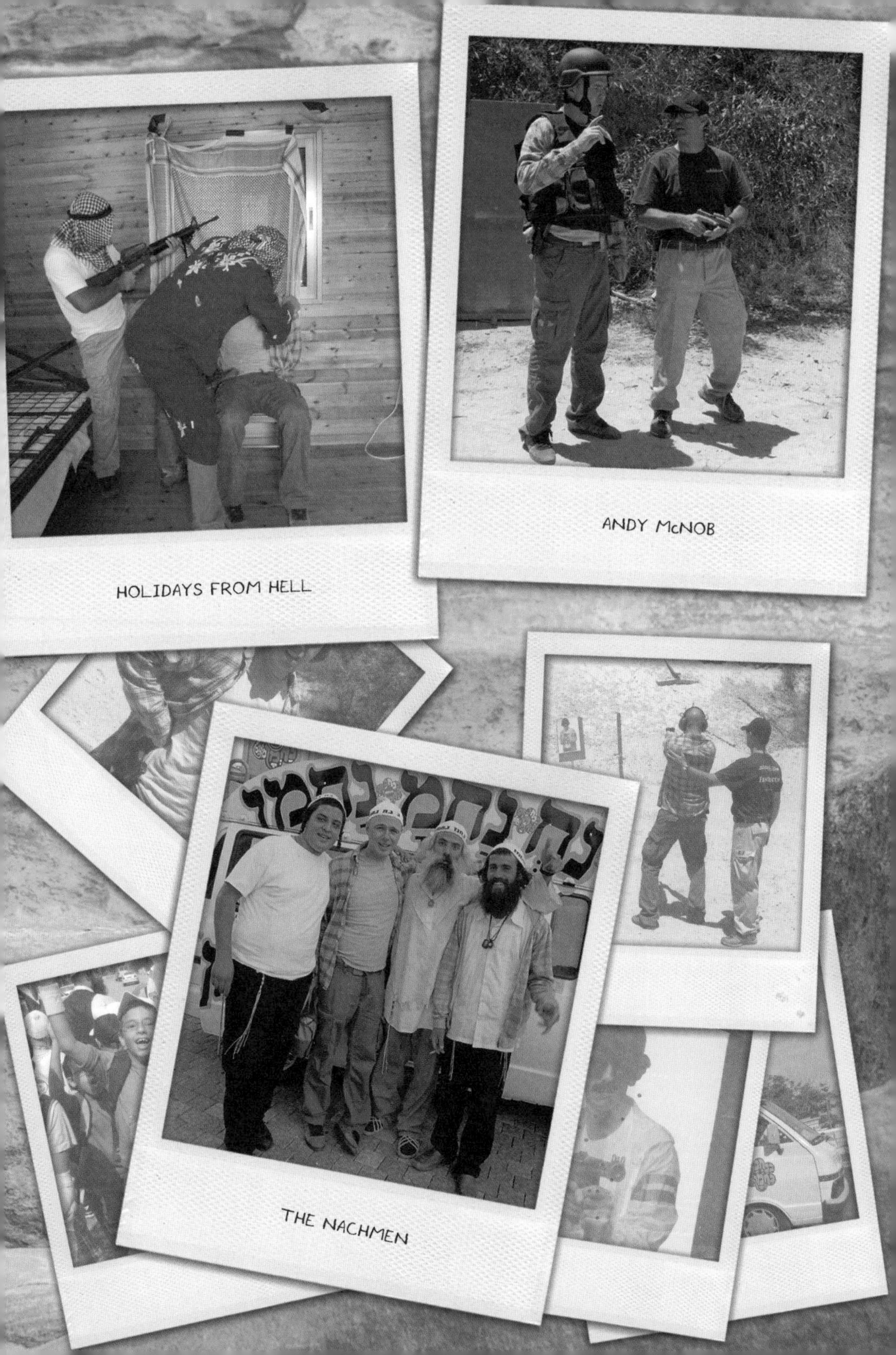

HOLIDAYS FROM HELL

ANDY McNOB

THE NACHMEN

Once I got back in the van I noticed I had a voicemail message from Steve:

ALRIGHT, KARL. IT'S STEVE, MATE. I DON'T WANT TO WORRY YOU, BUT I'VE BEEN TALKING TO SOME OF THE HEALTH AND SAFETY PEOPLE, AND OBVIOUSLY YOU ARE IN QUITE A VOLATILE REGION. WE'RE A BIT WORRIED BECAUSE YOU ARE WITH A TV CAMERA CREW, YOU MIGHT BE SEEN AS A JOURNALIST AND YOU COULD PERHAPS ATTRACT SOME UNWANTED ATTENTION. AT THE FAR EXTREME THERE'S THE DANGER THAT YOU COULD BE KIDNAPPED AND TAKEN HOSTAGE, AND YOU COULD BE USED AS A BARGAINING CHIP. THAT COULD BE A BIT OF A DOWNER FOR THE SHOW. SO YOU SHOULD HAVE SOME EXTREME SCENARIO TRAINING, AS A PRECAUTION. THEY'LL TEACH YOU A FEW THINGS SO IF YOU ARE IN ANY TROUBLE YOU'LL KNOW HOW TO DEAL WITH THE SITUATION. AND THE OTHER THING IS THAT IT WILL GIVE YOU A FLAVOUR OF WHAT A LOT OF ISRAELI MEN OVER 18 HAVE TO DO EVERY YEAR. YOU KNOW YOU HAVE TO DO MILITARY TRAINING IN ISRAEL? THEY DO THREE YEARS, YOU'LL BE DOING HALF A DAY OR SOMETHING. NO NEED TO PANIC, BUT I WOULD TAKE IT VERY, VERY SERIOUSLY INDEED. ALRIGHT? BYE.

It would have been nice to get that message a little earlier.

We travelled on to Jerusalem in the afternoon. There were young soldiers everywhere carrying guns – big guns. It looked like a scene from *Bugsy Malone*. There were people in all sorts of religious clothing. I went down one alley and was faced with a mob of monks coming at me so turned to go the other way when I was faced with a pack of nuns. I nipped down another alley where there were more soldiers marching towards me. It was like playing Pac-Man.

I saw a famous wall called the Wailing Wall. I'd never heard of it before today. It's a really old wall that Jewish people love. They use it to pray at. There was a big section of it for men and a smaller section for women. Not sure why they can't share a wall. They'd had to build another wall to divide the wall.

There seem to be lots of walls here. It's a good place for a bricklayer to live. We're not a fan of walls back home. I'd say we have fewer walls than ever. Open-plan offices and open-plan homes seem to be all the rage. No wonder Banksy, the graffiti artist, tends to do more stuff abroad these days.

I watched people pray for a bit. Some read from bibles, some kissed the wall and some pushed handwritten notes into the cracks. I met a Jewish fella called Dov. He told me that people write down their sins or wishes and place them into the wall for God to see. Every little crevice had a note shoved in it. It looked like a local postman had had enough of his round and had just dumped everything in his bag. I'm sure there was even junk mail in some of the cracks, from insurance companies and pizza delivery shops.

I had a bagel and left.

Steve called me this evening.

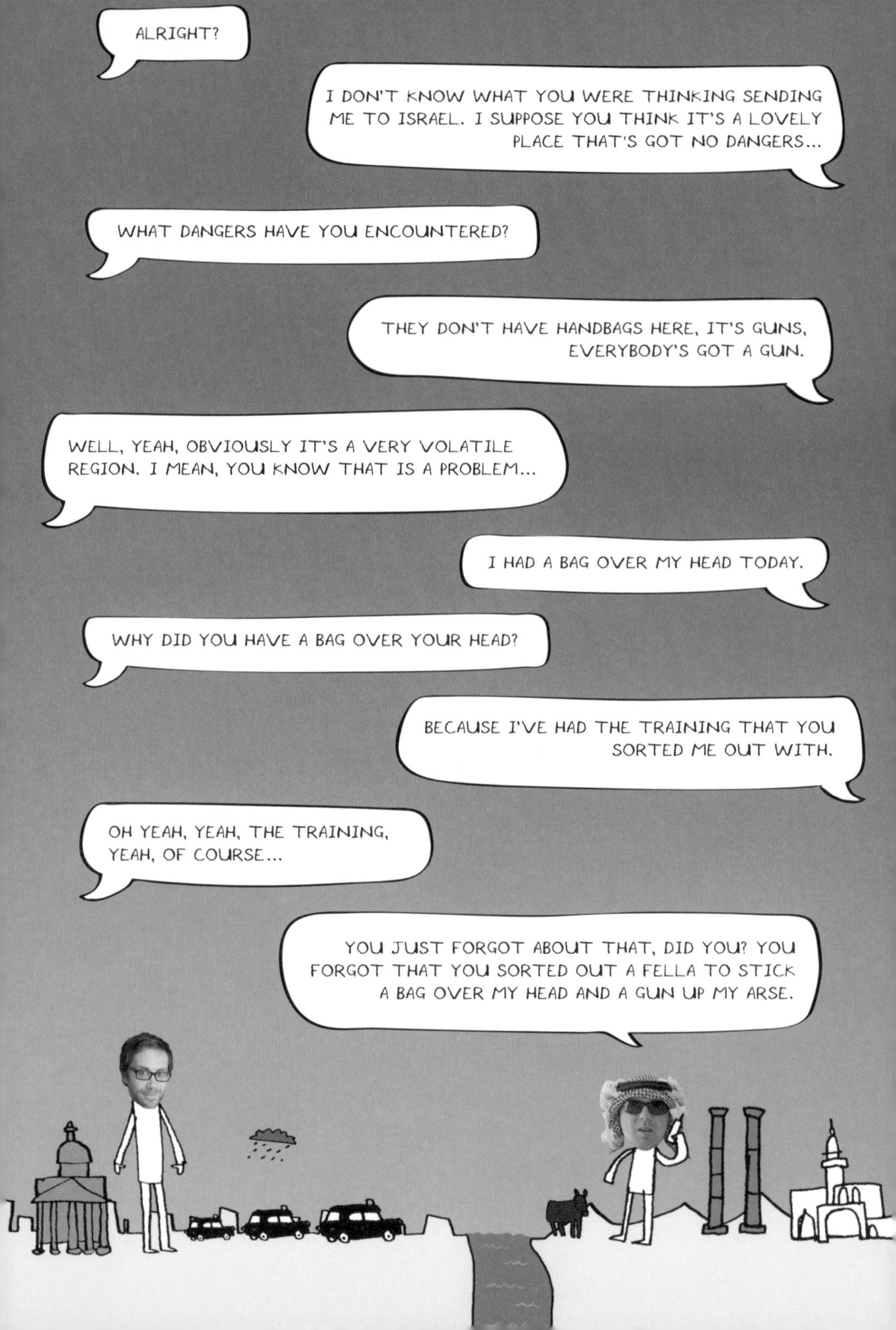
ALRIGHT?
I DON'T KNOW WHAT YOU WERE THINKING SENDING ME TO ISRAEL. I SUPPOSE YOU THINK IT'S A LOVELY PLACE THAT'S GOT NO DANGERS...
WHAT DANGERS HAVE YOU ENCOUNTERED?
THEY DON'T HAVE HANDBAGS HERE, IT'S GUNS, EVERYBODY'S GOT A GUN.
WELL, YEAH, OBVIOUSLY IT'S A VERY VOLATILE REGION. I MEAN, YOU KNOW THAT IS A PROBLEM...
I HAD A BAG OVER MY HEAD TODAY.
WHY DID YOU HAVE A BAG OVER YOUR HEAD?
BECAUSE I'VE HAD THE TRAINING THAT YOU SORTED ME OUT WITH.
OH YEAH, YEAH, THE TRAINING, YEAH, OF COURSE...
YOU JUST FORGOT ABOUT THAT, DID YOU? YOU FORGOT THAT YOU SORTED OUT A FELLA TO STICK A BAG OVER MY HEAD AND A GUN UP MY ARSE.

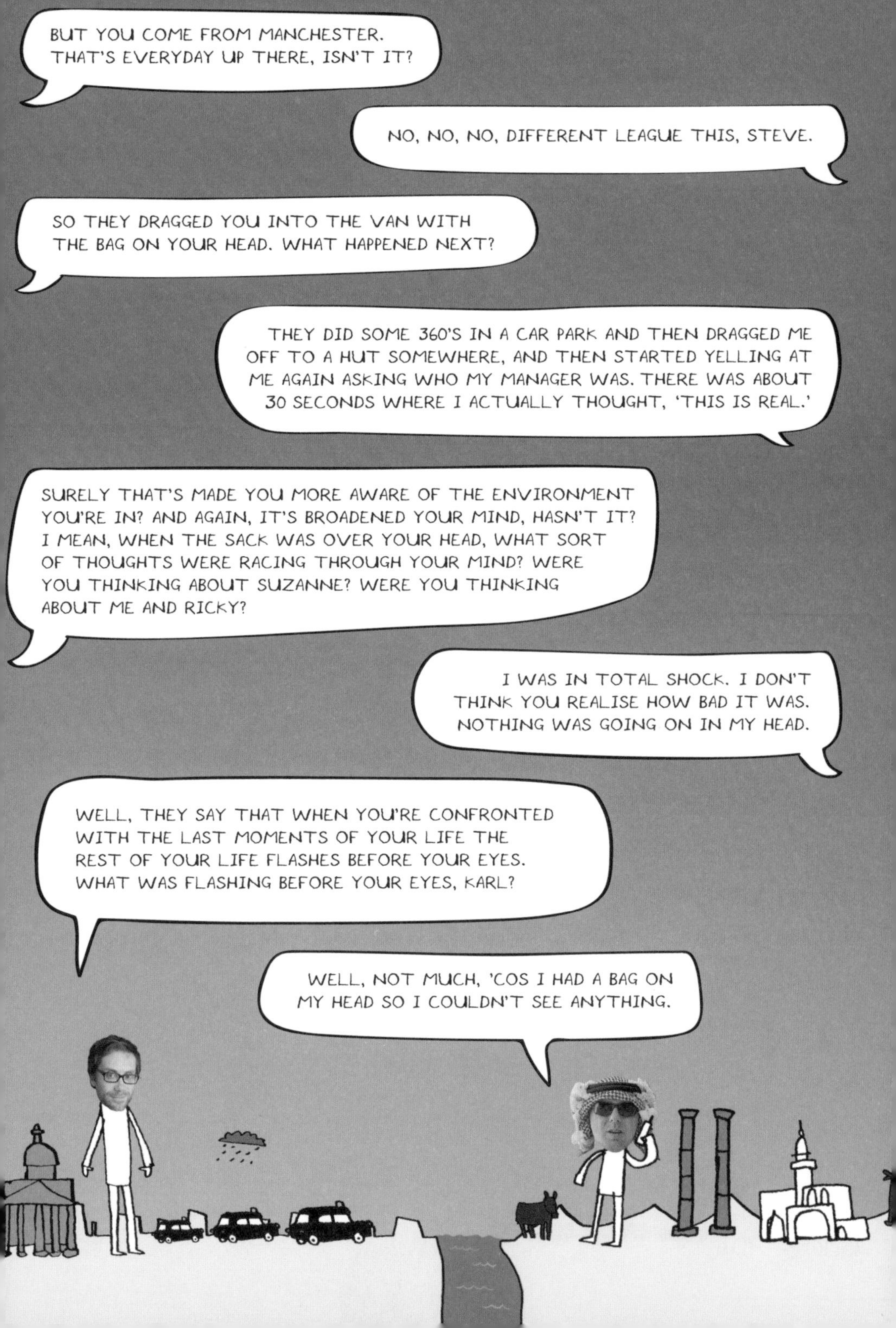
BUT YOU COME FROM MANCHESTER. THAT'S EVERYDAY UP THERE, ISN'T IT?
NO, NO, NO, DIFFERENT LEAGUE THIS, STEVE.
SO THEY DRAGGED YOU INTO THE VAN WITH THE BAG ON YOUR HEAD. WHAT HAPPENED NEXT?
THEY DID SOME 360'S IN A CAR PARK AND THEN DRAGGED ME OFF TO A HUT SOMEWHERE, AND THEN STARTED YELLING AT ME AGAIN ASKING WHO MY MANAGER WAS. THERE WAS ABOUT 30 SECONDS WHERE I ACTUALLY THOUGHT, 'THIS IS REAL.'
SURELY THAT'S MADE YOU MORE AWARE OF THE ENVIRONMENT YOU'RE IN? AND AGAIN, IT'S BROADENED YOUR MIND, HASN'T IT? I MEAN, WHEN THE SACK WAS OVER YOUR HEAD, WHAT SORT OF THOUGHTS WERE RACING THROUGH YOUR MIND? WERE YOU THINKING ABOUT SUZANNE? WERE YOU THINKING ABOUT ME AND RICKY?
I WAS IN TOTAL SHOCK. I DON'T THINK YOU REALISE HOW BAD IT WAS. NOTHING WAS GOING ON IN MY HEAD.
WELL, THEY SAY THAT WHEN YOU'RE CONFRONTED WITH THE LAST MOMENTS OF YOUR LIFE THE REST OF YOUR LIFE FLASHES BEFORE YOUR EYES. WHAT WAS FLASHING BEFORE YOUR EYES, KARL?
WELL, NOT MUCH, 'COS I HAD A BAG ON MY HEAD SO I COULDN'T SEE ANYTHING.

IT DOESN'T LITERALLY FLASH BEFORE YOUR EYES. IT'S NOT EVERYONE FROM YOUR LIFE DOING A LITTLE DANCE IN FRONT OF YOU: 'OH, THERE'S AUNTY MORD. I HAVEN'T SEEN HER SINCE 1973.' THAT'S NOT WHAT THEY MEAN, THEY MEAN IN YOUR MIND. ANYWAY, LISTEN, TALKING ABOUT EXPERIENCING THE EXTREMES OF LIFE I'M VERY EXCITED FOR YOU TO MEET SOMEONE TOMORROW WHO BELIEVES THAT HE IS JESUS CHRIST. YOU'RE IN A VERY SPIRITUAL ENVIRONMENT.
SO WHEN YOU SET THAT UP, WHAT WERE YOU THINKING? WHY IS THIS GOOD FOR ME?
OK, THERE IS A PSYCHOLOGICAL CONDITION KNOWN AS THE JERUSALEM SYNDROME IN WHICH PEOPLE WHO TRAVEL TO THAT MOST SPIRITUAL OF PLACES ARE OFTEN SO OVERWHELMED WITH THE SENSE OF SPIRITUALITY THAT THEY START TO BELIEVE THAT THEY HAVE A SPIRITUAL POWER, OR THAT THEY ARE SOMEHOW CONNECTED TO THE RELIGION TO WHICH THEY SUBSCRIBE. IT MIGHT BE VERY INTERESTING TO TRY TO UNDERSTAND HOW THAT CAN IMPACT ON SOMEONE. YOU'RE LIVING AT THE EXTREMES OF LIFE HERE, KARL. THIS IS EXCITING, MAN. TODAY YOU THOUGHT YOU WERE KIDNAPPED AND YOU WERE GOING TO BE DONE FOR, TOMORROW YOU'RE MEETING SOMEONE WHO'S PUSHING AT THE VERY PARAMETERS OF CONSCIOUSNESS. THEY'VE ALWAYS TALKED ABOUT THE SECOND COMING... HOW DO WE KNOW THAT THIS ISN'T THE BIG MAN HIMSELF?
HAVE YOU GOT ANY QUESTIONS FOR JESUS?
HAVE I GOT ANY QUESTIONS FOR JESUS?
YEAH. WHAT WOULD YOU ASK HIM IF YOU WERE IN MY SHOES? I DON'T WANT TO ANNOY HIM.
WELL, I DON'T KNOW IF YOU COULD ANNOY HIM. I IMAGINE THAT EVEN IF IT ANNOYED HIM HE'D FORGIVE YOU.
THAT'S TRUE.

THERE'S NOT MUCH THAT WOULD ANNOY THE BIG JC, I WOULD HAVE THOUGHT.
WHAT DOES THE 'H' STAND FOR? PEOPLE ALWAYS SAY JESUS H. CHRIST – WHAT'S HIS MIDDLE NAME?
I'M NOT SURE THAT'S PART OF THE OFFICIAL MYTHOLOGY, TO BE HONEST. I THINK THAT MIGHT HAVE BEEN INTRODUCED LATER. I MEAN, YOU CAN ASK HIM THAT. BY ALL MEANS ASK HIM – HE MIGHT HAVE A GOOD ANSWER. I'VE ALSO HEARD THE PHRASE 'CHRIST ON A BIKE'; YOU MIGHT WANT TO ASK HIM IF HE'S GOT A BIKE.
ALRIGHT THEN.
WELL, GOOD LUCK, MATE. I HOPE YOU HAVE AN INFORMATIVE TIME TOMORROW.
YEAH, I THINK IT COULD BE ALRIGHT, QUITE INTERESTING – BUT HE'S NOT MENTAL?
IF YOU BELIEVE THAT YOU ARE JESUS CHRIST, YOU'RE NOT GOING TO BE A DANGEROUS MAN, ARE YOU? YOU'RE GOING TO BE A PEACEFUL PERSON.
BUT ARE YOU SAYING THAT THIS SYNDROME MEANS THAT HE CAN'T SWITCH OVERNIGHT? HE COULDN'T BE SOMEONE ELSE TOMORROW, COULD HE? IT'S A SYNDROME WHERE YOU'RE DEFINITELY JESUS ALL THE TIME – TOMORROW HE'S NOT GOING TO TURN UP AND SAY 'I'M JOE PASQUALE TODAY'?
NO, HE'S NOT GOING TO WAKE UP AND GO 'HELLO, I'M SIMON COWELL'. I DON'T THINK THAT'S A PROBLEM.
I'M JUST CHECKING.

MONDAY 24TH MAY

I wondered if I'd have any nightmares after being attacked yesterday, but I had a good night's sleep.

At breakfast, Luke told me we would be meeting Jesus in the market today. It sounded daft, but I suppose he's got to shop just like anyone else.

When we got to the market I asked various people if Jesus was around and got some pretty mixed reactions. Some people pointed me to where he normally hangs out, others said I was wasting my time and that he was a crazy man. I passed quite a few men with long hair and beards, but I suppose when you live in a place near where Jesus lived, you might copy his style in the same way a lot of kids tried to look like Noel and Liam Gallagher in Manchester when I was growing up.

I kept asking around until finally a young lad told me he was also waiting for him. I asked him if he had an appointment with him and he told me he meets Jesus every day. I was just asking what I should call Jesus when a motorbike swerved up onto the foot path, driven by a man in robes with long hair and a beard. The motorbike had blankets covering it. The young lad I was stood with told me this was Jesus and that he tries to make the bike look like a donkey.

Jesus parked, got off his bike and rolled out a mat and sat on it. A crowd of around forty or so people started gathering and before long an argument broke out between Jesus and a woman. From what I could make out it was something to do with a holocaust. I pushed my way to the front of the crowd and told him that Steve had sent me.

'Hi, I'm Karl. How you doing? I'm here to see you. Can I sit down?'

'You're a very brave man,' said Jesus.

'Why am I brave?' I asked.

'Brave because you sit here and you can see the crowd – they don't like prophets.'

'Why not?'

'Why? Because I'm telling them bad things, of course, and they hate me because of it. They don't like me, period.'

'Can't you give them some better news than "there's a holocaust coming"?'

'Yeah, but I've said that there's a way to prevent it – by changing their hearts.'

'And they don't like it?'

'No, they don't like it.'

At that point he started shouting something in various languages that seemed to offend quite a few people. I tried to yell louder than everyone else to keep the conversation going.

'Do you have any days where you just think, "I can't deal with having to do this"?'

'Huh?' I'd lost him.

I tried again, even louder this time.

'People yelling at you all day? I think if I was you, I'd sort of be like "Oh, I can't be bothered with this". Do you know what I mean?'

'I don't have any other option.'

The shouting carried on in Hebrew. Jesus sat and took it whilst lighting a Marlboro cigarette.

A tourist called out to him, 'Messiah, Messiah, I have health problem, let me touch your vest and cure me.'

'Leave me alone, you crazy French guy.' Jesus shouted back.

'May I touch your vest, Messiah?'

'Don't touch my nothing!'

I left, as I felt I was never going to get a proper one-to-one with Jesus. Maybe if the real Jesus were still around this is what it would be like for him – people either abusing him or hassling him. Even though modern life is better than biblical times, people need help more than ever. I recently noticed a helpline on a bottle of HP brown sauce. I called it to see if anyone was there. There was, so I hung up as I didn't actually need any help.

I was standing in the shade, out of the sun, when a lad came over who had been watching us film. He asked me to go with him. He led me to the car park where he had a camper van with a massive speaker on the roof. Rave music blared from it. Him and four of his mates danced. They asked me to join them. So I did, for a couple of songs. I then said I had to get back to the hotel and they offered me a lift.

As we drove, one explained to me that they are known as the Nachmen. They believe in spreading happiness through the power of dance. I was polite and said 'very good' as I just wanted to get back to the hotel. They then pulled up at some traffic lights that were on red and jumped out and started dancing again. The drivers around us looked puzzled, but smiled.

The Nachmen told me they cheer up hundreds of people stuck in traffic jams every day. I said that it's probably them who are causing the traffic jams. At this point the lights went to green. The drivers around us suddenly didn't look so happy. They were beeping their horns, asking us to get a move on. Five hundred yards down the road at the next set of lights the same thing happened again. All the Nachmen hopped out and danced on the main road and on top of the van like the kids from *Fame*.

'I get my kids to join in with me. They love it, it makes them so happy,' one of them explained to me.

'But aren't they late for school every day when you're forever saying, "Get out! The lights are red!" "But Dad . . . I'm missing English!"?'

'No, no. It is good for them', the Nachman assured me.

They pulled up on a roundabout quite close to where the hotel was for a long dance. Two of the guys were on the roof, and the music was louder than ever. So loud that we didn't notice the police siren until the police car had pulled up next to us. The police got out and told us we couldn't film next to the main road because it was a distraction to the other drivers. The fact there was a van with several people dancing on the roof with music blaring apparently wasn't an issue.

I left them to it.

TUESDAY 25TH MAY

We went to another big wall today. It was massive and went on and on as far as the eye could see, separating Israel from Palestine. It's a horrible-looking wall. Big slabs of concrete with barbed wire on the top. I had to go through a check point and show my passport.

When I got to the other side I met a local Palestinian man called Kais, who took me to Bethlehem. He took me into a church to show me the spot where Jesus was supposed to have been born.

Kais had brought some flutes with him because the story goes that the shepherds came to Jesus's birth carrying flutes. But we were told by the man in charge that we couldn't play them, which was a blessing in disguise to be honest, as they are the most irritating-sounding instruments.

We had to wait our turn to see the special spot, while other visitors went in and cried. Some people placed beads and crosses on the spot, and one guy placed his mobile phone on it as if he was hoping it would charge the battery. I really can't see how they know this is the exact spot. My mam doesn't even remember the hospital bed number at Wythenshawe hospital where I was born and she was there, so I doubt this was right. It wasn't what I'd imagined either – I thought I was going to see a little hut with straw and a cradle, but it looked like a fireplace.

With me not being religious I didn't get anything from the moment. Although when I get a Christmas card with a little image of the nativity scene on it at least I can say I've been there.

On the way back to the wall I saw some graffiti done by Banksy. I knew he'd love it here.

WEDNESDAY 26TH MAY

We're finally headed into Jordan today. It was a long old trip. We drove through nothingness for hours and then we eventually reached the Dead Sea. I'd seen pictures of it in the guidebook. There is so much salt in it there was a photo of a man floating on his back while reading the paper. I asked Luke if we could stop off so I could have a go. He said okay. I think he still felt bad about the prank hostage incident.

I read a sign that said the Dead Sea was the lowest point in the world. It didn't feel any different and the sun didn't look that much further away, though Ben, Luke's assistant, said something about not having to wear suntan lotion as the UV rays don't reach this far. But now I think about it, Ben's job is to make sure we don't go over budget, so it wouldn't surprise me if this was his way of making sure we didn't buy suntan lotion for everyone.

The Dead Sea was very muddy looking and it wasn't very sea-like. It was more like a lake. I was up for getting in it, though, as I have a little bit of eczema on my leg and the mud and salt are supposed to be good for the skin. Hippos roll about in mud all the time and you never see them with eczema so there must be some truth in it.

I waded in, but it was hard to stand up as the dark green mud sucked you down. Straight away the salty water started to sting all the cuts on my wrists and knees that I got from being kidnapped. I didn't realise I had so many cuts. It's like when you only find out you have a paper cut when you eat a bag of salt-and-vinegar crisps.

I was the youngest person in there by a mile. Everyone else looked to be in their seventies. Maybe this is why they call it the Dead Sea – all the visitors are close to death. Having said that, it could just be that they're here on holiday and other than float about in the sea there isn't much to do. So maybe they're young but really wrinkly from being in the sea all day.

I lay back and floated. It was really good. Well, that was until Luke pointed out that I had something in my belly button. At first I thought it was a fag end until I flicked it out and got a closer look. It was phlegm. I glanced around and saw that a lot of people seemed to be blowing their noses and coughing up phlegm, especially when they had accidentally got a mouthful of saltwater. I started to wonder if the dark green mud was mud or snot.

Ricky called as I was floating:

WHAT'S GOING ON?
I'M JUST IN THE DEAD SEA.
FLOATING AROUND?
YEAH, JUST FLOATING AROUND WITH SOMEONE'S GOB.
WHAT?
I'VE JUST HAD A BIT OF GOB ON ME.
URGH.
THERE ARE OLD PEOPLE IN HERE JUST, Y'KNOW, CLEARING THEIR THROATS AND THAT. I JUST HAD SOME IN MY BELLY BUTTON.
OH, THAT IS DISGUSTING!
MAYBE THAT'S WHY I'M FLOATING AROUND. 90% CATARRH OR WHATEVER IT IS.
I WAS GOING TO SAY TASTE IT, TO SEE HOW SALTY IT IS – BUT DON'T. WHAT HAVE YOU BEEN DOING?
PRETTY STRESSFUL HERE.
Gervais
14

WHY? YOU SEEM TO BE OK, FLOATING AROUND LIKE YOU'RE ON HOLIDAY.
NO, THIS IS THE FIRST DAY I'VE DONE SOMETHING RELAXING.
HMMM. IT'S LIKE YOU'RE IN A SPA OR SOMETHING, BUT WITH PHLEGM. NEW PHLEGM TREATMENT: 'DO YOU WANT THE AROMATHERAPY OR THE OLD PEOPLE'S GOB TREATMENT?' 'I'LL HAVE THE AROMATHERAPY PLEASE.'
NOW, DID YOU ENJOY THAT CAMEL RIDE IN EGYPT?
YOU KNOW I DIDN'T.
WAS IT UNCOMFORTABLE?
YEAH, IT'S THE WORST ANIMAL YOU CAN SIT ON, INNIT? IT'S GOT A LUMP IN IT.
YEAH, WELL, I THINK YOU'RE GOING TO NEED TO GIVE IT ANOTHER GO BECAUSE, Y'KNOW, YOU'VE GOTTA GET USED TO IT, HAVEN'T YOU?
WELL, I DON'T MIND HAVING ANOTHER QUICK GO.
YEAH, YOU SAY A 'QUICK GO', BUT I THINK THE WONDER OF PETRA IS ABOUT TWO DAYS AWAY ON A CAMEL.
TWO DAYS?
Gervais

YEAH. SO, I MEAN, RELAX IN THAT LOVELY, SALTY, GOB-RIDDEN WATER BECAUSE YOU ARE GOING TO HAVE A SORE ARSE IN A COUPLE OF DAYS' TIME. SO I'D SOAK IT IF I WAS YOU.

WHAT? WE'RE GOING THE WHOLE WAY ON A CAMEL?

WELL, YOU MIGHT AS WELL. SILLY TO CHANGE, INNIT?

BUT WHAT'S THE POINT?

CAMEL, DIRECT, NO CHANGE. MUCH BETTER THAN, Y'KNOW, 'OH, LET'S GET A TRAIN, LET'S GET A BUS, LET'S GET A COACH, LET'S GET A HELICOPTER.' NO, LET'S JUST GET ONE CAMEL ALL THE WAY.

WELL, THIS CALL IS COSTING ME MONEY EVEN THOUGH YOU CALLED ME, SO THERE'S NO POINT ARGUING.

KARL. GET OUT OF THE DEAD SEA, PUT SOME CLOTHES ON AND DO SOME FUCKING WORK. YOU'RE NOT ON HOLIDAY.

I'VE BEEN DOING WORK FOR FOUR DAYS. THIS IS GOOD FOR THE PROGRAMME. I'M EXPLAINING TO PEOPLE HOW THERE'S LOADS OF SALT IN IT, YOU FLOAT ABOUT AND IT'S GOOD FOR YOUR SKIN.

IT'S NOT GOOD FOR YOUR SKIN IF YOU'RE COVERED IN OLD PEOPLE'S VOMIT AND SICK AND GOB AND PHLEGM AND SNOT. I'VE NEVER SEEN THAT ON ANY ALAN WHICKER OR MICHAEL PALIN SHOW.
EXACTLY. THIS IS THE TRUTH.
WELL, CAN'T YOU TALK ABOUT THE WONDERS?
WELL, IF YOU WOULD'VE FUCKING SENT ME THERE! YOU SENT ME TO ISRAEL! LET'S GET TO THE WONDER, I AGREE WITH YOU. JESUS! OH YEAH, I MET HIM YESTERDAY. I MET JESUS YESTERDAY.
DID YOU?
YEAH. COULDN'T GET A WORD IN EDGEWAYS. I COULDN'T GET THROUGH TO HIM.
YOU'LL SEE HIM JUST WALK PAST YOU IN A MINUTE. AT LEAST JESUS WOULD ONLY GET OLD PEOPLE'S GOB ON THE BOTTOM OF HIS FEET.
SEE YOU LATER.
Gervais
14

I had to go through another checkpoint on the way into Jordan. They opened my suitcase and I immediately felt guilty even though I had nothing to be guilty about. They went into my toilet bag and pulled out loads of ear buds. I don't think they had seen them before 'cos they looked confused as they passed them around.

We got to the hotel at 8 p.m., but the staff couldn't find the key for my room. They took me to another room but the door only opened a quarter of the way before jamming, so I couldn't get my case in. They eventually gave up and took me to a posh room. They opened the door and asked me if the suite would be okay. I said it would, but the knickers and bra on the bed are not my type. The room was already being used.

They eventually got me a room at 9.15 p.m. It overlooks the entertainment area, where a fat man was singing 'My Way'. He's still singing now as I type this at 10.30 p.m.

I just looked in the mirror and noticed that I've burnt my back in the sun, so Ben was talking through his arse about the UV rays.

THURSDAY 27TH MAY

I was up early today. Luke asked me to meet him at the front of the hotel with my luggage, as we would be making our way over to the Ancient Wonder of Petra.

Luke introduced me to a man called Mr Mohammed. Mr Mohammed asked me to get in one of two pick-up trucks parked outside. They were really old and battered and each one had a camel strapped in the back. He put my case right next to a camel's arse. Mr Mohammed said we would be crossing the desert on the camels, but we would need to drive to the edge of the desert first. I asked Mr Mohammed about what Ricky had said – that it would take 48 hours to cross the desert. He said it would, and I couldn't help looking back at the camels, who looked old and seemed to be moaning already.

Mr Mohammed got in one van and I got in another, which was being driven by a young lad. Then the driver's dad climbed in and squeezed down next to me. The camels had more room than I did! The dad was an old-looking fella with a big moustache, and he wore a gown with a suit jacket on top. His name was Saba. He didn't speak much English. I tried to explain a bit about my life. I told him I was from London and had a girlfriend called Suzanne, who I had been with for 16 years.

Within two minutes of leaving the hotel car park the van I was in broke down. Maybe that's why they have a camel in the boot – it's an emergency mode of transport. The young lad whipped the bonnet open and sorted it like it was something that happened quite often.

It took about an hour to get to the desert. When we arrived, Mr Mohammed gave me some clothes to wear that made me look like a proper desert adventurer. Before getting on the camel I popped some sun cream on my face. Mr Mohammed asked what it was. I told him it was suntan lotion; he then told me that proper Bedouin people rub their face with sand to stop getting burned. This was to be the first of many things I was told by Mr Mohammed that sounded like a load of bollocks. A lot of what he said as we crossed the desert didn't seem right to me. For example, he told me that the area we would be staying in that night had a shop and I would be able to buy a Twix. Really?

I tried different topics of conversation with him, but he didn't understand me. In the end, he started to sing so I left him to that while I just looked around. There was nothing going on. There was literally no one else around. All I saw in about five hours was two beetles.

I was expecting us to do an hour or two in the desert, and then be told by Luke that that is all we need for the programme. Six or seven hours later I realised that that wasn't going to be the case. At about the eight-hour point the camel that Mr Mohammed was on started to moan quite loudly, and kept sitting down, and then, eventually, it just gave up altogether.

The vans had to be called and the camels were loaded into the back once again. Saba, the man with a big moustache I sat next to on the way to the desert, was not happy. It turned out the camels belonged to him and he was annoyed that we had been out on them all day. I said I thought these animals were meant to be the ships of the desert. If so, we'd ended up with the *Titanic*.

I had to share a lift with Saba. I couldn't tell if he was ignoring me because he was annoyed or just because he didn't speak much English.

It turned out that I would be staying with him tonight at his tent, along with his family of 14 kids, in the middle of nowhere. I wasn't too bothered as I was so knackered that I could've slept anywhere. I asked Mohammed what time everyone would be going to bed, but he said they would be staying up later tonight as they have a guest to entertain. I said they shouldn't worry on my account and that we should all go to bed, but he explained that Saba was preparing food.

As Saba made dinner the rest of the family sat around smoking something that made their eyes big. I thought it was drugs but it was just strong tobacco. Mr Mohammed said that as the guest I should have some, but I refused. He said that this was rude and would annoy Saba. I tried to explain that I don't smoke and am not planning on starting now. It felt to me like we were bonding.

We sat down for food. They brought a massive plate that had some animal head in the middle with rice and milky type sauce poured over it. They call it mansaf. I ate some as I didn't want to be rude, but I wasn't really liking it. I like my meat quite well cooked and this wasn't. Mr Mohammed then said that Saba had insisted that the guest gets the best bit – the best bit being the eye. Two things worried me: firstly, I didn't want to eat an eye, and secondly, what sort of animal only has one eye?

Mr Mohammed said I'd offend Saba if I didn't eat it, but as far as I was concerned we had already fallen out over me not smoking the tobacco so what was the point? I gave the eye to a cat that was wandering around the tent.

Before I nodded off that night I told Mr Mohammed that we shouldn't hang about in the morning as I don't think Saba likes me very much. Mr Mohammed then explained that Saba wasn't happy that a man of my age was dating a 16-year-old girl. It turned out he'd misunderstood me in the car when I said I had been with Suzanne for 16 years.

FRIDAY 28TH MAY

I didn't sleep too well last night. I was aware of the insects that came out of the sand and crawled all over me. In the morning I got up and tried to use the toilet. I still couldn't do the crouching toilet. I don't know why. I've been to quite a few countries now and yet I still haven't mastered it. We had tea for breakfast with some bread, and then left.

Mr Mohammed wanted to carry on by camel now that they had rested, but I persuaded him to go by car. I say 'persuaded'; he tried to get me on a camel, but I refused and sat in a pick-up truck until he agreed to drive.

Finally, we got to the Ancient Wonder. Almost there now. The trip is almost done . . . or so I thought.

I'd barely had a chance to take it in when Ricky called. He told me I'd be staying in a cave tonight. I asked him why and he just said, 'It would be funny', and then the line went dead.

So I called Steve.

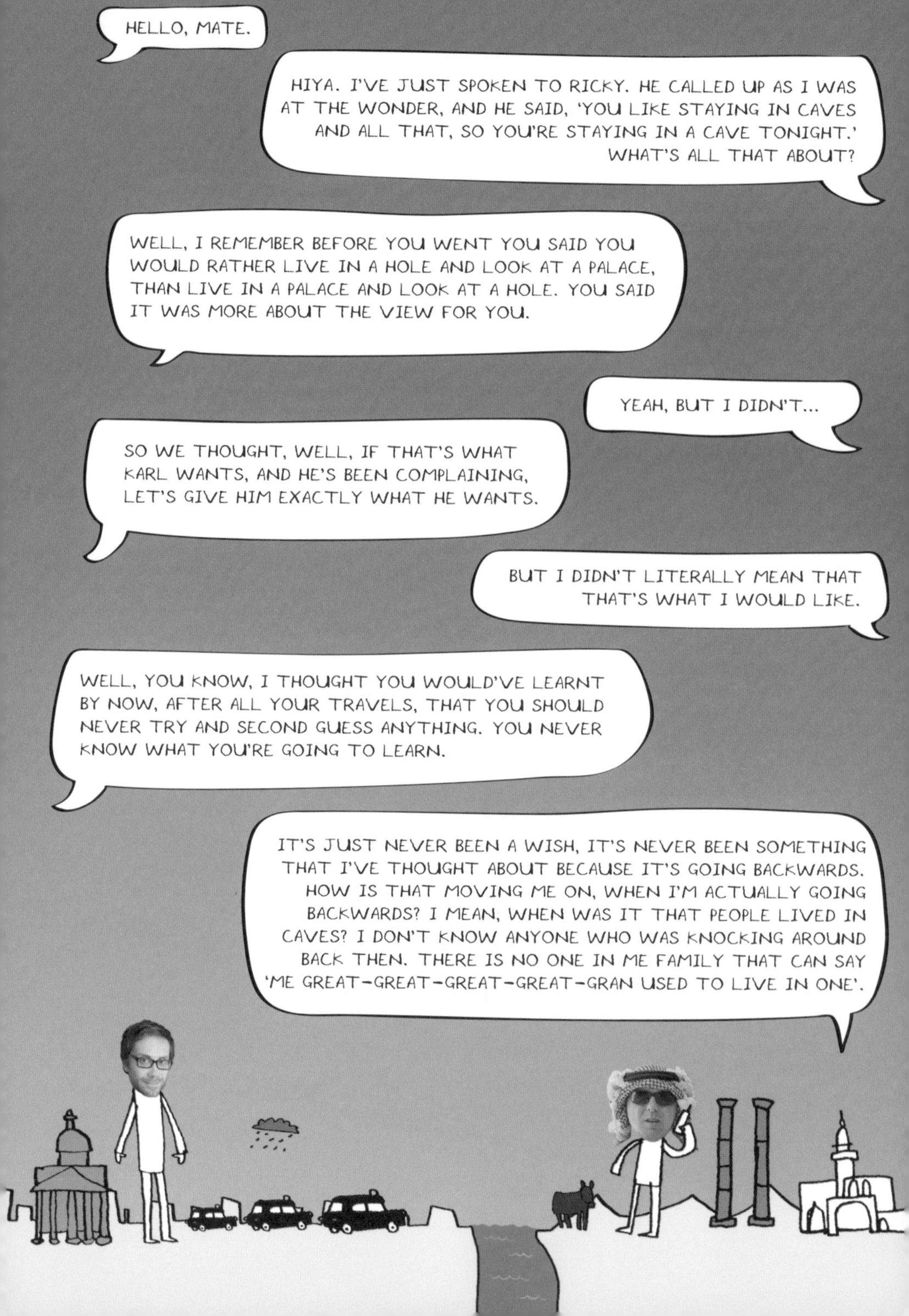
HELLO, MATE.
HIYA. I'VE JUST SPOKEN TO RICKY. HE CALLED UP AS I WAS AT THE WONDER, AND HE SAID, 'YOU LIKE STAYING IN CAVES AND ALL THAT, SO YOU'RE STAYING IN A CAVE TONIGHT.' WHAT'S ALL THAT ABOUT?
WELL, I REMEMBER BEFORE YOU WENT YOU SAID YOU WOULD RATHER LIVE IN A HOLE AND LOOK AT A PALACE, THAN LIVE IN A PALACE AND LOOK AT A HOLE. YOU SAID IT WAS MORE ABOUT THE VIEW FOR YOU.
YEAH, BUT I DIDN'T...
SO WE THOUGHT, WELL, IF THAT'S WHAT KARL WANTS, AND HE'S BEEN COMPLAINING, LET'S GIVE HIM EXACTLY WHAT HE WANTS.
BUT I DIDN'T LITERALLY MEAN THAT THAT'S WHAT I WOULD LIKE.
WELL, YOU KNOW, I THOUGHT YOU WOULD'VE LEARNT BY NOW, AFTER ALL YOUR TRAVELS, THAT YOU SHOULD NEVER TRY AND SECOND GUESS ANYTHING. YOU NEVER KNOW WHAT YOU'RE GOING TO LEARN.
IT'S JUST NEVER BEEN A WISH, IT'S NEVER BEEN SOMETHING THAT I'VE THOUGHT ABOUT BECAUSE IT'S GOING BACKWARDS. HOW IS THAT MOVING ME ON, WHEN I'M ACTUALLY GOING BACKWARDS? I MEAN, WHEN WAS IT THAT PEOPLE LIVED IN CAVES? I DON'T KNOW ANYONE WHO WAS KNOCKING AROUND BACK THEN. THERE IS NO ONE IN ME FAMILY THAT CAN SAY 'ME GREAT-GREAT-GREAT-GREAT-GRAN USED TO LIVE IN ONE'.

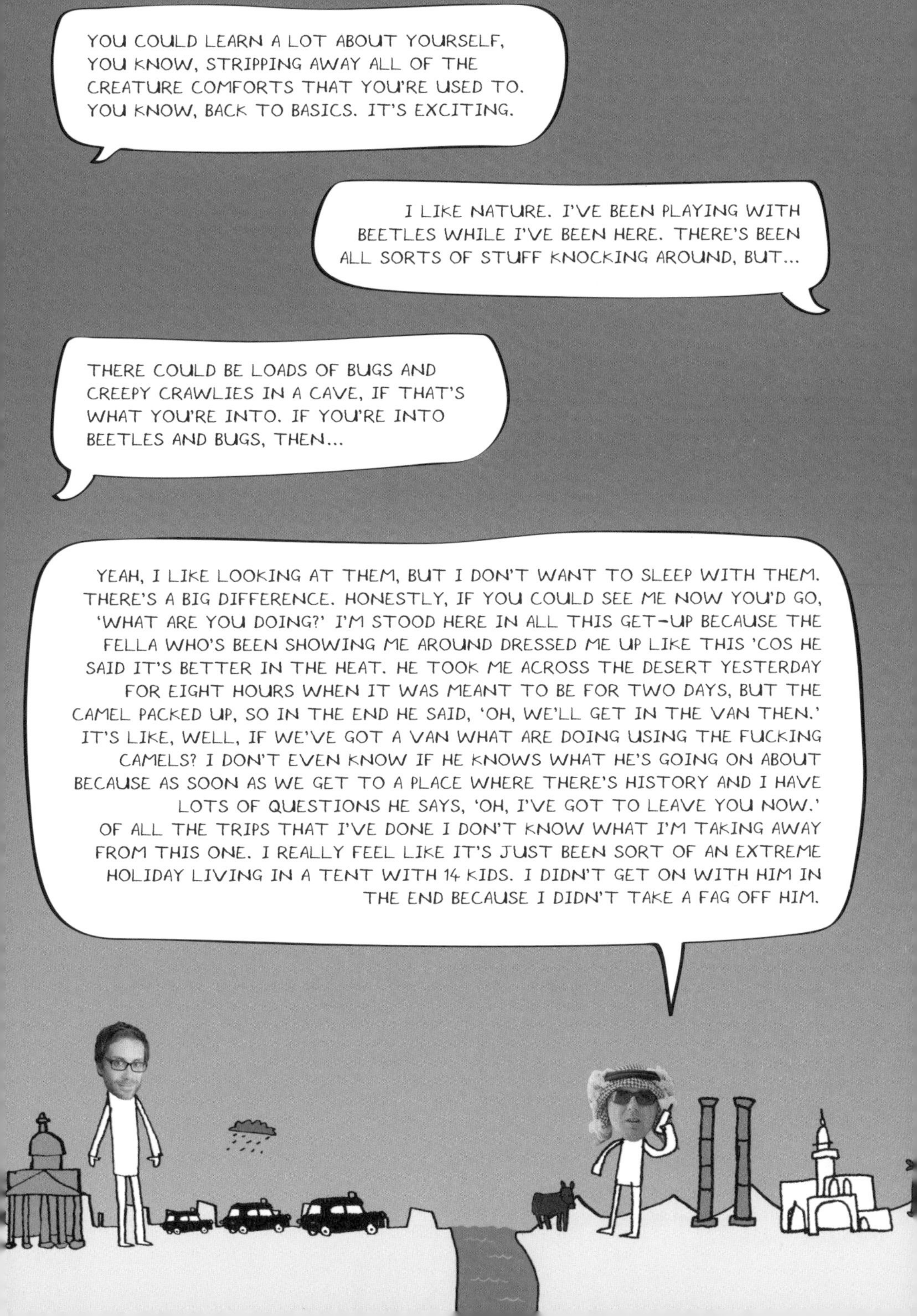
YOU COULD LEARN A LOT ABOUT YOURSELF, YOU KNOW, STRIPPING AWAY ALL OF THE CREATURE COMFORTS THAT YOU'RE USED TO. YOU KNOW, BACK TO BASICS. IT'S EXCITING.
I LIKE NATURE. I'VE BEEN PLAYING WITH BEETLES WHILE I'VE BEEN HERE. THERE'S BEEN ALL SORTS OF STUFF KNOCKING AROUND, BUT...
THERE COULD BE LOADS OF BUGS AND CREEPY CRAWLIES IN A CAVE, IF THAT'S WHAT YOU'RE INTO. IF YOU'RE INTO BEETLES AND BUGS, THEN...
YEAH, I LIKE LOOKING AT THEM, BUT I DON'T WANT TO SLEEP WITH THEM. THERE'S A BIG DIFFERENCE. HONESTLY, IF YOU COULD SEE ME NOW YOU'D GO, 'WHAT ARE YOU DOING?' I'M STOOD HERE IN ALL THIS GET-UP BECAUSE THE FELLA WHO'S BEEN SHOWING ME AROUND DRESSED ME UP LIKE THIS 'COS HE SAID IT'S BETTER IN THE HEAT. HE TOOK ME ACROSS THE DESERT YESTERDAY FOR EIGHT HOURS WHEN IT WAS MEANT TO BE FOR TWO DAYS, BUT THE CAMEL PACKED UP, SO IN THE END HE SAID, 'OH, WE'LL GET IN THE VAN THEN.' IT'S LIKE, WELL, IF WE'VE GOT A VAN WHAT ARE DOING USING THE FUCKING CAMELS? I DON'T EVEN KNOW IF HE KNOWS WHAT HE'S GOING ON ABOUT BECAUSE AS SOON AS WE GET TO A PLACE WHERE THERE'S HISTORY AND I HAVE LOTS OF QUESTIONS HE SAYS, 'OH, I'VE GOT TO LEAVE YOU NOW.' OF ALL THE TRIPS THAT I'VE DONE I DON'T KNOW WHAT I'M TAKING AWAY FROM THIS ONE. I REALLY FEEL LIKE IT'S JUST BEEN SORT OF AN EXTREME HOLIDAY LIVING IN A TENT WITH 14 KIDS. I DIDN'T GET ON WITH HIM IN THE END BECAUSE I DIDN'T TAKE A FAG OFF HIM.

OH DEAR, YOU'VE BEEN INSULTING LOCAL PEOPLE BY NOT ENGAGING WITH THEIR CUSTOMS AGAIN.
YEAH, BUT I SAID 'NO THANK YOU'. I WAS DEAD POLITE.
WELL, THINK ABOUT HOW HE'S GOING TO FEEL IF YOU TURN DOWN HIS CAVE.
WELL, I DON'T KNOW. I'D HAVE THOUGHT CAVEMEN WOULDN'T GET UPSET THAT EASILY.
I DON'T KNOW IF HE'S A CAVEMAN. THAT WAS A MORE GENERAL TERM. JUST BECAUSE YOU LIVE IN A CAVE, YOU'RE NOT A CAVEMAN.
WELL, WHAT IS IT THEN? WHERE'S THE LINE THEN? YOU'RE A MAN, YOU LIVE IN A CAVE. OK, I'M GOING TO DO IT BECAUSE I'VE GOT NOWHERE ELSE, BUT I HONESTLY THOUGHT THIS WAS IT.
GOOD ATTITUDE.
ALRIGHT. I'LL LET YOU KNOW HOW IT GOES THEN.

LOOK WHAT SABA GOT FREE WITH HIS NECTAR POINTS.

MR MOHAMMED

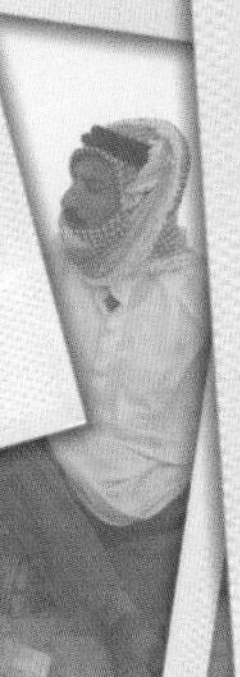

BIN THERE.

I met Ibrahim in a cafe. He had quite a caveman-type face and hair style. The only thing that ruined the look was the fact he seemed to have that 'wet look' gel in his hair that Michael Jackson used to use. Either that or his cave is really, really damp. He was a nice fella, though. He gave me a tour of the caves. There were loads of them. It was like *The Flintstones*.

A lot of them are now empty after the government moved everyone out in the 1980s, to protect the archaeological site. I could really imagine what it was like to live there back in the day. I can picture myself coming out of a little hole in the morning, armed with just a club, thinking, 'What am I going to do today?' I would probably spend my time inventing things 'cos it would have been a lot easier to do that back then. It's really difficult to come up with ideas now. I designed a see-through toaster, the idea being that you don't have to keep popping the toast up to see if it's cooked to your liking. Then I looked online and found that someone had already done it. I also came up with the idea of luminous tissue paper after not being able to find the tissues in the dark one night when I had a cold. I looked that up online, too, and it already existed.

The only thing that would get on my nerves if I lived here is this sort of 'open door policy'. Not having a door doesn't help. Anyone you know could walk past and see that you're in and keep nipping in. That's one thing that might mess up the invention thing. You might be thinking of something really good and people are constantly popping in going, 'Oh, alright Albert, how's it going?' 'I had an idea for something just then and it's gone now. Go away!'

Ibrahim took me to the cave where he was born and the one he lived in when he was younger. It was nice big cave with a living room his bedroom just off that. He then took me across the path to where they moved to when he got a little bit older and needed a bigger place. He was showing me around like he was on some property programme: 'Here's the living space; this area was where we cooked.' It all seemed quite normal until he pointed out the tomb in the lounge. The presenter would have told him to keep that bit of information to himself if he was selling it.

We eventually got to the cave he now lived in. It was simple but nice. I was imagining a dark damp place with sharp rock everywhere,

KARL'S FACTS

PETRA WAS FOUNDED BY A NOMADIC ARAB TRIBE KNOWN AS THE NABATAEANS. IT WAS THE CAPITAL OF THE NABATAEAN KINGDOM FROM THE 4TH CENTURY BC, AND WAS THEN CAPTURED BY THE ROMANS IN THE 2ND CENTURY AD.

PETRA MEANS 'ROCK' IN GREEK.

THE CITY WAS REDISCOVERED IN 1812.

PETRA WAS USED AS THE LOCATION FOR *INDIANA JONES AND THE LAST CRUSADE*' IN 1989.

but it was all nice and smooth. In fact, the walls in my bedroom when I was a kid were sharper 'cos my dad went through a phase of Artexing everything. It was trendy in the 1980s to have prickly walls. I used to wake up every morning with scratches on my arse.

Had some chicken that Ibrahim cooked on a fire. It was some of the tastiest chicken I had ever had.

I think being a caveman would have suited me down to the ground. I think my brain would have suited that time more as it can't keep up with stuff these days.

I think I was born too late.

I fell asleep watching geckos run across the ceiling. Suppose that was one good thing with Artex – the sharpness kept the geckos out.

SATURDAY 29TH MAY

I slept really well in the cave and only woke up once, when a cat wandered in. This is another problem when you haven't got a front door.

The night in the cave was my favourite experience since being here. Ibrahim made me feel really at home. I felt like I could do what I wanted. Suzanne always says I'm rubbish at making people feel relaxed 'cos I 'm always saying 'take your shoes off', or 'put your cup on a mat'. But when you live in a cave you don't worry about things like this.

We're going home tomorrow so I used the last day to have a walk around and see more of the Petra site. Ibrahim told me I should make the effort to go and see the monastery. It was one hell of a climb, over 800 steps. It looked very similar to the site that I had seen on my arrival, but bigger. It had a fancy, carved-out front, but it was all a bit damaged and chipped. People say that that's because it's so old, but I wonder if it ever looked perfect. You only get one go at chipping at rock so if the fellas who did it made a few mistakes it could have looked like this from day one.

And as impressive as the entrance was, it was still a cave. Yes, it has good 'kerb appeal', but once I stuck my head inside there really was nothing to it. If you add that to the fact that it was out of the way and you had to climb over 800 steps to get to it, it's fair to say that if it was on *Location, Location, Location* it wouldn't be on my shortlist. It wasn't as cosy as Ibrahim's place where we stayed last night, either.

I noticed there was a cave across from it so made my way over and sat in it. And it was there that I finally proved my point to Ricky and Steve. It was much better to look out of a hole at a palace, than live in the palace looking at a hole. I think the same rule applies with humans. I think I'd rather be an uglyish looking person than a beautiful one, as how often do you have to look at yourself? If you're quite ugly and you're sat facing someone who is pretty at work, who's got the better deal?

SUNDAY 30TH MAY

We flew home today. I checked in with Richard at the TV company and asked if he'd been told what the emergency code word was. He had no idea what I was talking about.

INDIANA JONES
GIFTS SHOP
INDIANA JONES
GIFTS SHOP

CHAPTER SEVEN

MACHU PICCHU

'IN THE VARIETY OF ITS CHARMS AND THE POWER OF ITS SPELL, I KNOW OF NO PLACE IN THE WORLD WHICH CAN COMPARE WITH IT.'
HIRAM BINGHAM
(DISCOVERER OF MACHU PICCHU)
'MAGNIFICENT. I AM SPEECHLESS.'
KARL PILKINGTON

ECUADOR
COLOMBIA
Iquitos
AMAZON
Santa Rosa
Rio Javari
Spent 2nights here
breakfast
Watch out!
PERU
BRAZIL
SOUTH PACIFIC OCEAN
Lima
Machu Picchu
Ollantaytambo
Cusco
BOLIVIA

MONDAY 14TH JUNE

It took ages to get to where we were going. The first flight went from Heathrow to Madrid. It was full of Spanish people – angry Spanish people due to it being delayed. The Spanish are already quite animated as it is, but even more so when they are annoyed. A man sat next to me was flapping his arms about so much the pilot could have turned the engines off and we'd have stayed in the air.

We had a burger and chips in Madrid airport and then got a night flight from Madrid to Lima. I'm not a fan of night flights. I worry the pilot isn't at the top of his game. I'd prefer it if the cockpit wasn't closed 'cos at least you could keep an eye on him and make sure his eyelids weren't dropping. I could go and have a chat with him like you can on a bus. I don't think it helps that all the controls are so close either. Surely it would be better to give him more space and maybe put some of the controls a bit further away so he has to get up now and again to wake him up a bit.

Once in Lima we had to get another flight to a place called Iquitos.

We were staying at a hotel there for the night. I was given a room on the top floor. It was really, really hot due to the fact that the roof was made out of tin. There were also some big windows that helped to increase the heat and the aircon unit was so old it seemed to give off more heat than cool the place down. I ended up sleeping on the floor, as heat rises and it was the coolest place I could find.

TUESDAY 15TH JUNE

I was woken up at 3.45 this morning and taken to an army base to catch another plane. Turns out it was one of them small planes that takes off and lands on water.

In fact, it was the smallest plane I have ever been on. It sat about ten people. It was also the first plane I've ever been told to leave due to an emergency. Freddie the soundman complained about heat coming off

FUERZA AEREA DEL
SERIES 300

the engines when they started them. I didn't really notice after my hotel room experience last night. But Freddie was right to be worried. One of the engines was on fire so we had to wait while about six men opened it up and put it right.

Then we all got back on again. It stank of petrol fumes, which started to give me a headache. I was sat behind the pilot, who was called George. I asked him if everything was okay. He did that hand signal which means 'so-so'. It wasn't the signal I wanted to see. Pilots in the film *Top Gun* always gave each other big smiles with a positive thumbs-up. George looked like his head was somewhere else. If this plane goes down so will mine.

Everyone was fairly quiet on the flight. I just watched as George flicked switches, pulled levers and ate home-made sandwiches from cling film. Now and again he would go to pull a lever only for his co-pilot to grab his hand before he had the chance to pull it. A man sat behind him doing some kind of paperwork. Maybe it was coordinates for the flight. Maybe it was just a Suduko. Maybe it's best not to see what the pilot is up to during a flight.

We flew over miles and miles of trees. I was looking out the window for any sort of activity when the plane took a dive and landed in a river. Turns out it was the Amazon. Richard the director told me I would be staying in the jungle to get a real taste of Peru. At least it'll make a change from petrol.

We unloaded our kit and got on a long thin boat. We had two of them between us. We were in the middle of nowhere. The plane left us. I had no phone signal. Richard the director could see I didn't look too happy. He told me I should be excited because I was standing next to the Amazon. I was just worried about what Ricky and Steve had arranged for me while I was there.

I had a wee in the Amazon. Until Richard told me I should be careful because there are some tiny fish that can swim up from the water through my urine and into my knob! Is that how amazing the Amazon is? The fish in there would really rather live in my knob than the river.

Richard then played me a message on his phone that Steve had recorded telling me that if I was going to experience the jungle then I would need my jungle bag which had been packed with all the survival kit I would need to get me through. I looked in my jungle bag. The first thing I found was a small torch and a whistle which didn't look of a high standard – more like the type of thing you'd get in a Christmas cracker. Next was a first aid kit. By the look of things it had already been used. The aspirin, Imodium and plasters had already been taken with just the wrappers left behind. There was also a pair of cycling shorts and a box of flavoured condoms; not sure what they are for. I know I needed protection from mosquitoes and rabies and typhoid, but condoms? I wondered if Steve had made a mistake and given me his gym bag instead of the jungle bag, until I found a pair of leech protectors. These were like big socks that I would have to wear over my trousers to stop the leeches sucking my blood. But things like this will just make the leech evolve to have stronger jaws and teeth, in the way that the giraffe grew a long neck to reach food that was high up. We are our own worst enemy when it comes to stuff like this.

There was also a book that contained loads of horrible pictures of people who had been bitten and eaten away by some jungle creatures. There were no details of what the creatures looked like or what to do if you got bitten so I presume he had put it in just to worry me. It did. I remember seeing a programme on the telly going on about something called a botfly which lays an egg under your skin and then it grows to the size of a cola bottle sweet and you can see it wriggling about under your skin. Why do they have to do that? All the space in the world and they're laying eggs under humans' skin. A while back I heard bears have to stick leaves up their arse to stop ants crawling up there and biting them! I know the world is getting overpopulated but it isn't that crowded that things have to live up an arse. No wonder Paddington Bear left Peru for London. When you've got bears wanting to leave the country it makes me wonder what I'm doing here.

Richard introduced me to a man named Matt who was on the other boat with all the camera equipment. He was our paramedic, apparently. This just worried me even more. Sometimes I think it's good not to know where I'm going or what I'll be doing, but having small nuggets of information like 'that's our own paramedic' makes my mind go into overdrive and I start to worry even more. It's like my mind likes to worry me. It never thinks of the good things, it just likes to stress me out.

We eventually pulled up. Wilder, who was travelling with us and knows the jungle like the back of his hand, said this is where we would stay as it would be dark soon and we still needed to clear an area to set up our tents and start a fire.

I was knackered, hot and dizzy, and when I got off the boat I fell straight into the clay-type mud on the banks of the river. Any energy I did have was now being sapped by the mud that was trying to suck me in. I really wanted to go home, more than I've ever wanted to on any other trips, but I had no option. We made our way through the jungle. As Wilder chopped away at the trees with a machete to make a path, he kept telling me to be careful where I was walking and to look out for snakes. He then stopped suddenly in front of a tree. It had big spikes sticking from its bark. He warned me not to touch it. What the hell am I doing here, I wondered, in a place where you can't even trust the trees?

Just as I was about to say I couldn't walk any further, Wilder announced that we had got to our base. I sat while the tents were set up. Wilder told me to make sure nothing had crawled onto or into my bags before putting them in the tent. I tried, but it was hard to tell, and then I made my bed. I say 'bed'; I had a tent mat from Halfords (a place not known for jungle survival gear) and a bag of socks for a pillow.

I went to bed at 7.30 p.m. Lots of insects were already crawling and flying around my small one-man tent. I don't ever remember going to bed as early as this in my whole life but I just wanted the day to end.

WEDNESDAY 16TH JUNE

I think I had about 30 minutes' sleep last night. It was really hot in the tent and I couldn't open the zip as more creatures and mosquitoes would have got in. The only time I let any fresh air in was when I had to empty my plastic water bottle which I had peed into three times throughout the night – some of which ended up on my Halfords mat as I couldn't see when it was getting full and I was just going by the sound. Suzanne had packed me some hand wipes. This made me laugh as I was sweating

WILDER WAITS FOR MY VERDICT ON THE COOKED WORM.

MY PRESENTATION TO THE DRAGONS DEN.

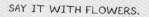

SAY IT WITH FLOWERS.

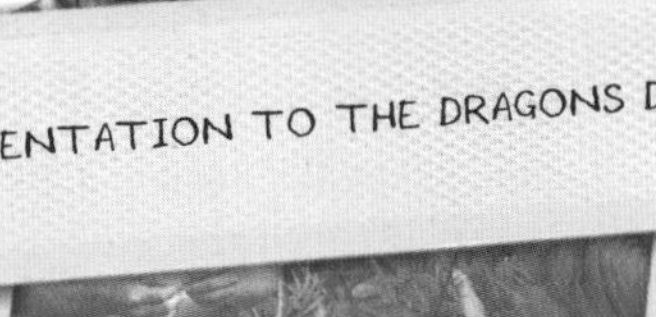

like an ape, was kneeling in my own piss and was covered in mud from when I fell over earlier – and I had baby wipes.

I remember being terrified in the night by a noise that sounded like a gorilla yelling. I don't know if there are gorillas round here but it must have been a big animal to make such a deafening noise. My tent was at the end of the row, and I was sure I was going to attract the gorilla with all the piss I had poured out near the entrance to my tent. I lay there listening to my heart pounding in my head. It was amazing that I could hear my heart as the sounds in the jungle at night were so loud. I'm not surprised there are a lot of nocturnal animals and creatures in the jungle, they have no choice but to be awake at night due to all the bloody noise.

I heard the gorilla growl again. It seemed closer this time. I looked at the time and it was only 2.22 a.m. It was one of the longest nights of my life.

Three hours later I got up. Just getting dressed took so much more effort than normal due to lack of space. I put on the clothes I'd worn yesterday as I didn't know how long I'd be in the jungle for, and if I couldn't wash there was no point putting fresh stuff on.

I left my tent and Matt the paramedic shouted me over. He had found a scorpion under his rucksack. Wilder came over and picked it up with his machete and a stick. It looked pretty evil. It looked like Batman's car. Flat, black and evil. Wilder went and chucked it into the woods. I thought he would have picked a camping area that was safe from these types of creatures, but obviously not.

Wilder then offered me some breakfast of worms he had caught. I said no, thanks. Half a cooked rat was his next offer. I had my boil-in-the-bag beans and sausage.

I got my small camera out and went looking for insects and creatures on my own. I watched hundreds of ants climbing up and down a tree. I saw a black snake but didn't turn on the camera fast enough so missed it. Things that don't look like insects sometimes are insects so a lot of the time I found myself filming something thinking it was a stick insect for it to turn out to be just a stick.

Richard the director was talking to the cameraman and soundman so I thought that this was a good time to get out my toilet that I had taken with me. I say 'toilet'; it was a camping chair that I had cut a hole into where I could place a bin bag. I went to my tent to get it to discover it wasn't there. I went mad at Richard telling him that it wasn't funny and wanted to know who had taken it. He said he didn't know what I was talking about. I asked Wilder and he acted the same way. I then went and looked in every tent but couldn't find it. I asked Wilder again and said if the others had told him to hide it he must tell me where as I had gone to a lot of trouble buying, altering and carrying it to the jungle. He took me into the woods where a path had already been cut and the chair set up. I thought he had done it especially for me until I noticed a small M&S bag next to the chair. Someone had already used it. I thought it may have been a joke and that the bag just contained soil so picked it up to check. I hadn't even undone the knot fully when the stench hit me. Someone had used it. No one would tell me who, but it smelt English to me.

I got another bag and told everyone to leave so I could try out my invention for myself. When I sat down in it the hole ripped and I fell right through. I'd brought this over 6,000 miles and it couldn't handle one sitting. I was fed up.

Wilder then took me on a boat down the Amazon. I think he could sense I needed to get away from the base. I had a go at piloting the boat, which was good. I got covered in mud again when I got off for a pee, and saw more giant ants and some pink dolphins. He had mentioned that there were dolphins in the water when we were on our way to our base yesterday, but I didn't believe him. In the end we saw about five or six. Richard the director and Freddie the soundman were particularly excited about seeing them. Dolphins tend to do this to people. I get sick of hearing people say they are really intelligent. People don't say they are intelligent for a fish, they just say they are intelligent as if they could wire a plug and do well on *University Challenge*. It annoys me 'cos I constantly get called a div and an idiot by Ricky and Steve and others, and yet dolphins are being called intelligent. They can't all be bright. Out of this group of six there must be two or three stupid ones.

When we got back to camp Richard told me that he had an electronic device that he has to hit a button on each day that sends a message to London giving them our location so they know that we are okay. It would be nice to be able to speak to Suzanne as she is good at

Mexican lunch

calming me down when I'm fed up. In the last 16 years I haven't gone more than a day without talking to her at some point.

I went to my tent and passed Richard on the way. I noticed he had left the satellite phone that was for real emergencies near the entrance and he wasn't there, so I tried calling Suzanne but it didn't work. Not sure if I was doing it wrong or if it just didn't work. I wanted to tell Richard that it didn't work but then he'd know that I'd tried to use it so I couldn't.

I asked Matt the paramedic if I could try his hammock tonight as my tent was too small. He gave me a spare one that he had. It took me about 30 minutes to put up. It was nice having a little job to do to take my mind off things. It was one that you get inside and zip up. It slowly swung from left to right. Quite calming in a way. It was probably the closest feeling you can get to being back in the womb. That was until a mosquito started whizzing round my head. It must have got in when I did. I had a quick nap in the hammock but decided I couldn't sleep in one all night so gave up on it.

Later I sat in the gloom round a fire and had boil-in-the-bag casserole while trying to shoo away a spider that looked dangerous.

Went to bed around 8.45 p.m. There was quite a big spider in my tent but it was busy catching smaller flies and insects that will probably bite me when I'm asleep, so I decided to leave it be.

I woke up around 10 p.m. to the sound of something heavy landing on top of my tent. No idea what it was. I then had an urge to go to the loo. I couldn't go into the woods as it's just too dark to see what might be crawling around me. So I ended up doing it in my tent into a carrier bag.

This was a new low point.

THURSDAY 17TH JUNE

When I woke up I looked for the spider that had been in my tent. It had gone, which seemed strange. There is a fact that says most people will accidentally eat ten spiders in their lifetime while sleeping. I've probably had my lifetime allowance since I've been here.

I looked for more insects this morning with my small camera. I filmed some ants. I decided to focus on one ant to see what it was doing. It walked along and then attacked another ant, then that ant started to fight back so another ant came along to stop it, and the one that started it all then sneaked off, and then more ants got involved in the fight. Within seconds there was a full-on riot going on, and yet the one who started it was now nowhere to be seen. Nature is amazing, but it goes to show, you get thugs in all walks of life.

I'm starting to get sick of eating boil-in-the-bag food. Someone back at the London office didn't know that Spotted Dick was a pudding so we're having to eat them as a main course.

I took some Ginger Crunch biscuits with me into the jungle as a treat. Suzanne had bought me some Happy Faces biscuits, which are my very favourite, but you don't get many in a packet, plus I didn't think it would be wise to have a biscuit with a smiling face looking all smug when there was a chance of feeling quite low in the jungle. I'd made my way through half the packet of Ginger Crunches when Wilder called me over with a sense of urgency. He had caught a boa constrictor close to my tent. It was about six feet long. It took Wilder about fifteen minutes to catch it using his hands and a stick. These are the snakes that have mouths that expand, which means that they can eat things that are bigger than them. I've never understood this. I saw one on YouTube that ate a hippo. It just lay there, bored, probably feeling a bit sick, not being able to move, with this hippo inside it for weeks while it digested it. It looked like a hippo in a snakeskin sleeping bag. I tried to give this one that Wilder had caught some Ginger Crunches but it didn't seem keen. Wilder managed to take it away from our base.

Later I stripped down to my underpants and let Dr Dolittle (aka Matt the paramedic) look at my bites to see if anything looked bad. He didn't seem too concerned about anything. But then again he never does. I'm sure he's just treating this like a bit of a holiday.

MY OPPONENT IN THE WORLD STARING COMPETITION.

IF THEY HAD SUDUKOS HERE, THIS SORT OF THING WOULDN'T HAPPEN.

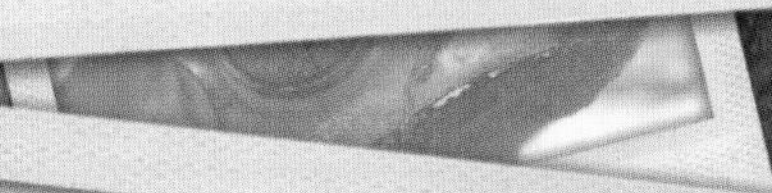

THE SLOTH MOVED AS FAST AS IT DOES IN THIS PHOTO.

SEVEN-NIL TO ME.

FRIDAY 18TH JUNE

Richard played a message to me this morning that Steve had recorded before we left the UK. He said I'd be going to see a tribe today further down the river. He said they were once cannibals. I think this was meant to scare me, but it didn't. I don't think it's that weird that people used to eat people. I asked Richard if there was any possibility that they would eat me. He didn't know. I think I'd be okay about eating a person but I think I'd like to know about them before I tucked into them, a bit like the way we like to know if the chicken we eat is free range or not.

Maybe it's what they do once one of the tribe dies. Someone dies, and they go 'Right, Molly was a lovely woman. Stick her in the oven', and then while she's baking – don't know how long that would take – everyone could be chatting about her. 'Molly was such a lovely woman, wasn't she? You know she had her faults, like everyone else' . . . chatting away about her. Get her out the oven. Still talk about her, 'She had a good arse, did Molly', 'Yes, she did, let's have a bite'. To me that is more respectful than just sticking them in the ground. You're saying you love them that much, you're prepared to eat them. You can't do more than that.

We loaded up the boats and set off in search of the tribe. After a little while the river suddenly got thinner and I felt like I was being watched. I then noticed we were being watched by men with orange-painted faces, straw skirts and spears. I waved. They didn't wave back. Maybe they didn't notice, so I waved again. They still didn't wave back.

I got off the boat and fell into more mud. The tribesmen still didn't give off any emotion. I climbed up from the river and noticed the whole village seemed to be lined up. I wasn't sure if this was to make me feel welcome or to worry me that there were more of them than us. I didn't know where to look when I was introduced to the women as they didn't bother with wearing anything on their top half. I thought I'd just keep my head down and look at the floor as I walked by, but even though I did this I could still see the breasts of the older women.

They took me to a spot where I could put up my tent. All the kids sat and watched. The older people all seemed to get on with their jobs, apart from one woman who looked a bit mad and was wandering around on her own swinging an axe. It's funny how no matter where you live there's always a local nutter.

Just as I got the tent up, the clouds opened and it chucked it down. I got my soap out and had a shower in it. I could see the tribespeople watching me through the doorways of their straw huts. I might have been playing a dangerous game, thinking about it; if they were cannibals, taking my clothes off and washing my body is like prepping some meat before cooking it. It was nice to feel clean though.

They lit a fire as it grew dark. If I was going to get eaten, now was the time.

I put my diary away, as I thought I should keep my eyes on the locals.

SATURDAY 19TH JUNE

I woke up this morning to find myself still in my tent, not in a pot. I slept okay, other than being woken early by a spraying sensation from a dog peeing on my tent. I thought it was waterproof. Turns out it wasn't.

I had a wander about round the village. A kid had a toad on a bit of rope as a pet; another kid showed me his baby sloth. He kept putting it on the floor, and it would try and crawl away, but what chance has one of the slowest-moving creatures on earth got of getting away?

I then saw the locals annoying a frog. They had suspended it by four sticks and some string and were rubbing its glands with another stick. This made the frog sweat. They then collected all the sweat before releasing the frog to use again at a later date. Then a local man called Eric had the sweat put into a cut on his skin. He sat and waited. Then he was sick. The tribespeople believe the frog sweat makes you throw up all your weaknesses and gets you pumped up ready for the hunt. They use frog sweat like we use Lucozade.

The local women then took my shirt off and painted me and dressed me in their dress. They covered me in red spots to make me look like a panther. With all my mossy bites I didn't need much make-up.

They took me to the woods and taught me how to use a bow and arrow. I had about fifteen goes but didn't manage to hit the target.

We went back to the camp. It felt like the blokes had lost a bit of respect for me since seeing my skills with an arrow. This was confirmed when they all went to hunt but left me behind. Not that I was too bothered, as I don't like the idea of killing stuff.

I got quite bored as there was nothing to do. The women were all sat around chatting. I wonder if this is why sloths evolved to move slowly. There's no point in moving fast when living somewhere like this as nothing needs to be done in a rush.

I ended up playing Connect 4 on my own. I played this when I was a kid. I pick which colour I think will win then place all the discs in with my eyes closed. Once all the pieces are in I open my eyes to see if I picked the winning colour. The kid who had the sloth came over, and I tried to teach him how to play but he didn't seem to get it. He just liked putting the pieces in the holes.

Once he'd wandered off I went and cleaned my clothes in the Amazon as they stank. Some of the younger people from the tribe were down there fishing and cleaning pots and pans. As I was washing my clothes I remembered reading about a tribe that only used the numbers one, two and three. Apparently they had no real need for the number four onwards. Maybe this was why the kid didn't understand the game Connect 4.

When I got back to the tent the men were back from the hunt and were setting up a fire again. It looked unsafe to me. All the wood was leaning to one side. Kids were playing around the side where the wood was leaning and everybody was wearing straw skirts. It was a disaster waiting to happen. Just when I thought it couldn't get any more dangerous a man came walking up with a small crocodile on his back. He popped it on the floor next to the kids, who were next to the fire, which was next to the people in flammable clothing. All we were missing was the local mad woman with her axe.

The men then danced around the fire as a woman chopped up the crocodile. They offered me some. I said I was okay, thanks, as I'd had some Spotted Dick for tea.

I went to bed at 9.30ish once the fire had died down and there was no chance of it spreading to my tent.

SUNDAY 20TH JUNE

We left the tribe this morning and made our way down the river for about four hours to a place called Angamos where we would be staying the night at a hostel. We got to the hostel and decided we would be better off staying in our tents as the rooms were rotten. The mattress had more stuff living in it than the jungle we had just left. We ended up just taking one room (Room 5) to put all the equipment into. The plan was that we could all use the toilet and sink in that room.

We had some food in a locals' place. Richard said it was a café, but I think it was just a normal house where the owner was making some money from us. I thought this for two reasons: 1) we were the only ones there; and 2) our table was next to the bedroom.

Got back and went to use the loo in Room 5 and was shocked at the state of it. Christian the producer was not well and had made a mess of it and the walls surrounding it. Even the cockroaches were running out the door. For the first time in my life I was aware that my face did a disgusted look. I decided I'd rather do it on the street than sit in there.

I couldn't believe I'd just about done a week in Peru. It had been perhaps the longest week of my life. If a doctor ever tells me I only have a month left to live I will return and do this trip again as it'll feel like I have lived a lot longer.

MONDAY 21ST JUNE

I had to get on another small plane again today. Wilder was flying with us. He is terrified of flying as he's already been in two plane crashes. He had to take some Valium to prepare himself for the flight. The news that they were using our flight as a training exercise for a young pilot to learn how to fly while carrying a heavy load due to all our kit didn't help to calm him either. To be fair, this made me nervous too.

We ended up in a nice hotel in a place called Cusco, which is a bit closer to the wonder of Machu Picchu. Cusco is so high up there is 30 per cent less oxygen here. I had to take altitude tablets otherwise I could have died. Just walking a few steps was really tiring. I'd like to see the sloth from the tribe live here. It would never move. It would be like an ornament with a heartbeat.

We booked into a hotel. There were oxygen tanks in the room but you had to pay to use them. I normally avoid taking anything from hotel minibars due to the mark-up on the price but they really have you with the oxygen tanks. I had to break the seal and have a go to make sure I knew how to use it, in case I woke up out of breath in the night. I know Machu Picchu is supposed to take my breath away, but not like this.

I was aware of my heart working harder and I was getting a slight headache behind the eyes, which is another symptom of altitude sickness. I also have a bad stomach. Not sure if it's due to the altitude or just that my body has relaxed since leaving the jungle and tribe. Hopefully it will clear up before I have to do the trek up to Machu Picchu.

Called Suzanne after not speaking to her for five days. She said she had missed talking to me but it has reassured her that if I was dead she could cope without me. I'm glad she's got something out of my travels. £1.50 a minute for that little bit of information.

I called Ricky too.

HOW'S IT GOING?
ALL RIGHT. YOU OUT OF THE JUNGLE?
YEAH, JUST ABOUT, LEFT YESTERDAY. IN CUSCO NOW, THERE'S 30 PER CENT LESS OXYGEN.
BECAUSE OF THE ALTITUDE?
YEAH. IN ME ROOM THERE'S A BOTTLE OF OXYGEN, JUST IN CASE I GO A BIT DIZZY AND THAT.
HAVE YOU FELT SICK OR DIZZY?
YEAH. I'VE FELT DIZZY, GOT THE SHAKES, GOT A LITTLE HEADACHE BEHIND ME EYES, I'VE GOT PINS AND NEEDLES IN ME FEET AND ME BRAIN WORKS SLOWER BECAUSE LESS OXYGEN IS GETTING TO IT.
JESUS, I THINK YOUR BRAIN WORKING SLOWER IS A PROBLEM. THANKS FOR POINTING OUT YOUR HEADACHE IS BEHIND YOUR EYES. I THINK YOU'LL FIND THAT IS WHERE YOUR BRAIN IS AND THAT'S WHERE MOST HEADACHES ARE.
NOT ALWAYS. I SOMETIMES GET THEM JUST BELOW MY EARS.
SURELY THAT'S A NECKACHE. YOU WOULDN'T SAY I'VE GOT A HEADACHE IN MY GUMS, WOULD YOU? YOU'D SAY I'VE GOT TOOTHACHE.

IT TAKES IT OUT OF YOU, THIS. THE PLANE GOING OUT TO THE JUNGLE SET ON FIRE, THAT WAS A GOOD START. I HAD TO JUMP OUT QUICK BECAUSE SMOKE WAS COMING OUT OF THE ENGINE. THAT'S JUST WHAT YOU NEED, THAT'S A NICE LITTLE PANIC ON THE HEART, JUST WHEN YOU ARE GOING INTO HIGH ALTITUDE, MORE PRESSURE ON IT.
WHERE WAS THE PAIN IN YOUR HEART? JUST BEHIND YOUR RIBCAGE OR IN YOUR CHEST?
I'M JUST AWARE OF IT SORT OF THROBBING AT THE MOMENT. I CAN HEAR IT IN MY EARS MORE. I'M MORE AWARE THAT I'M ALIVE.
OH WELL, THAT'S A BREAKTHROUGH.
WELL, IT'S NOT GOOD THOUGH, IS IT? YOU'RE MEANT TO HAVE A SLOW HEARTBEAT LIKE A TORTOISE, THAT'S WHY THEY LIVE FOR EVER. BUT JUST STOOD HERE NOW TALKING TO YOU I'M BREATHING MORE. I'M NORMALLY A REALLY QUIET BREATHER BUT I'M AWARE OF MY BREATHING. I'M AWARE OF MY HEART.
ONE STEP AT A TIME. YOU'VE DESCRIBED WHERE YOUR HEAD IS, YOU KNOW WHERE YOUR HEART IS, SOON YOU WON'T HAVE TO CONCENTRATE ON BREATHING. A LOT OF PEOPLE DO THAT INVOLUNTARILY, SO ONCE YOU GET THAT UNDERWAY AND YOU KNOW YOU'RE AWARE YOU'RE ALIVE THAT'S GOOD. SO, ALL IN ALL, THIS HAS ALL BEEN WORTHWHILE.

YEAH, BUT I TELL YOU WHAT, YOU COULDN'T HANDLE IT. I WOULD LOVE TO SEE STEVE HERE. I WOULD LOVE TO SEE HIM DEALING WITH THIS.
STEVE CANNOT AFFORD TO LOSE ANY BLOOD TO INSECTS. HE'S GOT TO BE ANAEMIC ANYWAY. HE IS THE PALEST PERSON; I'VE SAID IT BEFORE, HE'S LIKE ONE OF THOSE SMALL FISH. IF YOU TOOK HIS SHIRT OFF, I THINK YOU WOULD SEE HIS HEART. SO YOU WOULD DEFINITELY BE AWARE OF HIS HEARTBEAT.
THE THING WITH STEVE IS, I THINK HE HAS ALTITUDE SICKNESS ALL THE TIME, WITH HIS HEIGHT.
(LAUGHS)
SO ANYTHING ELSE BEEN GOING ON AT HOME? BECAUSE I'VE HAD NO PHONE CONTACT WHILE I WAS IN THE JUNGLE I DON'T KNOW WHAT'S GOING ON.
WHAT DO YOU WANT TO KNOW?
I DON'T KNOW. HAS ANYONE DIED? I DON'T KNOW... JUST SOMETHING.
I HAD A MEETING WITH EVERYONE, AND THEY WEREN'T SURE ABOUT THE TITLE 'KARL PILKINGTON'S SEVEN WONDERS'. I CAME UP WITH AN IDEA THAT THEY REALLY LIKED WHICH THEY'RE PUSHING THROUGH. I WANTED TO RUN IT BY YOU: 'AN IDIOT ABROAD'.

WELL, NO, WE DIDN'T SAY ANYTHING ABOUT THAT. WE SAID IT'S 'KARL PILKINGTON'S SEVEN WONDERS'.
YEAH, BUT THEY WERE SAYING, WHO'S KARL PILKINGTON?
YEAH, BUT WHO'S THE IDIOT ABROAD?
YOU'RE THE IDIOT ABROAD. THEY LOVED IT, THEY ABSOLUTELY LOVED IT.
WELL, THEY WOULD BECAUSE YOU SAID IT. YOU KNOW WHAT THEY'RE LIKE. THEY ALL SIT THERE GOING, 'YEAH, RICKY, THAT'S GREAT. YEAH. YEAH, WE'LL DO THAT.' WE'RE NOT HAVING AN IDIOT ABROAD. IT'S KARL PILKINGTON'S SEVEN WONDERS. I'VE BEEN THROUGH A LOAD OF SHIT HERE. YOU'RE SAT THERE GIVING THEM BLOODY SHIT TITLES. WE'RE NOT HAVING AN IDIOT ABROAD, WE'RE NOT HAVING IT. IT'S THE ONE THING THAT I SAID I'M HAPPY WITH. I DON'T WANT PEOPLE THINKING I'M A DIV. IT'S KARL PILKINGTON'S SEVEN WONDERS. I'M BACK IN A COUPLE OF DAYS. WE'LL HAVE ANOTHER LITTLE MEETING ABOUT THAT. WAS THERE ALL CROISSANTS THERE AND FREE COFFEE? ALL SAT ABOUT ON THEIR ARSES, 'YES, RICKY, ANY OTHER IDEAS? ANOTHER COFFEE?' I'M SICK OF THAT LOT. YOU'VE GOT MY HEART GOING MORE NOW.
(LAUGHS) I'LL SEE YOU LATER.
ALL RIGHT, SEE YA LATER.

TUESDAY 22ND JUNE

Richard bought me some walking shoes today ready for our walk up to Machu Picchu. I said all shoes are for walking in.

I met a man who gives spiritual advice to anyone who is about to climb the Wonder. He was a local man who lived in the hills. His name was also Richard. I met him in the middle of a field in the middle of nowhere. He sat me down and did a little ceremony. He opened up a small parcel full of bits and pieces. There was all sorts of tat in it. String, chunks of plastic, seeds, powders, paperclip . . . at one point I'm sure I saw a used ear plug. He was mixing them all together like some sort of mad witch. He then rubbed the package all over my body (well, up to my shoulders as he couldn't reach above them). He then got a guinea pig from a box and rubbed my body with it. He said all the badness from my body was being transferred into the guinea pig. God help it. He then took the package of tat and said he would bury it in the hills. Sweet Jesus, if he's doing that every day that hill is a right landfill.

Machu Picchu

WEDNESDAY 23RD JUNE

Up at 4 a.m. today to start our walk on the Inca trail up to Machu Picchu.

My stomach is still bad so just had two hard-boiled eggs for breakfast. We had to get a train from where we were staying to the bottom of Machu Picchu. When we got to the station we were told that Michael the cameraman could not get on the train as the ticket that had been booked was in another cameraman's name. Richard suggested we leave him to sort it out so that we would not lose time. Freddie the soundman stepped in to do the camera and Christian, Richard's assistant, took on the job of sound. It was like some kind of work experience day. The way I felt, I fancied letting the train driver do my job.

Freddie started using loads of sayings he had probably picked up from working with other cameramen; words like 'focus' and 'white balance'. I don't think he really knew what he was doing though. Richard must have thought the same. He said we should wait for Michael even though we had no idea what time he would get to us as there was no phone signal. He eventually turned up an hour and half later.

After a quick toilet stop we set off. We had four or five porters with us. These are men who help carry heavy loads. They can carry as much as a donkey. Even though they were carrying a lot of gear they were still hard to keep up with.

I'd only been going for 30 minutes and felt shattered. No wonder there is 30 per cent less oxygen here. I think it's due to all the tourists climbing this hill to the Wonder. More exercise means more breathing. If they sorted out a lift or some escalators to the top I think there would be a lot more oxygen to go round.

I had to let everybody else go ahead as my stomach was rumbling again. I had to crouch behind a bush. Never mind the Inca trail, I've left a Pilkington trail.

We passed old buildings made of rock that were constructed without the use of cement. I don't know if that was always the plan or if the man who was supposed to deliver the cement refused to carry it all this way. The buildings looked like bungalows to me, which seems odd when the whole idea of living in a bungalow is less stairs, yet they've been built on a hill.

I caught up with the porters, who had stopped to eat. They were tucking into some squashed guinea pig packed with green pesto. I think that's what it was; maybe it was the guinea pig that was used to soak up all my badness yesterday. There were a couple of porters who were not eating but were sat playing a flute. Why on earth, after walking for hours and hours in a place where there is 30 per cent less oxygen, would you start playing a wind instrument?

Richard asked me if I was excited about getting closer to Machu Picchu. I said I wasn't. How could I be? I was still ill, hot and exhausted. The views were amazing, we were on top of the world, but why people would live up here just doesn't make sense. My mam and dad have retired to Snowdon in Wales but they're sick of it being a 15-minute drive to the local Spar supermarket. Living high up just isn't practical.

We had been walking for about eight or nine hours. We got to a point called the Sun Gate that looked down onto Machu Picchu. It looked like more of the same that I'd seen earlier. Bungalows made from rocks with the roofs missing. I wonder if these were ever finished.

KARL'S FACTS

MACHU PICCHU TRANSLATES AS 'OLD MOUNTAIN'.

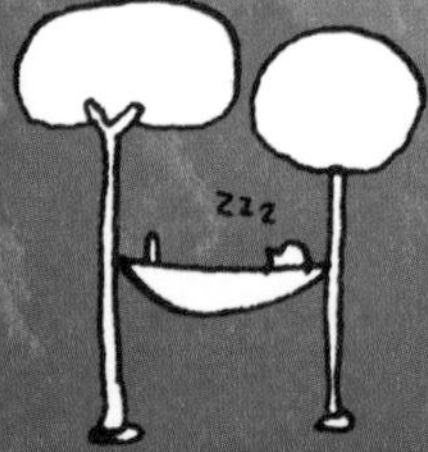

WHEN MACHU PICCHU WAS 'REDISCOVERED' IN 1911 A GROUP OF QUECHUANS WERE FOUND LIVING ON THE SITE. A BUNCH OF FEMALE MUMMIES WERE ALSO DISCOVERED.

THE INCAS DIDN'T USE ANY KIND OF MORTAR TO STICK THEIR STONES TOGETHER. INSTEAD THEY CUT THE STONES WITH SUCH PRECISION THAT THEY LOCKED TOGETHER SO TIGHTLY THAT YOU COULDN'T EVEN PUT A THIN KNIFE-BLADE BETWEEN THEM.

MACHU PICCHU STANDS 2,430 METERS ABOVE SEA-LEVEL.

'THE SECRET OF THE INCAS', STARRING CHARLTON HESTON, WAS SHOT ON LOCATION AT MACHU PICCHU IN 1954. THIS WAS THE FIRST TIME THAT A MAJOR HOLLYWOOD STUDIO HAD FILMED ON LOCATION.

I don't think they corroded away, I just think they couldn't get people to live in them so didn't bother completing the project.

I was really tired and was concerned that by the time we got to the Wonder it would be totally dark. I told Richard I thought it was pointless going any further. He said I had to go for the programme. I think he was worried the Sky bosses would be angry if we went back home with no footage.

I called Steve to try and get him on my side.

HELLO. HOW'S IT GOING?
ALL RIGHT, MATE. WHERE DO I FIND YOU?
I'M KIND OF AT THE WONDER.
KIND OF AT THE WONDER? OR AT THE WONDER?
I'M AT THE WONDER, BUT, ER, LISTEN, IT'S A LONG STORY, BUT YOU KNOW I'VE BEEN IN THE JUNGLE.
YOU'VE BEEN IN THE JUNGLE, YEAH. DID THAT GO ALL RIGHT?
ER, YEAH. IT SEEMS AGES AGO. I DID THAT. I'VE DONE THE TRIBE THING. I DID ALL THAT. I'VE BEEN REALLY ILL. AND THEN I GET TO THIS THING THINKING THAT I'M JUST GONNA BE SEEING MACHU PICCHU, RIGHT, BUT THEN I FOUND OUT I HAD TO WALK UP A MASSIVE HILL. I GOT UP AT FOUR O'CLOCK THIS MORNING. THERE WAS A PROBLEM WITH THE TRAIN. I'VE ONLY JUST GOT HERE. SO, I'VE BEEN WALKING ABOUT EIGHT HOURS. NOW I'M AT A POINT WHERE I CAN SEE THE WONDER, THE CAMERAMAN CAN SEE THE WONDER. THE SUN IS GOING DOWN. IF WE TRY AND WALK THERE IT IS GOING TO GET DARK AND WE'RE NOT GONNA SEE ANYTHING. BUT RICHARD, WHO IS IN CHARGE, IS WORRYING SAYING 'SKY WANT TO SEE THE WONDER'. I THINK WE CAN SEE IT FROM HERE. HAVE YOU GOT A PROBLEM IF WE JUST SEE IT FROM HERE? HAVE A LOOK FROM HERE AND GO?
WELL, HOW FAR AWAY ARE YOU FROM IT?

WHAT, IN WALKING TIME OR WITH ME EYES? WITH ME EYES I CAN SEE IT.
NO, I MEAN HOW FAR AWAY IS IT? CAN YOU SEE IT, LIKE, WITH ALL ITS DETAIL?
YEAH.
I'M NOT SURE I'M HAPPY ABOUT THIS, KARL. LET ME JUST TELL YOU MY CONCERNS, MATE. I WANT TO SEE THE WONDERS OF THE WORLD IN HD. I FEEL RESPONSIBLE, YOU KNOW. I'VE GOT YOU THIS GIG WITH RICKY ON SKY1. IT'S A MAJOR THING. THEY ARE PUTTING ALL THEIR MONEY BEHIND THIS. THIS IS MAKE-OR-BREAK FOR THEM. 24 HAS FINISHED NOW. THEY'VE GOT NOTHING ON SKY1, MATE. DO YOU KNOW WHAT I MEAN? YOU HAVING A HAZY SHOT THROUGH SOME HAZY LIGHT OF THE WONDER I AM WORRIED ABOUT. CAN YOU NOT JUST BED DOWN FOR A FEW HOURS? GET A BIT OF KIP? SET OFF TOMORROW EARLY AND MAKE IT TO THE WONDER?
NO, I'M NOT DOING ANY MORE OF THAT. HONESTLY, YOU CANNOT SEE WHAT I CAN SEE. I AM TELLING YOU NOW, IF WE GO OVER THERE THE VIEWERS OF SKY1 WILL BE SEEING OLD ROCK IN DARKNESS. IT WILL BE VERY CLEAR DARK. IT WILL BE THE CLEAREST DARK THEY'VE EVER SEEN. BUT I HAVE BEEN WALKING FOR EIGHT HOURS AND THE VIEW FROM HERE IS MAGNIFICENT. AND I'M NOT JUST SAYING THAT BECAUSE...
ARE YOU JUST SAYING THAT? ARE YOU BEING HONEST WITH ME?
I THINK IT LOOKS MAGNIFICENT.

KARL, I HAVE NEVER HEARD YOU USE THE WORD 'MAGNIFICENT' IN MY LIFE SO I AM SUSPICIOUS.
THE SUN IS SORT OF BOUNCING OFF A MOUNTAIN AND GOING THROUGH THE ROCK. AND YOU CAN SEE THE GREEN. FROM HERE IT LOOKS GOOD. WHAT I AM WORRIED ABOUT IS IF WE GET UP CLOSE AND IT DOESN'T LOOK GOOD. IT'S LIKE A PERSON'S FACE. FROM A DISTANCE YOU GO 'THEY LOOK ALL RIGHT', BUT UP CLOSE YOU GO 'BLOODY HELL'. SO, I RECKON, THIS IS THE LAST EPISODE SO LET'S JUST FINISH ON A BEAUTIFUL LONG-DISTANCE SHOT. HONESTLY, I THINK THIS WORKS. THIS IS THE WAY TO END IT. JUST A NICE SHOT WITH THE SUN GOING DOWN. IT WORKS A TREAT. I'M TELLING YOU. I AM SPEECHLESS.
TELL ME WHAT YOU CAN SEE OF THE WONDER RIGHT NOW. WHAT IS YOUR GENUINE REACTION? FORGET THAT YOU'VE GOT TO WORRY ABOUT WHAT'S GOING TO BE ON THE TELLY. WHAT'S YOUR REACTION RIGHT NOW?
WELL, IF I AM BEING HONEST, I AM PISSED OFF, AREN'T I? I'VE BEEN UP SINCE 4 O'CLOCK. I'VE HAD TWO HARD-BOILED EGGS AND THE SHITS. SO IT'S NOT THE GREATEST WAY TO SEE IT. BUT I'M JUST THINKING ABOUT THE VIEWER HERE. I AM NOT BEING SELFISH. AND I RECKON FOR THE TV PROGRAMME, AND THAT'S WHAT THIS IS ABOUT, THIS IS WHAT SKY WANT, THE SEVEN WONDERS OF THE WORLD...
KARL, WHAT WOULD MICHAEL PALIN DO IN THIS SITUATION?

HE'D PROBABLY DO A VOICEOVER. HE PROBABLY WOULDN'T BE HERE NOW AT THIS STAGE. THERE IS NO WAY HE WOULD WALK UP THAT HILL. YOU WOULD SEE A CLOSE-UP OF IT AND HE WOULD BE GOING 'MACHU PICCHU, HOME OF THE INCA. HUNDREDS OF YEARS AGO THEY LIVED HERE...' AND SO ON. I CAN DO THAT BACK IN LONDON. IF THE CAMERAMAN TAKES A LOAD OF PICTURES OF IT NOW, WHEN I GET BACK TO LONDON I WILL WRITE SOMETHING UP. AND I WILL SELL IT TO THE VIEWER.
KARL, YOU KNOW WHAT, YOU HAVE GROWN AS A HUMAN BEING THESE PAST FEW WEEKS. I FEEL LIKE PERHAPS AT THE BEGINNING I COULD HAVE BULLIED YOU INTO GOING OVER THERE. NOW I FEEL LIKE YOU ARE GOING TO DO WHATEVER YOU WANT TO DO, MATE. YOU'RE A DIFFERENT PERSON. I'M NOT SURE I KNOW THE REAL YOU ANYMORE. SO, IF YOU FEEL LIKE YOU DON'T WANT TO GO OVER THERE, IF YOU FEEL THE VIEWERS OF SKY ARE NOT GOING TO BE DEPRIVED, THEN I TRUST YOU.
MMM.
'COS I KNOW YOU'RE NOT GONNA LET THEM DOWN, YOU'RE NOT GONNA LET ME AND RICKY DOWN, AND YOU'RE CERTAINLY NOT GOING TO LIE.
NO.
I TRUST YOU.
IT WILL BE GOOD. STEVE, HAVE A GOOD ONE AND DON'T BOTHER TELLING RICKY OR ANYTHING. I WILL SPEAK TO HIM WHEN I GET BACK.
ALL RIGHT.
SEE YOU.

The MUSE

EL PERU

EL PERU

CAMINO SAGRADO
CHACHABAMBA
KM 104
WELCOME TO INKA TRAIL

An Idiot Abroad

The Final Questionnaire

By Ricky Gervais and Stephen Merchant

1. Travel broadens the mind, or so the phrase goes. Bearing in mind that you already have a perfectly round head, how much broader does it feel now you've visited all these amazing countries?

IT DOESN'T FEEL THAT DIFFERENT. I'VE JUST PUT SOME NEW MEMORIES IN THERE WHICH MEANS I PROBABLY HAD TO LOSE A FEW OF THE OLDER ONES FROM WHEN I WAS A KID, WHICH IS ANNOYING AS THEY WERE HAPPIER MEMORIES THAN THE NEW ONES FROM THIS TRIP.

2. Was there anything you saw that you wish you hadn't?

THE NAKED BODIES ON THE NUDIST BEACH IN BRAZIL. WHAT I DON'T GET IS THAT BRAZILIANS HARDLY WEAR ANYTHING ANYWAY. I CAN ALMOST UNDERSTAND NUDISM IN THE UK BECAUSE MOST PEOPLE HAVE TO DRESS UP FOR WORK – WEARING SHIRTS AND SUITS ETC –. SO MAYBE IT'S NICE TO FEEL FREE FROM CLOTHING. BUT IN BRAZIL THEY NIP TO THE SHOPS IN A G-STRING AND FLIP FLOPS ANYWAY, SO WHY THE NEED TO GO STARK BOLLOCK NAKED?

3. In retrospect, what one thing would you take to each place to make life easier?

A CHEMICAL TOILET.

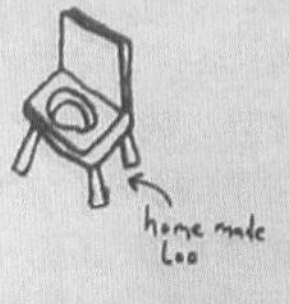

4. Who would win in a fight between the students at the Shaolin Kung Fu School in China and El Porky, Shocker and their friends at the wrestling arena in Mexico?

SHAOLIN KUNG FU SCHOOL WITHOUT A DOUBT. LEO THE HEAD MAN PUT ME ON THE FLOOR JUST USING HIS LITTLE FINGER! MY LITTLE FINGERS DON'T DO ANYTHING, THEY'RE JUST OBSERVERS TO WHAT MY OTHER FINGERS ARE DOING.

5. Ox's bollocks, blood cake, ash, crickets, donkey, worm, spicy rabbit, toad, Monster Munch . . . you've eaten some pretty tasty things on your travels. Which was your favourite?

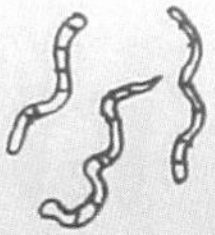

I TOOK MONSTER MUNCH CRISPS AS A TREAT IN CASE THE LOCAL FOOD WASN'T NICE, BUT IN THE END I ATE SO MANY BAGS OF MONSTER MUNCH THAT I AM NOW SICK OF THEM, SO ALL THIS TRAVEL HASN'T REALLY BROADENED MY MIND, ALL IT HAS DONE IS TAKE SOMETHING AWAY THAT I ENJOYED BEFORE I STARTED MY JOURNEY. SO I'M WORSE OFF.

6. If we could move one of the Seven Wonders of the World to the end of your road and rebuild it, piece by piece, which would you choose?

NONE OF THEM, AS IT'S HARD ENOUGH GETTING A PARKING SPACE AS IT IS WITHOUT HAVING LOADS OF TOURISTS CLOGGING ME STREET UP.

7. If Michael Palin was heading off to visit the Seven Wonders of the World, what advice would you give him?

I'D JUST TELL HIM NOT TO GO ON ANY TRIPS TO PLACES THAT RICKY AND STEVE HAVE SUGGESTED. I'D TELL HIM NOT TO BOTHER WITH THE 'WONDERS' AND TELL HIM TO JUST SIT BACK AND WATCH RATHER THAN GO CHASING SPECIFIC EXPERIENCES. INDIA WAS A MAD PLACE. IT'S LIKE WHEN YOU USE A DYSON VACUUM CLEANER ON A FLOOR THAT LOOKED QUITE CLEAN, BUT THEN YOU REALIZE THERE WAS ALL SORTS OF DUST AND MUCK ON IT. INDIA IS LIKE THAT – IT SEEMS NORMAL, BUT WHEN YOU LOOK CLOSER LOADS OF ODD STUFF IS GOING ON.

8. What do you think of Britain now?

THE UK SEEMS VERY WASTEFUL, BUT I THOUGHT THAT BEFORE I TRAVELLED THE WORLD. WE REPLACE INSTEAD OF REPAIR. WE BUY TWO FOR ONE WHEN WE ONLY NEED ONE IN THE FIRST PLACE. AND WE HAVE TOO MANY HEALTH AND SAFETY RULES. I DROPPED SOME FOOD ON THE FLOOR RECENTLY AND WAS TOLD THAT THERE IS A THREE SECOND RULE – IF IT'S BEEN ON THE FLOOR FOR LONGER THAN THREE SECONDS YOU SHOULDN'T EAT IT. AND YET HALF THE STUFF THEY EAT IN CHINA HAS BEEN CRAWLING ABOUT ON THE FLOOR FOR WEEKS OR MONTHS BEFORE THEY SWALLOW IT, AND IT AIN'T DONE THEM ANY HARM.

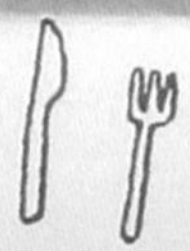

9. Do you whinge less now you have seen true hardship?

I DON'T WHINGE, I MOAN. THERE'S A DIFFERENCE. I LIKE MOANING, I THINK IT'S MORE NATURAL TO MOAN. BEING 'HAPPY' IS A MAN-MADE CONDITION. I THINK WE KID OURSELVES INTO THINKING WE'RE HAPPY. A MOAN IS GOOD FOR THE BRAIN, IT MAKES IT WORK HARDER.

10. What's the first thing you did when you got home from each trip?

I OPENED ME POST. WHEN I SAY POST, I MEAN BILLS. THAT'S ALL THE POSTMAN BRINGS ME THESE DAYS. TO BE HONEST, I'M HAPPY WHEN THERE'S A POSTAL STRIKE. SUZANNE WOULD THEN MAKE ME SOMETHING NICE FOR TEA. SAUSAGE, BEANS AND POTATO CAKES NORMALLY, THOUGH LIKE THE MONSTER MUNCH I'M GETTING SICK OF SAUSAGE, BEANS AND POTATO CAKES NOW.

11. Why were you so obsessed by writing about going to the toilet?

GOING TO THE LOO IS ONE OF MY FAVOURITE PASTIMES. IT'S 'ME TIME', OR AT LEAST NORMALLY IT'S 'ME TIME' BUT IN CHINA IT WASN'T AS IT'S AN OPEN-DOOR POLICY, ACTUALLY NOT EVEN OPEN-DOOR 'COS THERE ISN'T A DOOR, IT'S JUST A ROOM WITH A FEW TOILETS IN IT WITH EVERYONE CROUCHING. IT'S ODD HOW IT'S SOMETHING WE ALL DO IN THE WORLD, BUT WE LOOK AT IT IN DIFFERENT WAYS. IN BRITAIN WE TRY TO MAKE IT A PLEASANT THING BY HAVING COMFY TOILET-SEAT COVERS OR TOILET-ROLL COVERS. IN CHINA IT'S A GROUP ACTIVITY AND THEY HAVE NO SEATS OR TOILET ROLLS TO COVER.

12. Are there any customs you came across on your travels that you would like to introduce to the UK?

YES, I'D LIKE PEOPLE TO AUTOMATICALLY TAKE THEIR SHOES OFF WHEN THEY ENTER YOUR HOUSE SO I DON'T HAVE TO HAVE THAT AWKWARD MOMENT OF TELLING THEM TO TAKE THEM OFF 'COS I'VE JUST VACCED UP.

13. If your new friends Mahmoud, Carlos, Ashek, Leo and Wilder were coming to the UK for a week, which British 'Wonder' would you take them to see?

I THINK I'D TAKE THEM TO 'RIPLEY'S BELIEVE IT OR NOT' MUSEUM IN PICCADILLY CIRCUS. NO MATTER WHAT LANGUAGE YOU SPEAK, EVERYONE IS INTERESTED IN SEEING THE MAN WHOSE FACE WAS ON BACKWARDS, AND THE HORSE-FACED WOMAN.

14. Where are you and Suzanne going on your holidays next year?

SUZANNE WANTS TO GO ON A SAFARI, AND SEEING AS I HAD AN INJECTION AT THE START OF ALL THIS TO PROTECT ME FROM A DIRTY CHIMP, I MAY AS WELL MAKE USE OF IT.

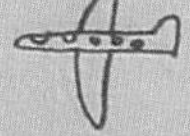

THANKS TO:

Jan Pester (main camera on all trips except for Peru); Rich Hardcastle (photographer); Freddie Clare (sound recordist and photographer); Richard Yee (Series Producer/ Director on Peru); Krish Majumdar (Director on Egypt, Brazil, China); Christian Watt (DV Director); Ben Green (DV Director); Luke Campbell (Director on India and Jordan); Jamie Jay Johnson (Director on Mexico); Barnaby Lankester-Owen (DV Director); Michael Timney (Main Camera in Peru); Emma Riley (Production Manager); Claire Pocock (Production Co-Ordinator); Rebecca Wadcock (Production Co-ordinator); Lynda Featherstone (Editor on India, Egypt and China); Gwyn Jones (Editor on Brazil, Jordon and Mexico); Sam Santana (Editor on Peru); James Cooper (Production Assistant); Dan Goldsack (Executive Producer); Simon Arnold (Assistant Producer); and Michael Andrews (Researcher).

PHOTO CREDITS:

RICH HARDCASTLE

The Pyramids: pages 6, 7, 14, 17, 20–21, 23 (all photos), 25, 28, 31, 33, 34–35, 37, 38–39

Christ the Redeemer: pages 41, 45, 46, 48, 52–53, 65, 69, 72–73, 74–75

The Taj Mahal: pages 76, 77, 81, 85, 86–87, 89, 96, 103, 105, 110–111, 112–113, 114–115

Chichen Itza: pages 116, 117, 123, 145, 147, 149, 151, 152–153, 155, 156–157

The Great Wall: pages 158, 168, 170, 172, 176–177, 180, 195, 196–197

Petra: pages 198, 199, 233, 234–235, 236, 239, 240–241

Machu Picchu: pages 242, 243, 270–271, 273, 274, 275, 280–281, 282–283

FREDDIE CLARE

The Pyramids: pages 13, 28

Christ the Redeemer: pages 40, 48, 59, 66, 69, 71

The Taj Mahal: pages 84, 91, 92, 103, 107

Chichen Itza: pages 121, 124, 131, 132, 135, 141

The Great Wall: pages 159, 163, 165, 172, 175, 182, 184–185, 186, 192

Petra: pages 205, 207, 213, 217, 218, 219, 226, 228, 233

Machu Picchu: pages 246, 249, 251, 254, 257, 260, 262–263

RAY BURMISTON

Introduction: vii, 1

OUT ON DVD
22 NOV
HIS FOURTH LIVE STAND-UP SHOW
RICKY GERVAIS LIVE IV
SCIENCE
RICKY GERVAIS LIVE IV SCIENCE
ANIMALS - POLITICS - FAME
ALSO AVAILABLE
RICKY GERVAIS LIVE
Animals
RICKY GERVAIS LIVE 2
POLITICS
RICKY GERVAIS LIVE 3
UNIVERSAL
DVD
VIDEO